The author

LLOYD SPENCER DAVIS is a zoologist, writer and filmmaker. He has been writing, producing and directing prize-winning documentaries for over twenty years and has numerous academic publications to his name. He is the author of *Penguin: a season in the life of the Adelie penguin* (1993) which won the Pen (NZ) Best First Book Award for Non-fiction, and *The Plight of the Penguin* (2001) which won the New Zealand Post Children's Book of the Year Award.

He has been the recipient of many fellowships, distinctions and awards including the Foundation for Research Science and Technology's Merit Award for Excellence in Scientific Communication. Lloyd is a former director of the world's first university course in natural history filmmaking, and now holds the Stuart Chair in Science Communication and directs the Centre for Science Communication at the University of Otago.

Also by the author

Penguin: a season in the life of the Adelie Penguin   1993

The Plight of the Penguin   2001

Penguins (with M. Renner)   2003

Smithsonian Q & A Penguins: the ultimate question and answer book   2007

LOOKING
FOR DARWIN

Lloyd Spencer Davis

To Chris & Alison
Best wishes

Lloyd Spencer Davis

Longacre Press

Published with the assistance of

ISBN 978 1 877361 22 7

A catalogue record for this book is available
from the National Library of New Zealand.

First published by Longacre Press, 2007
30 Moray Place, Dunedin, New Zealand.

Book design by Christine Buess
Cover design by Nick Wright
Cover photo by Daniel Davis
Map illustration by Katy Buess
Printed by Astra Print, Wellington

www.longacre.co.nz

Contents

Preface

This is as much a journey through the mind and heart as it is one through the world. Ever since a vicar, stoned on altar wine, lurched towards me when I was a twelve-year-old attending my first confirmation class, I have found it necessary to search for my own kind of God.

Charles Darwin, it seemed to me, offered a clearer alternative to the slurred words of that messenger from Christ; though, in fairness, once the vicar toppled over the pew it was always going to be difficult to hear what he was saying. However, as many an explorer to a new land has found, spying a landmark of interest in the distance is easier than the getting there. The journey for me has been a troubled one. I've often found myself going in different directions. On occasions I've lost my way. Yet, no matter how dark it's become, sitting there just above the horizon like my personal North Star has always been Darwin.

It would be wrong to assume that this is simply a travelogue about moving away from the Church. I have discovered that the vicar of Christ was right about some things that as a twelve-year-old I could never have believed: such as there are few pleasures in life quite as satisfying as a nice glass of red wine — or a whole chalice!

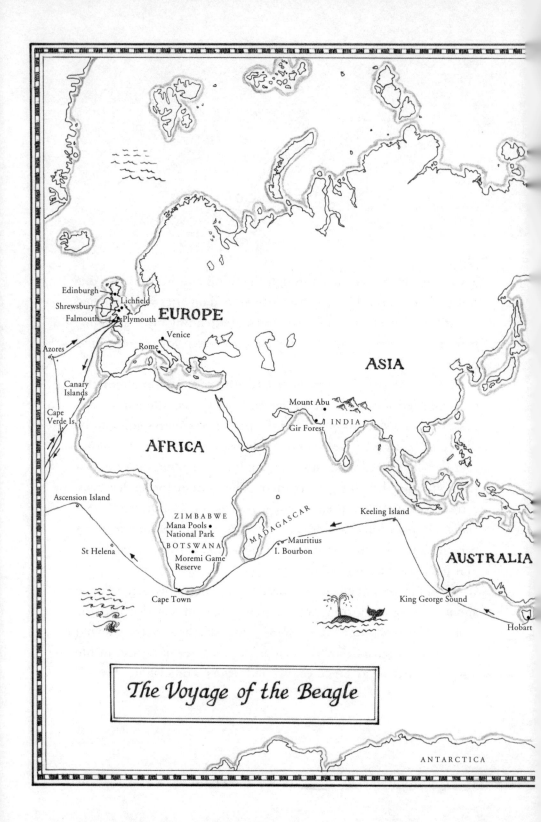

The Voyage of the Beagle

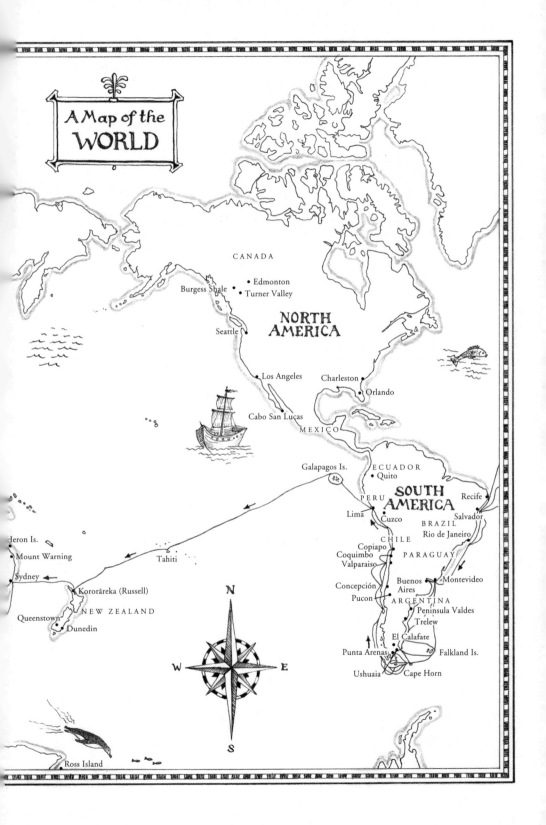

To Frances

From the Big Question
to the Missing Pope

– 1 –

Antarctica and the Big Question

There is a place in the Antarctic where only I have been. Not Scott. Not Shackleton. Not Mawson. Just me.

I stood beneath chiselled cliffs of ice, twenty, thirty times my height. Long icicles reached down from the slightly overhung top edge, like the pipes of an unlikely and chaotic cathedral organ. If any part of the giant glacier had broken away — for that was essentially what it was — I would have been crushed in an instant.

It was snowing. Heavily. Thick glutinous flakes that fell like parachutes and stuck wherever they alighted. The snow had returned the surface of the ice cliffs to a Colgate-white, covering the volcanic grit and stones that had been driven into them the previous day by winds strong enough to bowl over one hundred and seventy litre drums full of fuel. Beyond the cliffs, it was impossible to tell where snow-filled skies and ice-filled seas merged. The cloud, the ice floes, the snow and the small patches of sea between the floes all blended together, so that the view more than a hundred metres away was one of nothingness: a world without edges or horizons.

The ice floe on which I was standing had been blown into the base of the cliffs by the storm and, in a few hours, it would be blown back out to sea by another. For the time being, however, I was able to stand there, an alien in my yellow padded fibre-filled clothes, as out of place as I would have been on the moon. I watched a creature on a nearby floe move slowly towards me. It was about chest-height. Solid. Yet, despite its bulk and measured gait, it exuded a gracile beauty: its long slender bill with its fleshy pink pads; its yellow ear patches that faded to white on its chest so subtly that you would swear must have been done in Photoshop; its haunting call and the way it swung its neck when it cried out. All this, and the surety with which it carried itself, suggested that the emperor penguin was as much at home in this environment as I was a foreigner in it.

If the penguin was conscious of me and what I represented, it did not give any indication. I could have been just a strange snow-covered yellow rock for all the attention it paid me. And that is it — both our curse and our blessing. We humans have somehow ended up with the power of conscious thought. We can go where we were never intended to go. We can invent synthetic fibres to keep us warm. We can make planes, ships and helicopters to take us where we cannot walk. We can build shelters from the storms. And — perhaps most cruelly — we can question our own existence.

'What the hell am I doing here?' I asked myself. If I had taken off my clothes I would have died within a few hours. If I had stepped off the ice floe into the sub-zero waters I would have lasted for only marginally longer than if the ice cliffs had fallen on me. And yet, it was not *my* vulnerability that intrigued me, it was the apparent invincibility of this creature, this bird, in an environment that could smite me out in the time it took to unzip a jacket, to slip, or for gravity to deal to tons of ice.

The key word was 'bird'. This animal ambling towards me I knew to be a bird. It had feathers like a bird. It laid eggs like a bird. But thereafter, any obvious similarities with the sparrows that frequented my garden back in Dunedin became lost on me. For one thing, it was big. *Effing* big. It couldn't fly. Its wings resembled more the paddles of a canoe than a sparrow's fragile wings. It did not nest in trees, it nested on frozen sea ice. And, this was the really hard part to understand, it did not breed when 'spring has sprung and the grass is ris' like any self-respecting sparrow should; no, this emperor penguin bred in the heart of the Antarctic winter, in total darkness, when temperatures fell below minus sixty degrees Celsius and wind speeds of up to two hundred kilometres per hour took the wind chill factor down to levels where I could not survive for long even in my synthetic clothing.

Still, the biologist in me knew that the bones and blood vessels, the nerves and hormones of this emperor penguin were essentially the same as those of a sparrow. The emperor penguin, despite appearances, was nothing more than a modified sparrow. Yet, here it was, a modified sparrow indisputably at home in an environment that would kill a normal sparrow, let alone a naked, clumsy human. Or, one dumb enough to stand beneath the advancing face of the Mount Bird Icecap.

The Antarctic, more than anything, is a silent place. The occasional call from the penguin, the cracking of the ice in the cliffs, the muffled movements of the ice floes — they did little more than to underscore the deep silence that enveloped me. Consequently, when a seal, with a mouth that appeared to hinge at its anus, plopped out of the water next to me, I didn't so much leap out of my skin as catapult out of it. I won't say that I voided my bowels, but it was a close call. My sphincter teetered on the verge of massive, uncontrolled convulsions.

A leopard seal is what you'd get if you could graft the head of *Tyrannosaurus Rex* onto a torpedo. It was sleek — about four metres long — with an olive-green back and a pale underbelly spotted with black dots. But to be up close to a leopard seal is to notice only one thing: its mouth. Like a snake, this seal has the capacity to disarticulate its jaw, allowing it to kill penguins, other seals, and even whales. I stared into the twin arcs of pointed teeth and the massive pink tongue. Even in that moment of pending rectal collapse, I was able to reflect on how its dentition resembled that of a bear.

It is the darnedest thing that a creature so beautifully adapted to scaring the be-jesus out of any animal in Antarctic waters should share so much of its biology with a creature capable of scaring the be-jesus out of any land animals in Northern Hemisphere woods. From the bones that make up its flippers to the heart that beats in its chest, the leopard seal is a modified bear.[1]

There I was, standing in a snowstorm, surrounded by a modified sparrow and a modified bear, and back came the question, 'What the hell am I doing here?' Except that this time I was not indulging in self-criticism for my decision to go out onto the ice floe beneath the cliffs, I was questioning the wisdom of what a vicar had told me when I was twelve years old. And the 'I' in the question no longer referred to me, but to the whole world. *If some Superior Being really had created the world the way my alcoholic minister told it, then why — when creating the penguins and seals of Antarctica — would He have been restricted to using the body parts of flying birds and the body plans of land-based carnivores?* Why not just start with a new blueprint? It's like trying to build a submarine using only the parts that can be salvaged from a 1962 Oldsmobile: it's feasible in a *Junkyard Wars* kind of way, but why do it if you don't need to?

'*What the hell am I doing here?*'

That question became like the South Pole to me. To get to the answer I would need all the determination of the Antarctic explorers I admired. And if I could not tread in their footsteps — and they in mine — I had at least some pretty big footprints to follow.

---

[1] Some authorities now believe that while bear-like ancestors gave rise to some seals, others, like leopard seals, descended from ancestors that were more otter-like. Either way, the dentition would be similar, and let me just say for the record, that a two hundred kilogram otter would be no less scary to me than a bear.

- 2 -

Westminster Abbey and First Encounters

Charles Darwin was a man who did more to change the way we think about ourselves than anyone since Jesus. This was a man who as a scientist stood shoulder to shoulder with Newton and Einstein in terms of elucidating an understanding of our world. It is true that he was not the first person to contemplate questions similar to the one I had grappled with that day in Antarctica, and not the first to conclude that life on Earth must have evolved from one form to another; *but* what he gave us — those of us who ask the question — is a mechanism for evolution, an understanding of how it can happen without the divine hand of God creating all life. How strange should be our meeting place, then, the first time my size ten-and-a-half boots caught up with Mr Darwin's.

During that wonderful period, somewhere between 'Love Me Do' and Pink Floyd's *The Wall*, I suppose I had a naïve view of the world — or, at least, the world of the Church. I had been brought up High Anglican, attending a church-led 'Young People's Union' twice a week and church proper on Sundays. Yet somehow, whenever I heard that someone was buried in Westminster Abbey, it conjured up images of an English churchyard, with headstones on the surrounding lawn. When I went to Westminster Abbey for the first time, I was in my twenties, a longhaired graduate student enjoying a Christmas vacation in England. Walking down an aisle, I was spellbound, taking in the lofty drama of the centuries-old building — experiencing the same sense of humility that I had felt at the Grand Canyon, which I am sure was an intentional part of the design and something common to the grand houses of worship of most religions. The aim was to make you feel insignificant — or perhaps, the other way round, to at least make you feel that you were in the presence of something far more significant than yourself. And it was working. I was in awe.

The floor was somewhat uneven and my toe caught on one of the stones. I looked down to discover that I was standing on a black stone with the inscription:

BROUGHT BY FAITHFUL HANDS
OVER LAND AND SEA
HERE RESTS
DAVID LIVINGSTONE

Then it struck me: I was standing on David Livingstone. I WAS STANDING ON DAVID LIVINGSTONE! I quickly discovered many other luminaries dotted throughout the Abbey and, in a corner, next to the black and much-inscribed stone of astronomer Sir John Herschel, there was Charles Darwin. Darwin's contrasting pale stone was marked simply:

CHARLES ROBERT DARWIN
BORN 12 FEBRUARY 1809
DIED 19 APRIL 1882

It didn't seem quite right to me. I couldn't bring myself to stand upon Charles Darwin, though thousands of tourists did. But it wasn't just the sacrilege of standing on his grave (funny word that — there I was in a church and I felt sacrilegious about what the Church had done). No, I felt uncomfortable that he should be there at all. By now I had embarked on a career in biology, a newly anointed doctoral student in the church of evolution, with Darwin as its patron saint. Had Darwin sold out in the end? He was seventy-three years old. His lifetime's work had rocked the Church. At the time of his death his views on evolution were bitterly opposed by the Church. Yet here he was interred with the devout. It intrigued me that his wife of over forty years, Emma, had chosen not to attend the funeral service.

Nearby, in front of the ornate choir screen, was the grave of Sir Isaac Newton and a monument to Sir Isaac exquisitely carved from white and grey marble. At its centrepiece the monument depicted Sir Isaac Newton reclining on books representing his great works. There was a long Latin inscription, which, translated, read in part:

> Here is buried Isaac Newton, Knight, who by a strength of mind almost divine, and mathematical principles peculiarly his own, explored the course and figures of the planets, the paths of comets, the tides of the sea, the dissimilarities in rays of light, and, what no other scholar has previously imagined, the properties of the colours thus produced. Diligent, sagacious and faithful, in his expositions of nature, antiquity and the Holy Scriptures, he vindicated by his philosophy the majesty of God mighty and good, and expressed the simplicity of the Gospel in his manners.

Where was Darwin's monument? Why not a marble effigy of Darwin reclining on *On the Origin of Species*? Why was the grave of this person, described as the most influential scientist since Newton, so lacking in embellishment, like a whisper engraved into the stone floor? Was it that he had not 'vindicated by his philosophy the majesty of God mighty and good'? Oh sure, six years after his death, Darwin's family, like an afterthought, erected a bronze memorial showing the head and shoulders of a bearded Darwin in the north choir aisle, but the wording on it makes his grave's inscription seem positively loquacious — it says simply: 'Darwin'. Somehow, it seemed that after having opted for burial in this holiest of holies, either the Church, Darwin, or both, had done it only half-heartedly.

This ambiguous relationship between Darwin and the Church should not, I suppose, have been unexpected. Darwin was not a stranger to the Church. He was brought up as a Christian and at one time was even headed for a career in the clergy. Admittedly, Darwin had begun his life under quite different circumstances to mine, but as I stood in Westminster Abbey looking at his gravestone, with prayers from an ongoing service being chanted behind me, I could not fail to see glimpses of my own life in his: we'd both been devoted church-goers who had eventually withdrawn from the teachings of the Church.

A decade later, when back in New Zealand as a family man, there came a day when I was playing the game donkey with my young son on the lawn.[2] During repeated excursions into the garden to retrieve balls that had, in my judgement, been thrown nowhere near me, I played mental catch with myself — tossing up the perennial question 'What the hell am I doing here?' and never quite gloving a satisfactory answer either. I resolved then and there that I needed to know more about the enigma that was Darwin. It seemed to me that a good starting place might be his early years and what had led to his questioning the religious doctrine to which we had both been exposed. Did some pissed priest put him off, or was it a slow pained separation like that between two lovers who hang onto the threads of their relationship even while they know they are not right for each other? I decided to go back to the other side of the world, to Britain, to get at Darwin's beginnings and — somehow in the process — I hoped to get at my own.

---

[2] The game requires two individuals to toss a ball to each other. Each time someone fails to catch the ball they get assigned consecutive letters from the word donkey, starting with 'd'. The first person to complete the word donkey (i.e. miss six catches) is the loser.

- 3 -

England and the Influence of Fathers and Grandfathers

England had given birth to two Darwins famous for evolution. There was Charles, of course, but before him, his grandfather, Erasmus.

Erasmus Darwin is, in many ways, the logical starting point when trying to unravel the developmental influences that would lead, ultimately, to his grandson proposing a theory of evolution that would so rile a contemporary Christian, such as the superbly-monikered St George Jackson Mivart, that he should feel compelled to attack it as the province of 'half-educated men and shallow thinkers'. Erasmus was both a celebrated physician and, during his lifetime, Britain's foremost poet.

In every way, the Darwins were larger-than-life characters. For one thing, they were big. One has only to look at portraits of Darwin's father and grandfather to realise that had they been alive today and not given to medicine, both could probably have found employment as defensive guards for the San Francisco 49ers.

The London of the Swinging Sixties and Swaggering Seventies had long since given way to the grunge of the Nineties and the new millennium by the time I arrived back there, but it was still a time when pigeons packed Trafalgar Square and the policemen all looked like Enid Blyton characters. I cleared a way through the pigeons and headed for the nearby National Portrait Gallery, which had on display an oil painting of Erasmus done by Joseph Wright in 1770.

Room Thirteen, *Science and Industry in the Eighteenth Century*, given the size of the topic, was a surprisingly small room — maybe six by eight metres — with a high stud and lit from above by a large skylight. Hanging from the olive-green walls were portraits of James Watt, who refined the steam engine that propelled the industrial revolution, looking suitably dark and contemplative; the beautifully-named Benjamin Stillingfleet, a botanist who advocated the Linnaean system of classifying the natural world; and, given pride of place, set into an alcove in the wall, was the visage of Sir Hans Sloane, President of the Royal Society from 1727 to 1741.

But it was the portrait of Erasmus Darwin that I had come to see. And I was mildly disappointed to discover that it was a reproduction that was on display: the original residing (appropriately, one had to concede) in Darwin College, Cambridge. Nevertheless, it was supposedly an excellent copy of Wright's oil painting, described by eighteenth-century poet and friend of Erasmus Darwin, Anna Seward, as 'a simple contemplative portrait of the most perfect resemblance'.

To me, he looked kind of sad, almost worried. Something in the pinched mouth and the hangdog eyes suggested that he would rather not be there. The arc of his right hand made his fingers look unusually long and slender for such a fat man. But, if the painter had captured anything of his subject, it was that behind the wig, the frilly cuffs and the poignant expression sat a corpulent man apparently comfortable in his girth. His son Robert — Charles's father — was no shrinking violet either. Robert stood 1.87 metres (six foot two inches) tall and stopped weighing himself once he got to one hundred and fifty-two kilograms (three hundred and thirty-six pounds), after which, according to Charles Darwin, he got a hellova lot bigger. Actually, Darwin didn't quite use those words, but that is what he meant. However, as I stood rooted to the parquet flooring in the portrait gallery that day, staring at the copy of Wright's beautifully illuminated painting of Erasmus in his brown top coat — a much lighter brown than it appeared in all of the reproductions I had seen — I judged that Erasmus could have given Robert a run for his money in any sumo-wrestling contest.

Erasmus Darwin and Josiah Wedgwood — Charles Darwin's maternal grandfather, the successful potter who would build a dynasty of crockery — were close friends who attended meetings of the Lunar Society around Birmingham: a gathering of movers and shakers of *Science and Industry in the Eighteenth Century*, a sort of Room Thirteen personified. Here they hobnobbed with the likes of James Watt and Joseph Priestley, the discoverer of oxygen. In fact, Priestley's portrait hangs directly below that of Erasmus Darwin in Room Thirteen. It is a pastel drawing by Ellen Sharples and, either Priestly was an incredibly ugly man, or Sharples should have taken up basket weaving instead of art. Giving him a head far too big for the shoulders, she managed to make Priestly look like a mentally deranged murderer rather than a mental athlete.

To the right of Erasmus, on the other wall, hung a large portrait of a young Sir Joseph Banks, only thirty when painted by Sir Joshua Reynolds. Very dramatic and, of the three clustered together in the corner (Erasmus Darwin, Priestley and Banks), he looked like the one most likely to change the world. Indeed, Reynolds had underscored this by including a globe in the portrait. But it was the 'lunatics' who most intrigued me; so named because they met monthly about the time of the full moon to lessen the likelihood of being attacked by highway robbers when travelling to and from the meetings. Their society was the birthplace, the incubator, and the nursery of industry, chemistry, medicine and, from one member at least, the neonatal whisperings of such new and daring ideas as evolution.

– 4 –

Lichfield and the Darwin Family Tree

From the little English village of Litlington, I set off with long-suffering friend Andy Wroot — the only one good-natured enough to accompany me to Lichfield and the home of Erasmus Darwin: the fat man with a way for words and a belief that life on Earth must have evolved from simple animals to more complex beasts.

We drove across to the M1, then picked up the M6 to Birmingham, where we skirted the city. Birmingham still wore the bruises of its industrial past — the steel girders, the large power transformers, the untidy waste of all that manufacturing. Unsightly perhaps, but these were also the by-products of what had made Birmingham the powerhouse of industrial England in the late eighteenth and early nineteenth centuries, and as unlikely as it seemed, the nurturing grounds of great minds like Darwin, Wedgwood, Watt and Priestley. We carried on to Lichfield through a veritable minefield of speed cameras, in such a density that it felt like Big Brother was not just watching you but reprimanding your every twitch of the accelerator too.

Lichfield Cathedral is notable for having three spires, but the city itself proved something of a disappointment: a red-brick town, which had grown so fast over the previous fifty years that it had out-stripped its history, it exuded about as much character as the glass of British wine I had tasted the night before. We parked near the cathedral and walked to Erasmus' house located in the close next to the cathedral — the irony of their juxtaposition just too choice not to enjoy. The cathedral was full of people waiting for the ordination of a large number of ministers. Its insides were austere and dark.

Outside, Erasmus' lovely gardens backed onto the cathedral grounds. A minister, about to be ordained and perhaps a little late, hurried past Erasmus' house in his grey clothes, black shirt and dog collar — like a child on the way to school running past a house where he suspected he may be tormented.

More charmer than tormentor, as it turned out, Erasmus Darwin and his lineage were undeniably fecund. Despite Erasmus' bulk, his pronounced stammer, and a face pock-marked by the after-effects of small-pox, he was by all accounts endowed with generous measures of animal and magnetism. As he wrote in his two-volume work *Zoönomia*:

> Wine, women, warmth, against our lives combine;
> But what is life without warmth, women, wine!

In later life it is said that he cut back on the wine but, like an eighteenth-century Meatloaf, his rallying cry must have been, 'two out of three ain't bad'. He fathered fourteen children: five by his first marriage, seven by the second, and two by his mistress, Mary Parker, while between wives.

My own paternal grandfather sired a bastard child. The only other thing I have been able to discover about this grandfather I never knew is that he was Polish. In many ways, this pleases me. A young Polish lady for whom I once harboured carnal thoughts, but who was herself given more to platonic considerations, divulged to me that there was no such thing as an unintelligent Pole because just to speak the language required extraordinary intelligence. Having tried to learn a few words of Polish in a misguided attempt to get, if not to her heart, then at least near her bra strap, I can vouch for the veracity of her statement. It pains me that my grandfather's intelligence, which I reasoned was my birthright, should have been so obviously diluted — but of course, that is fully in keeping with the genetics that underpin Darwin's mechanism of evolution. I am not my grandfather; I am a quarter of my grandfather. This no doubt accounted for my singular lack of success at conjugating verbs — not to mention with my conjugal intentions.

No such impediments, it seems, lay in the way of a wordsmith like Erasmus Darwin.

Mary Parker had been Charles Darwin's father's nursemaid. She was eighteen, Erasmus was forty. In addition to Erasmus' fourteen children, Darwin's father would have six, and Darwin himself sired ten. Furthermore, through Erasmus' close friendship with Josiah Wedgwood, the Wedgwoods and the Darwins became like factories producing spouses for each other.

Josiah, as was more acceptable then than now, married his cousin (also a Wedgwood) and set about having seven children. It would be his eldest daughter, Susannah, who would eventually marry Erasmus' son, Robert Darwin (Charles' father), in 1796, when he was thirty and she already thirty-one. Susannah's brother, Josiah II (Charles' uncle), would have nine children: his second child, Josiah III, married Charles' second sister, Caroline; the fourth, Charlotte, married a man Charles Langton who would go on to marry Charles' youngest sister, Catherine; and the ninth, Emma, would marry Charles. And Charles's older brother, Erasmus, had an affair it seems with another married Wedgwood cousin.

If the young Charles Darwin needed any notion that reproduction held the key to understanding evolution, he need only have looked at his own family for inspiration.

To an outsider, the incestuous links between the Darwins and Wedgwoods can appear even more confusing and convoluted than they really are, if for no other reason than both families were singularly unoriginal when it came to names. Erasmus' father was Robert Darwin. So was his eldest brother. As was his fourth child, who in turn demonstrated a little more originality: calling his eldest son Erasmus and his next, Charles Robert Darwin.

In keeping with something of a short family tradition (because in fact the Darwins had, like the Wedgwoods, risen from common beginnings not so very long before), Robert had studied medicine at the Edinburgh Medical School. Robert wasn't exactly chafing at the bit to be a doctor, but felt dutibound to do so after his eldest brother — named with the redundancy from which the Darwins suffered, Charles — died after developing septicaemia from a cut finger sustained while carrying out a post-mortem on a child (actually Charles Darwin was named after his dead uncle, otherwise it is likely that he too would have been simply Robert Darwin). Incidentally, Charles's brother, Erasmus, was named after their father's other dead brother, who drowned himself five years to the day before Erasmus was born.

Robert then established a large practice in Shrewsbury and, partly with Susannah's inheritance of twenty-five thousand pounds from Josiah Wedgwood (he died a year before her marriage to Robert), they built a large house on the edge of Shrewsbury called The Mount.

– 5 –

Shrewsbury:
Darwin's Birthplace

Andy and I arrived in Shrewsbury, where a clock-like one-way system meandered through the heart of the city, taking us in an inordinately large circle through a town of crooked old buildings falling over themselves with charm. Shrewsbury barely acknowledged that it had once been home to greatness: an almost illegible sign at a roundabout was the only indication I saw that the city in any way promoted its connection with Darwin. A visitor to Shrewsbury could easily spend the day there and not realise that the town was the birthplace of the world's greatest ever naturalist.

We drove up an incline until, at a rather anonymous entrance, we turned into the beautiful grounds of The Mount, dominated by a huge oak tree which I assumed had to have been there when Darwin was a boy. Perplexingly, The Mount is now the Shrewsbury Valuation Office, and while typically the office is closed on a Saturday, the presence of cars in the driveway led me to ring the doorbell. Three valuation office staff were doing overtime. One, a small-built Welshman called Colin, agreed to give us a quick tour of the house.

He initially showed us into the drawing room to the right of the main entrance, the high stud and twin pillars the only indication of its former grandeur. Otherwise the room was dominated by large grey filing cabinets and big black ring-binders — the accoutrements of the bean counter. I was not allowed to take photographs — not because of the significance of the place or, like at the National Portrait Gallery, the damaging effect that flash photography might have on the paintings, or because of copyright issues — but because of the perceived sensitive nature of the documents and information those filing cabinets and ring-binders contained.

There was the waiting room for Dr Darwin's surgery to the left of the main entrance; again, the high stud and a fireplace. Down the corridor to the left, the surgery itself, and, across the passage, the servants' quarters. Finally we traipsed up the staircase to a room overlooking the front lawn and the oak tree, the very room where Darwin was born on 12 February 1809. No attempt had been made to glorify it: three abandoned computers lay like corpses on the floor against the far wall. A desk was pulled up near the window and a small table lay along the near wall with a few more of the ubiquitous ring-binders. Colin allowed me to photograph the room, and Andy took one of me standing against the fireplace — but my overall feeling was one of bereavement that what should have been a shrine to the birthplace of such a great thinker should be so casually disregarded.

It was from The Mount that the young Darwin began his lifelong association with natural history. The River Severn ran along the edge of its grounds. Darwin was a quiet boy and from an early age would take long walks along its banks to fish, and like many children, to collect things.

Andy and I found our way to a pub that sat by the River Severn as it moved sluggishly through Shrewsbury on its way to Bristol. The Armoury was the only pub in Shrewsbury listed in *The Good Pub Guide* and it was vast by English standards. It was distinguished by having walls lined with books, an open fireplace and high, arched windows overlooking the river along which Darwin had wandered as a boy. We ordered two pints of a local real ale, Shropshire Lad, which one might have supposed had been named for Darwin himself were it not also the name of a collection of verse produced by Alfred Edward Housman a few years after Darwin might have rightfully claimed that title. It proved a deliciously bitter beer to swallow: hoppy and with a long aftertaste.

Andy ordered the 'Local Maynards Farm Shropshire sausage served with mash and onion gravy'. How anyone could call such a thing a meal was beyond me: when presented, it resembled nothing so much as a large turd curled atop a mound of brown-stained mash potatoes. Andy pronounced it 'mighty fine', but inwardly I was glad I had changed my order at the last minute to the safer 'Ploughman's lunch'.

Afterwards, we walked beside the River Severn. Slow moving and brown, its banks were covered in thistle. A few cows gathered at the water's edge. Boys in coxed fours rowed under a suspension bridge — built in 1922 according to the sign — while being shouted at through a megaphone by their coach, who rode along the banks of the river on a bicycle that looked like it had been made some time before the bridge.

I couldn't help thinking what it must have been like for a young Charles Darwin following the same path nearly two centuries earlier. How he must have paused to look at similar butterflies, similar tadpoles, similar flowers. How he must have picked up a stone — perhaps the exact same one, for the stone I held was at least two hundred years old — and thrown it onto the surface of the river to see how many skips it could do. From this, one got a sense of a child not so much alone, as absorbed in the natural world around him. I could relate to that: as a child I had spent hours alone lying on a riverbank shunning company for the pleasure of hearing the brook run or watching a heron spear a fish. There is a certain affinity that some people have for the natural world — it is the need to hear, as Aldo Leopold put it, 'goose music'. It is something that I think some of us are born with, encoded in our DNA from some primordial time when we were little more than amoeba, slug or song sparrow.

At The Mount such a fascination with natural history and the sciences were taken for granted. It was in this regard, rather than just because of the servants and the wealth (Robert Darwin was, in addition to being a physician, a skilled investor and financier — although he was never ostentatious with his money), that the Darwin household was most different to others. Not only had Charles's grandfather, Erasmus, been famous for his love of natural history, but his great-uncle had written a textbook on botany still used to classify plants in Darwin's day; and his father, Robert, had a keen interest in botany, ensuring that the garden at The Mount contained many exotic species. From his father, Darwin learnt to systematically record what was happening in the garden: a skill that would serve him well in later life as a naturalist.

A fondness for nature, however, does not make a family immune to its dictates. One consequence of the inbreeding so rife among the Wedgwoods was that many of them were subject to chronic ill health and Darwin's mother, Susannah, was especially prone to such suffering. In the end it was peritonitis that killed her at fifty-two after a wretched few days of stomach pains and vomiting. Charles was only eight at the time. But the truth is that to a large extent, even at that age, it was his three older sisters (Marianne, Caroline and Susan) who were most involved in caring for him — and they stepped up this role upon their mother's death. Caroline initially home-schooled Charles and his young sister Catherine. At eight he was sent to a small school run by the Unitarian minister Reverend George Case in Shrewsbury. During this period it seems that the young Darwin was prone to telling lies or using exaggeration for effect. For example, he would tell fibs about seeing rare birds, or, more fancifully, skite of an ability to change the colour of flowers.

Later in life Darwin would be able to recall very little of his mother. Probably more influential than her death was his being sent away to board in Shrewsbury School when he was nine. The school was already attended by his older brother, Erasmus, and although only fifteen minutes' walk from The Mount, the two Darwin brothers lived there under cramped, poorly ventilated conditions, exacerbated by the fact that the boys did not wash much: Darwin disgusted his sister Caroline by telling her that he washed his feet only once per month (in his favour, he apparently did so whether they needed it or not). Its headmaster was the strict Dr Samuel Butler, a man prone to the classics and to beating the boys — although, to give him his dues too, he said that he rarely beat the same boy twice in one week.

In one of those small twists that somehow appear to link us all despite the enormity of the world, Butler's grandson, also Samuel Butler, would go to New Zealand, a buggy ride from where I lived my early years, and write a book about his experiences, *Erewhon*, which satirised an ideal Darwinian world. The headmaster's grandson would eventually become a staunch critic of Darwin, accusing him in correspondence and at public forums of misinterpreting evolution and having done little more than plagiarise the works of Lamarck and his grandfather, Erasmus.

Andy and I left the Severn and climbed the path to Shrewsbury School. Leaving the law-abiding Andy at the gate, I ignored a warning about it not being a thoroughfare and entered the school grounds. Red brick buildings and a chapel set in neatly manicured green lawns lent the school a kind of elegance that the stuffy buildings probably did not deserve. In fact, a game of cricket was being played on the green, and with the boys dressed all in whites and shouting encouragement like, 'Well bowled, Anthony,' the whole school projected an air of gentility.

I asked a small boy walking towards me whether he knew anything about Darwin and what parts of the school he had occupied. The dark-haired lad said 'No,' then added that I should ask one of the older boys. I approached a tall boy with blond curls who was carrying a skateboard. After ascertaining that he really was a pupil, I asked him, 'What parts of the school did Darwin occupy?'

'I don't know,' he replied.

'Don't they teach you that sort of thing?' I asked incredulously.

'Yeah,' he said, 'but I don't find it very interesting.'

Another two boys playing football were no better informed. I took a photo of an exceptionally fine statue of Darwin, but was surprised to read that it had been made by Jemma Pearson in 2000. *What*? Had the school only started to appreciate the import of their most famous pupil as some sort of millennium project? The statue showed a young, vigorous Darwin standing on what I recognised as an especially good imitation of the lava rock of the Galapagos, surrounded by a marine iguana and other creatures that had been so seminal to the development of his theory.

Eventually I found a master of the school, who told me that the school had shifted to its present site before the turn of the twentieth century and that during Darwin's time it had been located in what was now the public library.

Frustrated, but with at least some certainty now that I was closing in on my quarry, I picked up Andy and we headed back to the one-way loop through the heart of town. Apart from a statue of Darwin in its forecourt — this one, far more traditional, showing a bearded older Darwin — there was really nothing to indicate that greatness had slept and studied books in what was now a library for a generation of snotty-nosed kids that wouldn't know a foramen magnum from a foraminifer unless it was something that David Beckham wore. Even the librarian seemed not to have the faintest notion of the connection between the building and Darwin.

Yet I saw enough in the old building to remind me of the oppression — masquerading as 'tradition' — at the hundred-year-old boys' boarding school I had attended. Although I was a day boy, I knew the boarders well enough to understand what a wrench living away from home can be for a thirteen-year-old, let alone a nine-year-old; and I saw enough of the cane to know that, even once a week, corporal punishment was no way to engender school spirit.

As a twenty-something prospective Ph.D. student (just prior to my pilgrimage to Westminster Cathedral), I had arrived in Edmonton, Canada, and had to briefly go into emergency housing, sharing a single room with twenty-two other males: conditions that were not unlike those at Shrewsbury School when Darwin boarded there. Our beds were so close together that if someone sneezed, the person two over got wet. But out of this, firm friendships were forged very quickly. So while there is no doubting that Darwin detested school — in his own words, 'Nothing could have been worse for the development of my mind than Dr. Butler's school...' — it would be wrong to paint a picture of a lonely, unhappy boy. Darwin did not want for friends and, most importantly, he had his older brother for company.

– 6 –

Early Experiments
in the Back Garden

Erasmus and Charles were very close. It was round this time, with the help of money from their father (a process they euphemistically called 'milking the cow') that they set up a chemistry lab in a scullery in the back garden of The Mount. Through this they acquired, as well as an interest in mineralogy and crystals, a level of appreciation for experimental methodology, for recording results systematically and for analysis.

Doing chemistry for pleasure holds about as much appeal to me as performing an auto-appendectomy. But from what I could see, certain segments of British society were — how can I put this — decidedly peculiar. They were, to my eye, less a nation of shop-keepers than they were a nation of trainspotters, pigeon fanciers and Morris dancers. In other words, some of them were completely bonkers when it came to devising pastimes. While Americans often get attributed with strange goings on — how often have I heard the expression 'only in America'? — when it comes to ludicrous ways to while away a few hours, the Poms have it all over them. Where else would lawn mower races, muddy canal swimming or darts be considered sports, let alone spectator sports? Perhaps, I thought, it was because the beaches and the weather were so abysmal that one could not simply grab a towel and lie under the sun with a good book; instead one had to be adding crystals of copper sulphate to hydrochloric acid, or the like.

Another famous Brit driven to such backyard experiments was William Hamilton. Said by many to have been the most important biologist since Darwin, he expanded Darwin's concept of Natural Selection to give us a variant of it called Kin Selection. And, in another of those unlikely links that make us comment 'it's a small world' (a phrase that I would eventually come to detest) the brother-in-law of my Polish girlfriend was a childhood friend of Hamilton's. Some years ago, I met Bill Hamilton and was driving him to a hut in Berwick Forest in New Zealand, where we were both attending a workshop on behaviour and evolution. I told him of my indirect connection to him — leaving out the bit about the firmly fastened bra — and Bill wondered whether it was the same friend who had been with him the day, he too, carried out a chemistry experiment in a shed at the bottom of his parents' garden. However, unlike Robert Darwin, Hamilton's father was not a practitioner of medicine, but a structural engineer: he built bridges and, during the Second World War, his expertise was used to help blow them up. As a consequence, the shed at the end of the garden held not glassware and copper sulphate, but dynamite.

'How did it go?' I asked. And, even negotiating the winding bends through the pine trees rally-style, I had time to glance across and catch Hamilton's wry grin as he held up his hand with its missing fingers.

I'm often amazed by the lucky escapes people have had. But of course, that is the marvellous thing about survival: you only get to talk to 'the fittest'. How many Charles Darwins or Bill Hamiltons might there have been that simply blew themselves up by adding too much nitro to glycerine, or drowned while fishing, or got hit by a cart crossing the road? That is not to mention the potential losses to disease: how many Charles Darwins died of septicaemia before they could reach greatness? Like Natural Selection and evolution itself, the progress of ideas and understanding also has elements of luck to it.

Perhaps Charles's greatest piece of luck was that his father decided to take him out of Dr Butler's school and ship him off to Edinburgh to study medicine with his brother Erasmus at the tender age of sixteen.

7

Edinburgh, Medical School and Exposure to New Ideas

I had tried to ship myself off to Edinburgh too. After completing my Ph.D. studies in Edmonton, I had gone to the UK with visions of recreating a sort of British *Easyrider* experience, cruising up to Edinburgh on a motorbike. There were several elements to this plan that I did not get right. First, my girlfriend refused to accompany me, calling the enterprise 'daft in the extreme'. Second, the only motorbike I was able to hire was a tiny Honda that barely had room for me let alone a biker chick. But, without doubt, my worst miscalculation was that it was November. To my credit I did get as far as the Lake District before a series of severe snowstorms drove me back into the unsympathetic but warm arms of my London-based friend. Anyone who has ever been on the M6 in a snowstorm, in the dark, on a bike with a cc rating even lower than the intelligence quotient required to have you out there in below-freezing temperatures, being passed within inches by huge lorries with articulated trailers, will know that it could have been Quasimodo waiting for me in London and I would still have turned back.

The two Darwin brothers were not nearly so stupid: they took a coach and arrived in Edinburgh after a couple of days, where they took rooms at 11 Lothian Street. Today it's a decrepit, run down area — but while it may not have been much better in Darwin's day, it was a relatively well-off part of a city that was overrun with the hovels of Irish immigrants.

It would be fair to say that Darwin did not exactly take to medicine the way his genealogy might have suggested he should. Of course this was a time when much of studying medicine consisted of observing cadavers being cut up. The university medical school and the competing private medical schools in Edinburgh had a great deal of difficulty getting sufficient bodies, so it seems that few questions were asked about their source and a local industry of grave robbers developed to supply the medical schools. Most notoriously, in 1828, the year after Darwin left the university, an Irish immigrant, William Burke, and his accomplice, William Hare, killed at least sixteen people who were then supplied to the medical schools for up to ten pounds a piece. As a final piece of brutal irony, Burke was executed for his crimes in 1829 and his body sent to the university anatomy school where it was dissected before a large audience.

However, it wasn't the dissection of cadavers so much as witnessing two particular operations that made Darwin realise that medicine was not for him. This was in a time before the use of anaesthetics such as chloroform and it seems that one operation involved a child and an amputation. Darwin ran from the theatre before the operation was complete and the screams of the child and the blood would haunt him forevermore.

The liberating effect of this was that Darwin, no longer concerned with medicine as a career, started to pick and choose the lectures he attended. Accounts of Darwin's time in Edinburgh vary. Some say this was a period when he was exposed to radical ideas — many of them emanating from Europe — which challenged traditional views of chemistry, anatomy, geology, and perhaps most pointedly, the immutability of species. He joined a group called the Plinian Society, which met regularly to read papers on natural history and he was exposed to rebellious views on religious ideology, particularly through a Plinian friend, Robert Grant. Others paint a picture of a studious, retiring young man, who spent much of his first year in his brother's company, before, in his second year, drifting somewhat aimlessly, almost instinctually, into concentrating on the natural sciences — largely as a consequence of his revulsion at surgery.[3]

How paradoxical then, that this should coincide with Darwin throwing himself into hunting as a pursuit. During the two months of the university vacation alone, his own records show that he killed one hundred and seventy-seven hares, pheasants and partridges at an average of three animals per day. He decided not to return to Edinburgh, but to go to Cambridge University instead, and like his great-uncle John, the botanist, read for the clergy. He reasoned that like his grandfather's brother, he could indulge his passion for natural history — especially collecting beetles — between ministering to his flock.

---

[3] After that first year, Erasmus left to go to London and the Great Windmill Street Anatomy School.

– 8 –

Cambridge University and Academia

I have been to Cambridge several times and have come to love it. Cambridge and its surroundings don't just represent 'a slice of history,' as the travel brochures say, they ooze it from every cobblestone, from every gated college courtyard, from every pub window; it is underscored by every doughty Englishman wearing a suit while pedalling around on an ancient bicycle, basket on its front. It can be a weird experience to walk down a narrow cobbled street and realise that Darwin, Rutherford and Watson probably went there before you, and that the place is essentially unchanged save for the hundreds of tourists in designer tracksuits. On one occasion, I presented a seminar to the Department of Zoology: midway through I had one of those rare outer-body experiences and watched myself struggling to captivate some of the best minds in the business. I was left, like the audience, hoping that it would all be over quickly and painlessly. At the end, I was pelted with a barrage of questions that made Pearl Harbour seem like an act of friendship.

Yet, it is this concentration of academic firepower that makes Cambridge University arguably the world's superpower of the sciences. It has the potential to be the cerebral equivalent of Normandy, Hiroshima and Desert Storm all rolled up in one. The cut and thrust of academic debate: it doesn't just kill bad ideas, it really tests good ones.

It was in such a culture that Darwin now found himself — a

member of Christ's College, in the footsteps of the likes of John Milton. Here he became close with the cleric and botanist the Reverend John Stevens Henslow, often accompanying him on his daily walks. This caused Darwin to be known as 'the man who walks with Henslow'. At Henslow's urging, Darwin accompanied Professor Adam Sedgwick to Wales, where he learnt all about geology.

By way of getting a taster of the college life, my wife and I left Andy and his wife, Sarah, in Litlington and travelled to Cambridge to attend a dinner with a friend's father who was then in a position of significance at Jesus College. Before dinner we enjoyed a glass of sherry with fellows of the college dining at the high table with us. I was introduced to Sir So-and-So and to Lord This-and-That. Anyone else that was not a knight of the realm seemed to be either an MP or a full professor. The food, it has to be said, was nothing special and the wine no more than pleasant. The conversation, too, was congenial enough, but like the food, a little bland. That is, until after the ceremony of dinner had been completed and we retreated to a smoking room where cigars were passed around beneath a huge portrait of Thomas Malthus — one of a long line of distinguished graduates of the college. At the beckoning of the Master of the college, a middle-aged man handed out glasses of port as if he were some sort of sycophantic servant. It was only later that my wife informed me that he was one of the world's leading paediatric neurosurgeons. I was given pride of place next to the Master, and for the next few hours, the conversation ranged widely: from medicine to anthropology, from seismology to biology, from particle physics to law. It struck me then, that this was surely the triumph of the British system of education at the elite universities like Cambridge and Oxford: the college system encourages, nay, insists upon, the exchange of ideas across a wide variety of disciplines. Scientists don't just speak to others in their narrow fields of speciality, but to all different kinds. And from this competition of ideas can emerge new ideas, new 'species' if you will. It is Natural Selection of the intellect in action.

It was this more than anything that I found unfathomable about Darwin's time at Cambridge. Living on such an intellectual battlefield, how could he succumb to the teachings of the Church? Whatever ideas on evolution Darwin had absorbed from his grandfather and during his time in Edinburgh — such as the heretical views of Frenchman Jean-Baptiste Lamarck — he apparently did not feel sufficiently conflicted to disqualify himself from a life of preaching the word of God. From preaching that the world was made in seven days. From preaching that God *created* all the animals and plants.

Of course, it must be remembered, neither did most other members of the Cambridge University fraternity; such was the unquestioned authority of the Church, especially the Church of England. In those days it would have been one thing to discuss ancient Thai civilisations with the Master of a college named after God's son, but quite another to proclaim that God does not exist.

Back in Litlington, enjoying a meal with Sarah, Andy and my wife — where my only contribution had been to add to the cooking time for the pork through my late arrival — I remained preoccupied with the thought that if the academic artillery at Cambridge was no match for the Church, how could the ideas of Darwin and evolution have ever found traction? Perhaps it was the shiraz we were drinking, but for whatever reason my deliberations flittered to images of a drunken vicar from All Saints Church in Taradale lambasting a young — but admittedly, precociously obnoxious — boy for simply mentioning the word evolution.

By now I was in my forties. I had done the God thing as a child and been a rabid proponent of evolution as a postgraduate student, but the more I matured the less the world seemed so black and white to me; like the hair I observed change in my mirror, my view of the world was turning to shades of grey. I began to think that if the Anglican Church were so intolerant, perhaps one should look to an alternative church if science and sermons were to comfortably co-exist. I started to wonder what the Catholic Church might have to say.

It turns out that the Catholic Church adopted a far more ambiguous position when it came to evolution. Among the 1,359 additions to the index of books banned by the Catholic Church during the nineteenth century, Charles Darwin and *On the Origin of Species* are conspicuously absent. It is true that they listed Erasmus Darwin's book *Zoönomia*, but that was more due to the lack of regard the Church had for its Italian translator, Giovanni Rasori, a politician with revolutionary rather than evolutionary inclinations. Of course, that is not to say that the Catholic Church was particularly liberal in its attitude to evolution during this period, and its *Syllabus of Errors* — published in 1864 and regarded by many as an unfortunate error in itself — essentially condemned science without ever mentioning Darwinism specifically by name. Even so, liberal elements in the Catholic Church sought a reconciliation between evolution and religious tradition. 'Christian evolutionism' battled with criticism from conservative elements, notably the Jesuits, throughout much of the next century. But then, in 1996, Pope John Paul II shocked the religious world by declaring in a formal statement sent to the Pontifical Academy of Sciences that 'fresh knowledge leads to recognition of the theory of evolution as more than just a hypothesis'.

In John Paul II it seemed that I had found my man. Infallible. Indefatigable. Dead certain. According to him religion and Darwin could co-exist. Natural Selection was a process but the hand of God was responsible for its operation and, most importantly, for our souls. Could I buy that? Perhaps. But first I determined that I had to see the man.

– 9 –

Rome: Catholic Viewpoints

So I flew to Rome for the weekend. I wasn't quite sure what I would find or how it could advance my search for meaning in a Darwinian world. I just knew that somehow I needed to know more about the context for John Paul II's position.

Arriving at the airport in Rome, I took the fast train into the city centre, armed with my copy of the *Lonely Planet Guide*. This suggested a number of modest hotels where I anticipated finding a pillow with my name on it. Alas, no one had mentioned that this was the Year of the Family — a time when Catholic pilgrims from around the globe descend on Rome to be blessed by Il Papa at Mass. As I wandered from two-star, to three-star and eventually to five-star hotels within walking distance of the Stazione Termini, I quickly learned that to be unhampered by any schedule or plans had its attractions, but getting a night's sleep in Rome was not one of them.

Exhausted, I sat down at a tiny table on the sidewalk in front of an expensive-looking restaurant and ordered a bolognaise and a large beer. I played the last card I had remaining: I called my wife on my cellphone. One advantage of having a wife who is part of a Catholic family is that, like a modern-day version of the Darwins, there are so many of them — and, indeed, my wife had a cousin who was living in Rome. She rang around, dug up cousin Peter's phone number and called me back. Yes, they would be pleased to have me.

I went to the bathroom to freshen up. The Italians have such design flair that even if things don't function as they should, which is often the case, it is impossible not to admire them. The tapware was exquisite and the air-dryers looked so sexy that you felt like hugging them. At least the taps worked, and wiping my hands on my jeans, I headed off to get the Metro.

The next day it rained like hell. Getting the Metro to the Vatican was like riding with a bunch of damp socks. By nearly all standards, the Italians are a beautiful race. It was the Latin look that I was to encounter elsewhere, and as I looked about the carriage, I could not help but be affected by the almost unanimous beauty of the women, at least the young women. And I noted that the men, too, were sexy. It wasn't just their olive skin and black hair, or the way they wore it long, it was the sensual nature of the way they carried themselves.

Darwin puzzled for years about what it is that makes one animal attractive to another. His answer was Sexual Selection, whereby traits that make an animal sexy get fixed in the population because they are more likely to mate and have babies with the same sexy characteristics. In that case, why don't we all look like Latin lovers? By what cruel twist of evolutionary fate am I not like Enrique Iglesias? Surely, if Sexual Selection led to the selection of favoured traits then I should have Jon Bon Jovi's hair, Tom Cruise's smile, Brad Pitt's body and I should be hung like Errol Flynn. But look around you — even on a Metro in Rome — and you will see variation. Was variation the key to understanding Darwin, or was it a point against? I was on my way to see a man who apparently had a direct line to a God that had made us all in His own image. *Is God infinitely variable too?* I thought.

When the Italians tried to put an underground through Rome they kept running into sites of antiquity. As a consequence, they have essentially only two lines, an A and B line, which intersect at the Stazione Termini. To get to the Vatican I had taken the A line train and, after disembarking with seemingly the train's entire manifest of passengers, I marched past brown stone buildings and what looked like a whole fleet of Mr Whippy ice-cream vans.

The street entering the Vatican was blocked off to traffic and I joined the crowds pressing forward over its slippery and cobbled surface. It should have been my first warning of how seriously I had underestimated the will of the faithful on this bleak day. Entering Vatican City I found myself unable to see anything but a throng of bodies sitting under a curved colonnade. People had brought camp chairs, chilly bins and, of course, umbrellas. But there was no festive picnic air about them, there was just the grim expression of the devout as they struggled to catch every word blasted over the loudspeaker system. At this stage I still had no real idea where those words were coming from, so I adopted another tactic. I retreated, and then, ducking low to avoid the spiky corners of umbrellas, I squeezed myself around the flanks of the crowd. Eventually I found myself at the very back of the crowd in St Peter's Square. A lamppost with a concrete base about half a metre high had observers standing on only three of the corners. I clambered up the vacant one.

I was so far from the dais that it was impossible to discern Il Papa with the naked eye. To my surprise, several of those on stage were wearing pointy hats of the type I associated with the Pope. Fortunately there were large screens like those found at pop concerts. And there he was, sitting in a chair, head tilted to one side as he seemed to struggle with the effort to keep it raised even that much.

But there was no doubting the strength of the devotion his audience had for him. I am not much good at estimating crowds. There were as many people there as can be packed into St Peter's Square. If I said one hundred thousand that might do him an injustice. It was as big a meeting of humanity as I had been in. Bigger than the All Blacks versus Australia for the Bledisloe Cup. Bigger than the Rolling Stones.

The Vatican was unexpectedly austere. Looking about at the solid grey and fawn buildings that flanked St Peter's Square it seemed to me more Stalag than Grand Canyon, more oppressive than uplifting. The strength of the buildings served only to emphasise the frail body of Il Papa, which had to be hoisted into the Popemobile at the conclusion of the mass. Then he drove through the crowd, to within eight metres of my perch on the lamppost, the adulation of the crowd — including my own involuntary excitement — left behind him as a cheering wake. If we were a wolf pack, then there was no doubting that he would be our alpha wolf. Part of my own submissiveness in his presence, I was sure, stemmed from my admiration of his absolute certainty. Here was a man who knew the answers to the big questions. He knew why I was here; he knew why we were all here.

The crowd began to disperse. For reasons I could not quite fathom, many in the crowd had used collapsed cardboard boxes to shield themselves from the incessant rain during the mass — perhaps it was the latest in deconstructed rainwear from the Armani winter collection? At any rate, discarded and stomped on, the rain-sodden cardboard left behind on the cobbled stones made St Peter's Square look like one hundred thousand puppies had crapped themselves before their alpha wolf.

I stood in a massive line of umbrellas waiting to get into the Basilica. Nuns and priests queued shoulder to wet shoulder with the devout and the tourist. By the time I entered the great doors I was completely soaked, dripping, more drowned rodent than curious canid.

The inside of the Basilica spoke to me of authority and power. It was dark, foreboding. Whereas cathedrals like the ones I had visited in England, like St Paul's and even Westminster, can be uplifting and joyous in a *Sound of Music* kind of way, this was more *Pulp Fiction*. It seemed to be saying, 'Don't mess with me you mother-fuckers.'

I made my way — carefully — across the ornate inlaid marble floors, past vast ornate confessionals that advertised the language in which one could atone for one's sins, past ornate tombs, past ornate statuary and, in an alcove, I discovered a simple slab of marble engraved with the names of popes interred in the Basilica, starting with Saint Peter (S. Petrvs) and ending with John Paul I (Joannes Pavlvs I) in 1978. As I scanned the list, I noted that the Catholic popes had been about as original as the Darwins when it came to choosing their professional names, with the same ones being used over and over. But for some reason, my eye registered that there were not enough Leos. Looking again, I realised that from Saint Leo IV in 855 there was not another Leo mentioned until Leo VI in 928. What, I wondered, had happened to Leo V? What had happened to the missing pope?

It turns out that there is not much known about poor Leo V. He was pope for a mere thirty days or so in the year 903. He had come from outside Rome, from Priapi, and despite Leo being an apparently good man, Christopher, the Cardinal Priest of St Damasus, led an uprising against him and threw him in prison. Christopher then became pope but is said to have been an anti-pope.

What is that, I thought, *is it like anti-matter, some sort of ecumenical black hole*? While I had not expected to find perfection in Rome, I was beginning to be worried by the signs of such papal flexibility rather than the notion of infallibility. Truth to me need not always be absolute, but it should never be arbitrary.

It turns out that there have been as many as thirty anti-popes in the history of the papacy: those who assumed the role without being duly elected. But Christopher didn't last long as either pope or anti-pope. Sergius III, who had been elected to the papacy in 897 but then excommunicated and driven into exile by Pope John IX, marched on Rome in January 904 and was reinstated. It is possible that Leo and Christopher were left to rot in some prison or monastery, but at least one source says that Sergius had Leo and Christopher strangled. If that seems a somewhat uncharitable way for a man of God to treat his fellow popes, it pales into comparison with the way Pope Formosus was treated by Sergius and others.

Formosus featured seven places ahead of Sergius III on the marble plaque I had found in the Basilica. Despite a troubled relationship with the Church that had seen him excommunicated too in earlier times, Formosus was elected pope in 891 and remained as such until his death in 896. Six months later, the then Pope Stephen VII brought Formosus' decaying corpse to trial for capital crimes, seating the body in a chair as the charges were read. When the ominously-named Cadaver Synod found the dead pope guilty, Stephen had three of Formosus' fingers cut off — the ones he had used for blessing — along with the pontifical vestments in which the body had been interred. Formosus' body was dragged through the streets of Rome before being thrown into the River Tiber. Fifteen months later, Stephen was overthrown in an uprising by the Romans, consigned to a dungeon and then strangled — as good as an example of poetic or should that be papal justice as one might imagine.

If Sergius modelled his treatment of Leo and Christopher on the method of Stephen's dispatch, he also showed some sympathy for Stephen's views. While Formosus' battered body, which had been found washed ashore, was eventually re-interred in the Basilica by Pope Theordore II (who mysteriously died himself after only twenty days in office), Sergius later reaffirmed the decision of the Cadaver Synod. It was left to Pope John XI to finally restore the standing of the unfortunate Formosus. Ironically, John XI was Sergius III's illegitimate son by Marozia, the fifteen-year-old daughter of his friend and the most powerful noble in Rome, Theophylactus. (John XI was only in his early twenties when elected pope and atoning for his father's hatred of Formosus.)

Of course, while the moral grounds for a pope having illegitimate children may have been somewhat shaky even then, that was before the Second Lateran Council under the wonderfully-named Pope Innocent II decreed in 1139 that celibacy was mandatory for priests. Yet even after that, at least six popes are known to have fathered children, starting with Innocent VIII, who was never quite able to live up to the austere dictates of his namesake and sired several children.

As I left St Peter's that day, I passed by heavy metal-studded doors, where grown men in blue, orange and red striped pyjamas held long spears. They were the Swiss Guards, the pope's personal bodyguards for the last five centuries. Ceremonial maybe, but somehow symptomatic of the Church: colourful, splendid, archaic and political with a dangerous, even lethal, potential. This did not seem like the seat of reasoning and compassion that I had come to see. Murders. Infidelities. Anti-popes. Uprisings. Could I really trust the pope to be believable, let alone infallible? As genuine as the man had appeared, as excited as I had been to see him, I wandered back through the streets of Rome wondering if it was reasonable that I should play gamma to his alpha.

Perhaps, like Darwin, I needed to get out and see the world. Get out and see how real wolves lived. Or whales. Or walruses. Or insects. Or orchids. I didn't have a *Beagle* but I could go where the *Beagle* went.

South America

– 10 –

FitzRoy and an Offer
Not to Be Refused

If Cambridge did not put Darwin off a career in the clergy, it at least gave him the opportunity to take his life in another direction. That opportunity came in the form of a proposition, via his walking companion Professor Henslow, to join the *Beagle* as naturalist on a voyage to South America and beyond.

Robert FitzRoy, captain of the *Beagle*, was no ordinary man. A direct descendent of Charles II, by way of the illegitimate son of the king's assignation with one Barbara Villiers, his family name, FitzRoy, actually means 'royal bastard'. But that is the thing about the British aristocracy: better a royal bastard be than a common man. Whereas my grandfather's bastard child and the lives of thousands of commoners were compromised by the unmarried status of their parents, the FitzRoys enjoyed lives of privilege as descendants of a royal bastard christened Henry but given the title of the first Duke of Grafton.

Royal blood and privilege are no guarantees to happiness, however, and the spectre of depression and suicide would haunt Robert FitzRoy all his life. His uncle on his mother's side, the hugely influential Viscount Castlereagh, MP, Minister for War, Foreign Secretary and Leader of the House of Commons, slit his throat with a knife: a method of despatch that FitzRoy would later employ to good effect for his own purposes. After graduating from the Royal Naval College at Portsmouth, FitzRoy ended up being posted to the

South American fleet, where in 1828, the captain of a small coastal ship on surveying duties in Tierra del Fuego — unable to cope with its frightful weather and desolate landscape — had shot himself with a pistol. At the ripe old age of twenty-three, then, Robert FitzRoy found himself promoted to the role of Commander of Her Majesty's sloop *Beagle*.

FitzRoy continued to chart the southern tip of South America before returning to England with three Tierra del Fuego natives in tow, but soon after was asked to go back and continue his mapping. Perhaps it was because of the lessons of his depressed uncle's demise, or the loneliness that could drive the *Beagle's* erstwhile Captain Stokes to blow his brains out — but either way, FitzRoy determined that he needed a companion, a gentleman, to accompany him. Which is where Henslow stepped in. Briefly considering the offer himself, for Henslow was only thirty-five, he offered the post initially to another student, Leonard Jenyns, before eventually recommending Darwin as an agreeable companion first, and competent enough naturalist second.

Darwin's secondment as naturalist aboard HMS *Beagle* suggests something that it was not: gainful employment. In fact, the Admiralty expected Darwin to pay for himself during the expedition, which in effect meant that his father, Dr Robert Darwin, had to foot the bill along with some £600 of expenses to equip his son before the ship even left the docks. To be sure, Darwin's father had been against the trip initially, albeit not because of the cost but because he felt it would be uncomfortable and likely to detract from Darwin's career as a clergyman. On both counts he would be proved right, but he relented after Darwin's uncle, Josiah Wedgwood, made a strong case for his nephew going.

So it was that on 27 December 1831, Charles Darwin set sail from Plymouth aboard the *Beagle* on a journey that would change not just him but every one of us too: he would do nothing less than change our understanding of the world.

– 11 –

Departures for the Americas

Darwin's departure from Plymouth had been delayed for nearly two months: first, by renovations and fittings to the *Beagle* that the fastidious FitzRoy insisted upon, and second, by the appalling weather. In the end, though, it would be the turbulence caused by Christmas celebrations, rather than a bit of wind or rain, that dogged Darwin's departure. The crew of the *Beagle* got so drunk that they were unable to set sail on Boxing Day and FitzRoy was forced to put some of the men in irons and flog four others, including thirty-one lashes given to my namesake, Elias Davis, for neglect of duty.

When under way eventually, Darwin and the *Beagle* headed directly to South America, stopping only at the Cape Verde Islands and briefly at a small archipelago called St Paul's Rocks, before making landfall in north-eastern Brazil at Bahia (Salvador as it is known now) sixty-three days after leaving England. In contrast, I needed to take a more circuitous route: my plan involved flying to the United States with my family before joining friend and fellow penguin researcher, Professor Dee Boersma, on a research expedition to Argentina.

Sitting next to my son on the Qantas flight to LA, while he made liberal use of every sick bag I was able to retrieve, hastily, from the seat pockets in front of us, I was reminded of the nightmarish journey Darwin had undergone from England to Brazil. He spent much of it being sick, either lying in his hammock or on FitzRoy's sofa. In fact, throughout the entire expedition of nearly five years, Darwin would look in vain for his sea-legs, as sick on the final stretch as he had been during those dreadful moments encountered soon after leaving Plymouth and entering the Bay of Biscay. 'I hate every wave of the ocean,' he wrote. Forevermore he would protest that he loathed and abhorred the sea and all ships that sailed on it. I can relate to that.

Like Darwin, I suffer from extreme seasickness, so I know what he must have been going through — or rather, what must have been going through him. I can get motion sickness on a skateboard let alone the Atlantic. Once, en route to a Subantarctic island, I spent three-and-a-half days strapped to the bunk of a small yacht, convinced at first that I was going to die, and then, concerned that I was not. I can be pretty sure that at a certain point the will to live would have deserted Darwin completely and it would have been only his inability to move that would have stopped him from seeking the Captain Stokes solution. Yet, if a goal is worth pursuing, the mind can put up with a lot. Although FitzRoy fully expected Darwin to part company at the first landfall, Charles Darwin, naturalist, even lying in his hammock with the shrieks of men being flogged echoing in his head and sickening him nearly as much as the movement of the sea, determined that he would not do so.

– 12 –

Disneyland and 'It's a Small World After All'

Coming into Los Angeles, the thing that strikes you most is not the need for a breeze to blow away the ever-present smog — yes, it really does hang above the city like a dirty halo — but how brown, how barren, how treeless it all is. Miles upon miles of square blocks with brown buildings and multi-level freeways. There may be dirtier cities around, but there can surely be none uglier than LA — at least from the air. It's like a giant cow pattie over which cars swarm like flies.

My children had insisted that I only got to go to South America if they got to go to Disneyland. It had seemed like a fair trade at the time. Besides, I told myself, it reduced any risk of getting thirty-one lashes for neglect of duty from my wife.

There was little in Darwin's background before he set foot on the *Beagle* to suggest that he was destined for greatness any more than for Disneyland. Friends at school remembered him as retiring and not especially academic. Henslow recommended him for the trip mostly because his breeding made him a suitable companion for the aristocratic FitzRoy, and even then it was only after first suggesting Leonard Jenyns, a graduate of Cambridge, and well-respected as a natural historian and entomologist. After a day spent considering the offer, Jenyns had turned it down on the grounds that he had just been appointed as curate to a parish at Bottisham and he felt disinclined to disappoint his new congregation. The mantle was passed to Darwin, whose chief strength at the time was that he was an avid collector — especially of beetles: an activity at which he both excelled and was, privately, quite competitive. He once confided to his cousin, William Fox, of one particular specimen that he was 'glad of it if it is merely to spite Mr Jenyns'. Competitive beetle collecting is not exactly tennis, but if it were, it seems that Darwin would have been the equivalent of a Wimbledon Champion.

Turn anybody out into a new environment and the ones that will find the gems are the collectors — and in this regard Darwin was not just well-qualified, he was one of the best. So it was that on the journey to South America, between bouts of seasickness and when conditions would allow, Darwin set about collecting. He trailed nets behind the *Beagle,* and to the amusement of the sailors, hauled in their contents and started dissecting, preserving and describing them. It was the beginnings of amassing a large collection, effectively a database of knowledge, of the animals and plants from areas of the globe that were hitherto largely unknown.

If an alien spaceship landed on Earth with some sort of Alpha Centaurian version of Darwin on board, if he were any good he would start making collections: of plants, of animals, even of us. As he dissected those of us unfortunate enough to be caught in his traps, he would notice variety in our stomach contents — from Big Macs to coquilles St Jacques — but otherwise our insides would all look pretty much the same: the same bones, the same muscles, the same blood vessels. On the outside however, he would note that we look very different. The colour of our skin, the colour of our hair. Our size. Our facial features. Darwin might have been happy with a couple of agoutis — why collect more, they all look the same — but an alien collecting humans, surely he would not stop at one or two; surely he would have to continue collecting until he could hold no more. And how would he classify us?

Those thoughts haunted me as I strode with my family through the gates of Disneyland and we were welcomed into the 'Magic Kingdom', for it struck me that if an alien wanted to make a collection of humans then the best place to set the trap would be at Disneyland. Streaming through those gates was as broad a cross-section of humanity as you could ever hope to see — all attracted to the home of a mouse and duck like moths to a lamp.

There is something about Disneyland that is quite surreal: everyone but everyone seems happy. Their girlfriend may have just left them, their parents may have had a fight, the dog may have died — it doesn't matter — put them in Disneyland and their cares disappear. It is hard to fathom why. The entrance price is not exactly cheap; you pay an exorbitant amount to stand in line for upwards of sixty minutes just to enjoy a ride of one minute, sometimes less. Of course, not all rides have such long queues, and maybe, that is the attraction of *It's a Small World*, which might just explain why we made a beeline for it. Personally, I blame my daughter.

I should have guessed from the hideous topiary or the chaotic pastel façade with its big happy face that this was not a place for someone who likes a bit of Dire with his Straits. I should have twigged when the boats came so slowly into view that this was not a one-minute ride: it was destined to seem like the rest of my life. But nothing, nothing at all, could have prepared me for the excruciating pain that surrounds you the moment your boat bumps through those doors: over three hundred animatronic dolls all singing in unison 'It's a Small World After All'.

In concept the exhibit is okay. Initially built by Disney for the 1964–65 New York World Fair and then transferred to the theme park in Anaheim afterwards, the ride purports to take you to different areas of the globe where dolls in their national dress sing the title song in a range of appropriate languages. I don't doubt that Darwin would have loved it — and not just because here at last was a boat he could ride on without feeling seasick, but because it was so darned egalitarian.

The Darwins and the Wedgwoods were very much out of step with many of their contemporaries in their humanitarian beliefs and their abhorrence of slavery. Both Darwin's grandfathers,

Erasmus Darwin and Josiah Wedgwood, were at the forefront of the abolitionist movement in the late eighteenth century. Wedgwood's factories even produced a blue and white cameo depicting a slave with the slogan, 'Am I not a man and a brother?' Slave trading had only been outlawed in Britain and its colonies about the time Darwin was born and it took until Darwin left on the *Beagle* to have slaves freed throughout the British dominions. Yet when Darwin got to South America he found slavery very much alive and legal.

1832 was a leap year and it was 29 February when the *Beagle* arrived in South America, landing at Bahia, Brazil. But if it were love that Darwin felt for the lushness of the tropics he found there, it was something else again for his first encounter with slavery. The Portuguese still allowed the transport of slaves from Africa to Brazil. By 4 April, the *Beagle* sailed into Rio de Janeiro and Darwin went ashore for three months, setting up house in a small cottage with the painter Augustus Earle, leaving FitzRoy to sail up and down the Brazilian coast to map it. No sooner had he landed than Darwin accepted an invitation to visit a plantation some one hundred and sixty kilometres from Rio. There he witnessed

> [...] one of those atrocious acts which can only take place in a slave country. Owing to a quarrel and a lawsuit, the owner was on the point of taking all the women and children from the male slaves, and selling them separately at the public auction at Rio.

Darwin was perhaps most moved by the cowering reaction of a negro whom he described as 'uncommonly stupid' and to whom Darwin raised his voice and gesticulated to make a point:

> I shall never forget my feelings of surprise, disgust, and shame, at seeing a great powerful man afraid even to ward off a blow, directed, as he thought, at his face. This man had been trained to a degradation lower than the slavery of the most helpless animal.

Darwin's appalled response to the treatment of slaves in Brazil led to a confrontation with FitzRoy who, while not condoning slavery perhaps, was less inclined than Darwin to condemn it. Darwin wore the humanitarian heart he had inherited on his sleeve. But it would be wrong to conclude that he was an egalitarian in all respects. All men may have had equal rights in his eyes, but they were not all equal. And, in that way, I suppose that his personal beliefs were nothing less than consistent with his scientific ones. Even so, philosophically he would have been comfortable with the Disneyland ride: unlike some of his contemporaries. Although Darwin was as capable of looking down on the next man as the next man, he never regarded even those he held in lowest regard as anything less than human: as anything less than members of his own species. Had he been from Alpha Centauri, he would have classified us all as *Homo sapiens.*

For some reason my daughter wanted to go around the ride three times: that's nearly a thousand freakin' dolls singing the lamest and most contagious song on the planet. The song burrows into your head and will never go away. It's the musical equivalent of a tapeworm. As I go to my grave, the last thing I will hear is a little voice inside me singing the refrain, 'It's a small, small world.' The exhibit was sponsored by Mattel, the makers of Barbie, and, honestly, by the end of the third lap I was ready to take anyone that worked for Mattel outside and shoot them. Heck, I was ready to shoot myself.

I couldn't get out of Disneyland fast enough. If I could have taken the Space Mountain roller coaster directly to Seattle and Dee I would have. All I wanted to do was jump on a plane and go to South America. I wanted to catch up with the *Beagle.* I wanted to catch up with Darwin. Sometimes the world is not small enough after all.

– 13 –

Diversions from New Zealand

'I just can't believe how smoothly it's all gone,' said Dee as we carried our bags into Seattle/Tacoma Airport.

A moment later we were standing at the business class desk where Dee intended to use a couple of upgrade certificates to get us moved out of 'sardine class' as she called it. The prospect of champagne and being pampered loomed large.

The girl behind the desk began to flick agitatingly through my passport. I was about to point out to her that she should get glasses as she'd already gone past my American visa when she said, 'I can't seem to find your visa for Argentina.'

The blood drained from my arteries.

'I don't need a visa for Argentina,' I said, 'my travel agent told me I didn't need one.' Even as I said the words, they seemed as weak and pathetic as the probability of his being correct. The first rule for travel of any kind should be: get yourself a good travel agent. Mine, I regret to say, is a cretin. Had he lived fifty thousand years ago, he would have given Neanderthals a bad name. That being said, I like my travel agent immensely. In part, I must admit, because he has a corporate box at Carisbrook Stadium and there is nothing quite like the thrill of watching Brian Lara being bowled by a member of the New Zealand cricket team, or the Springboks being given a good hiding by the All Blacks, to wash away the disquiet you once felt about finding yourself on an aircraft bound for San Diego rather than Santiago.

'Well our computer is updated daily and it says that if you are travelling on a New Zealand passport, you do. If I let you go on, you will be deported when you arrive in Buenos Aires and I will be fined three times the cost of your airfare.'

It was all I could do to hold back the pressure of the blood, which had seemingly pooled in my nether regions.

'What if I were on a British passport?' I asked desperately, knowing that I held dual citizenship.

She checked her computer and said, 'Citizens of the United Kingdom do not require visas...'

It just didn't make sense to me. I had stood in the Argentine cemetery at Goose Green in the Falkland Islands where scores, perhaps hundreds, of simple white crosses sat atop a bleak hill with nothing but the wind to accompany them. Many had just the inscription, 'Known only to God'. Whatever the rights or wrongs of the war, they had been ill-prepared Argentine boys and men hacked down by British soldiers. It was 1994 when I was there, more than ten years after the Falklands War, but a mere nine months before my visit, the Falkland Islands government had allowed the first and only plane load of Argentine relatives to visit the graves to mourn their dead. The crosses still bore the few remnants of that visit that the wind had not blown away — plastic flowers, rosary beads, the odd picture or note. I had been particularly moved by one cross to an unknown soldier around which had been placed two strings of rosary beads — one brown, one white — each with a small plastic cross. As the wind blew, the crosses tinkled together. It was the only sound you could hear above the wind: no birds, no insects. Just desolate.

'... I can let you on if you have a UK passport,' she finished up.

I reached into my bum bag where I kept my UK passport and then my fingers froze. I remembered that I had taken it out when packing for Argentina, thinking I would not need it.

Oh God. Our tickets had been bought through barely legitimate channels and were non-transferable and non-refundable. But there was nothing else for it, I would need to go to the San Juan Islands, where my family was staying, to get my British passport; I could not be back before morning. Dee would try to change the tickets.

'I'm sorry,' said the United Airlines clerk as we prepared to leave, 'UK citizens are okay without a visa, but not New Zealand ones.'

'Well that makes a lot of sense! Tell me who was it sunk the bloody *Belgrano*?' But my protests were to no avail.

To make matters worse, we missed the shuttlebus and there were no taxis, so we had to take a limo back to Seattle. It would have been cheaper to have bought the Lincoln. A family of five could have survived for a year on the fare.

• • • •

Darwin's time in Rio de Janeiro was made immeasurably easier by the company of Augustus Earle, the painter who had lived in the city for over three years during a previous journey as remarkable for the scope of his wanderings as the quality of his watercolours. It had taken him to such exotic locations as Tristan da Cunha and the colonies of New South Wales and New Zealand — all without the need for a bloody visa I was sure. Earle became Darwin's guide, showing him the exotic sights of Rio, from the ageing palaces to the young women.

Earle definitely had an eye for the ladies. While in New Zealand in 1827, he had lived for nine months with a Māori woman. He wrote a book about his time in New Zealand and a copy of his *A Narrative of a Nine Months' Residence in New Zealand in 1827* was carried on board HMS *Beagle* during Darwin's time on the small ship.

Earle was certainly smitten with New Zealand's young Māori women, waxing lyrical in his *Narrative* about their rounded limbs, beautiful eyes and long silky hair. He was taken, too, with 'the graceful and athletic forms of the men'. He contrasted the Māori with the Aborigines he had seen in the New South Wales area of

Australia, describing the latter as, 'the last link in the great chain of existence which unites man with the monkey'.

There was surely more to that disparaging remark than met the eye. Like Darwin's grandfather and Robert Grant in Edinburgh before him, Earle presumably exposed Darwin to the notion that species were not immutable, not inflexible creations, but things that could evolve, one to the other.

Ill health would later force Earle to leave the *Beagle* in Montevideo and be repatriated back to England, where he would die in 1838, two years after Darwin's own return and some twenty years before those seeds of Darwin's ideas on evolution, watered as the men sat around quenching their thirst in the heat of Rio, would flower.

• • • •

Traffic was very heavy on the I5 and I missed the five p.m. direct ferry from Anacortes to Friday Harbor, which meant waiting for the eight p.m. ferry that stopped everywhere it possibly could.

I had not eaten all day, so I figured I should be able to get something in Anacortes. It may well be the 'gateway to the San Juan Islands', but gastronomically speaking, it is the end of the road. There was one long street with a mess of low buildings and gas stations that, perversely, were all offset to varying degrees from the roadway, increasing the sense of untidiness. The only two places to eat seemed to be a McDonald's and a place selling 'submarines'. I'd never eaten a submarine, but as my stomach was telling me it wanted more than a cholesterol fix, I didn't have many options.

The sub was enormous. It had been cut in half and cleverly wrapped to stop all the food escaping. I was still eating when the ferry docked in Friday Harbor about ten-fifteen p.m.

Housing at Friday Harbor Marine Laboratories is about three kilometres from the township, nestled in woods. It's very beautiful, but also very isolated. My family were living in a trailer at the time, set some way back on the property and surrounded by trees that held deer, otters, racoons, foxes and possibly escapees from mental institutions who'd killed their sons with an axe. Hence, my wife's reaction to having someone knock on the door unexpectedly at ten-thirty p.m. was not one of joyous welcome.

'Who's there?' said a meek voice from behind the wooden door.

'It's me, Lloyd.'

'Lloyd who?'

Jesus. 'Lloyd your bloody husband!'

At least, I reflected, she hadn't said something like, 'Is that you Jack?' and opened the door naked with a red rose clenched between her teeth. I explained what had happened and went to get the brief-case from the closet that contained my British passport.

Taking the passport out, I breathed a sigh of relief and casually said to my wife, 'If only I'd had this with me it would have saved a lot of grief.'

And then, I swear, the passport fell open at the very page where a big oval stamp indicated that it had expired six months earlier.

Following the *Beagle* seemed more and more like an impossible dream.

• • • •

There was no other option for it: it was going to be easier to go to Miami to get a visa for my New Zealand passport than it would be to get my British passport renewed. I rang Dee. The earliest flight we could get on was one via Chicago, leaving Seattle at eleven-thirty p.m. Sunday night. We arrived at O'Hare Airport at three a.m. Seattle time and had two hours before leaving for Miami. Exhausted, Dee and I lay on the floor in front of the gate to our plane on the assumption that if we fell asleep they'd either have to wake us for boarding or walk all over us. There was little chance of sleep with the Airport CNN broadcast nearby. So we listened to frequent repetitions of a very limited supply of news, interspersed with much longer and seemingly limitless advertisements for CNN.

The Argentine Consulate required only that I pay them some money to get the visa issued. Why I couldn't have done that in Buenos Aires was never explained. But at last Dee and I were seated in Business Class in a United Airlines jet on the tarmac of the Miami airport waiting for clearance to take off for Argentina. Perhaps it was a frightfully busy day air traffic control-wise, or maybe it was simply the release from all the stress that chasing Darwin had engendered, but from memory I consumed seven glasses of champagne before the wheels even left the ground.

– 1 4 –

Punta Tombo and Evidence for the Modification of Species

I love South America.

Darwin's initial reaction to arriving in Brazil, a tropical paradise, was one of wonderment and love too.

He was particularly taken with being in the tropics. The sounds of the insects. The extravagance of organic forms. The wildlife. One aspect in particular caught his eye during those first few months spent in Brazil: mimicry. For in the South American jungle he found many instances where insects such as butterflies and moths resembled other insects, or leaves. If this were the work of a Creator, what sense did that make?

Darwin would dwell on these things before sailing down the Patagonian coast — Dee and I flew. We arrived at Punta Tombo, a wildlife reserve that is primarily known as the breeding ground for penguins. Given the demonstrably derived nature of penguins, it is surprising that Darwin hardly mentions them. He wrote to Professor Henslow about one night, anchored in the Rio Plata estuary near Buenos Aires, when he saw how penguins leaping through the water left long trails of phosphorescence in their wake. In his account of *The Voyage of the Beagle*, he describes them only once: when, at a point farther south on the Patagonian coast than Dee and I were now, one amused him as it tried to get to the water with him in the way. He described their ass-like call and how when they leap out of the water to breathe, 'I defy any one at first sight to be sure that it was not a fish leaping for sport'. But nowhere does he say how remarkable it was that this was a bird which to all intents and purposes had become like a fish again, at least as far as it could. Even in *On the Origin of Species*, he only refers to them once, when remarking that the flipper is an example of a modified bird's wing.

What he does describe, however, is the behaviour of the penguin that wanted to get to the sea when its way was blocked by Darwin: it turned its head from side to side. This is something I noticed too, the first time I encountered the Magellanic Penguins at Punta Tombo, and it is a behaviour peculiar to the banded penguins — the group of four species of penguins found mainly in the tropics and subtropics. The penguins I was familiar with from New Zealand and the Antarctic did not do that. I also saw the Magellanic Penguins engaging in bill duelling, a kind of ritualised dance, more tango than waltz, which includes moves where the two partners click their bills together like swords. Again, it was something that I hadn't seen in other penguins, but had seen in albatross. Could their behaviour hold clues to their evolution?

I did see some of the other animals that captured Darwin's imagination. An armadillo would come to eat from titbits supplied at the accommodation. Like a mini armoured tank, an armadillo is as strange a creature as you could ever hope to see. Guanacos, basically skinny looking llamas, wandered — sometimes alone, sometimes in small herds — through the low bush that carpeted the Punta Tombo reserve. Rheas, too, walked through the same parts, looking for all the world like skinny ostriches or cassowaries. And you had to ask yourself, as Darwin did in *The Origin*, if we didn't have the likes of penguins or rheas, could we have believed that a bird's wing could have other functions, other modifications? For if you accepted that they were modified birds' wings — the flipper of a penguin, the useless bits of fluff beside the rhea's body — then you had to accept that these birds had been derived from ancestors that at one time must have used those wings for flying.

Immersed in such thoughts, I was watching a pair of rheas make their way through the low scrub of the pampas to the south of Punta Tombo, when another creature caught my eye. It was a horse. As it came closer I could make out its rider: a gaucho. Well, to be honest, he was more Clint Eastwood than gaucho. He had the same moustache as the gauchos that Darwin described, the same poncho, the same knife tucked into his belt. But the long hair was cropped short and he wore a cowboy hat that could have come right out of *A Fistful of Dollars*.

· • • ·

Darwin and the *Beagle* did not follow a linear path around the South American coastline. After leaving Montevideo on the Uruguayan side of the Rio de la Plata in August 1832, they headed south to Bahia Blanca, then back up to Montevideo before turning southwards once again, past Punta Tombo and as far as Tierra del Fuego at the bottom of South America. A bit of a side trip out to the Falkland Islands and then it was back up the Argentine coast again to the area of the Rio de la Plata, which is straddled by Buenos Aires on its south-western side and Montevideo on the north-eastern one.

Ironically, Darwin's path was not dissimilar to the one taken by the penguins Dee and I were studying. The research we were doing involved putting little transmitters on the backs of the penguins that could be tracked by satellites when they were in the water. Our results, and those that Dee derived later from the Falkland Islands, showed that Magellanic penguins breeding on the Patagonian coastline and in the Falklands all head to the Rio de la Plata area in winter like waves of Pommie tourists heading for the Spanish beaches of the Costa del Sol.

The Rio de la Plata is really a huge funnel-shaped estuary formed by the confluence of the Uruguay and Paraná Rivers and it is especially rich in sea-life, fed as it is by more than fifty-six million cubic metres of silt and nutrients annually from a river system that drains one-fifth of all the land area in South America. The *Beagle*, like the seabirds, went there for nutrients too: it was a convenient staging post for mapping the Argentine coast and the *Beagle* made several trips taking supplies from Montevideo to points along the Patagonian coast.

Somewhat north of Punta Tombo is the town of El Carmen (Patagones) on the banks of the Rio Negro, which marked, in Darwin's words, 'the most southern position (lat. 41°) on this eastern coast of America inhabited by civilised man'. In August 1833, after a year of to-ing and fro-ing, literally, along the Argentine coast — and nearly twenty months since leaving home — Darwin found himself disembarking at El Carmen with the intention of making an inland journey of some eight hundred kilometres across the pampas to Bahia Blanca and then onto Buenos Aires.

But these were dangerous times. The local Indian tribes had reacted to the incursion of Europeans, civilised or not, by burning the farmhouses and slaughtering the farmers who had moved onto their ancestral lands. Thousands of soldiers under General Juan Manuel de Rosas were effectively at war with the Indians. Nevertheless, for Darwin the demands of geology could not be ignored, 'so that I determined to start at all hazards'.

He took with him a trader, a guide, and five gauchos. They travelled by horse, slept under the stars and ate nothing but meat — and Darwin loved it. He was full of admiration for the gauchos and their flamboyant dress, but wary of them too. They were very polite but with a dangerous edge like that of the knives they carried tucked into their waistbands. He thought, 'whilst making their exceedingly graceful bow, they seem quite ready, if occasion offered, to cut your throat'.

The party arrived at General Rosas' camp near the Rio Colorado, a conglomeration of guns, wagons and straw huts. 'I should think such a villainous, banditti-like army was never before collected together,' was how Darwin described it. And no one was more banditti-like than the ruthless Rosas, who requested a meeting with the young English naturalist.

Rosas dressed like a gaucho, rode like a gaucho but was said to be much more ruthless — especially when he laughed. Darwin had been told stories such as how the General had been known to laugh and then order someone staked out in the sun to become carrion for vultures. So it showed a certain sense of humour on Darwin's own part, that he recorded of his meeting with Rosas, 'My interview passed away without a smile.'

Darwin was actually favourably impressed with Rosas: 'He is a man of an extraordinary character, and has a most predominant influence in the country, which it seems probable he will use to its prosperity and advancement.' This was a view Darwin was later to retract — 'This prophecy has turned out entirely and miserably wrong' — in light of Rosas' maniacal rule once he became dictator of Argentina.

When Darwin eventually got to Bahia Blanca, one night a party of three hundred soldiers sent by Rosas stopped en route to seek retribution for the murder of Rosas' men at an outpost along the route that Darwin intended to take to Buenos Aires.

> It was impossible to conceive anything more wild and savage than the scene of their bivouac. Some drank till they were intoxicated; others swallowed the steaming blood of the cattle slaughtered for their suppers, and then, being sick from drunkenness, they cast it up again, and were besmeared with filth and gore.

If he had been at home and in the twenty-first century, he would probably have thought he had just encountered a group of Manchester United supporters, but then and there in South America, he was taken aback by the savagery of the men and the punishment they meted out to the Indians. The men and women were massacred. The children were sold to slavery. 'Who would believe in this age that such atrocities could be committed in a Christian civilised country?'

Darwin feared that the fate of the Indians was to be exterminated.

I think there will not, in another half-century, be a wild Indian north-ward of the Rio Negro. The warfare is too bloody to last; the Christians killing every Indian, and the Indians doing the same by the Christians. It is melancholy to trace how the Indians have given way before the Spanish invaders.

One day Darwin came across a soldier lighting a fire with a flint that he recognised as an arrowhead — an 'antiquarian relic' as he called it — from the time before the Spanish.

Earlier in the day, when walking out to the actual spit of land that is Punta Tombo, I had stooped to pick up an odd-shaped stone. Pointed and flat, with its edges clearly chipped away to sharpen them, I realised it was an arrowhead. Darwin had been right, but I realised, far too circumspect, for even south of the Rio Negro it did not seem that there was now an Indian in sight, just their antiquarian relics.

It was in this climate of murders and massacres, of deadly gauchos and sadistic soldiers, that Darwin, when riding near Bahia Blanca with a companion, spied three suspicious looking riders in the distance. His companion ordered him to load his pistols and they took evasive action, finding refuge behind a hillock. To their eventual amusement — and relief — the riders turned out to be women from General Rosas' camp, out collecting rhea eggs.

The rider that approached me now seemed completely uninter-ested in the rheas. He was polite. He may even have bowed. Pleas-ingly, he did not dismount and his knife stayed in his belt. As I went back to the accommodation hut to pack for our departure from Punto Tombo, I congratulated myself on having, like Darwin, a benign encounter with the 'banditti-like' characters that roamed the pampas — but I did so too soon.

• • • •

We left Punta Tombo in the early hours, when the sky was still dark and filled with so many stars that it was a statistical impossibility that there could not be a planet out there with intelligent life — at least one with enough intelligence not to get up at five in the morning. The road between Punta Tombo and Trelew is about one hundred kilometres long and filled with such emptiness that it was no less scenic for travelling in the dark. The ground is basically stony with a smattering of low, thorny bushes. Stocking rates, it seemed, could not possibly exceed about one sheep per ten thousand hectares and for that reason the ranches or estancias were the size of small European countries.

Suddenly, unexpectedly, here in the middle of nowhere there was a vehicle some way from the road with a huge searchlight. A small Indian — probably Bolivian, someone remarked — ran out onto the road waving his arms frantically, his instructions obviously to stop us. Fredrico, our driver, stopped as directed, but I noticed that he kept the engine running, the truck in gear, and his right foot hovering over the accelerator.

Out of the gloom came a dentist's nightmare. A large man, who looked like he had last shaved about three days ago with something no sharper than a brick, swaggered up to the driver's side window. The teeth he had left were pus-yellow and twisted. He didn't so much speak as spit words through them. If he'd thrown up cow's blood, I wouldn't have been surprised.

'What the hell are you doing here?!' he demanded in Spanish that Fredrico was to tell me later came not from the region. I couldn't understand the words, but I didn't need to: their meaning was clear.

'We're from the penguin reserve,' replied Fredrico submissively, the tension obvious in his voice.

The large man threw back his head to digest this and there was a long pause while he seemed to be contemplating whether it was going to be most convenient to shoot us now or later.

'Okay,' he said eventually, 'I'm the owner of this estancia.'

It was just too absurd. Here we were in pitch black, halfway to nowhere, surrounded now by four men who undoubtedly had guns (and there were at least two other men by their vehicle), whose only reason to be here could be at best to rustle sheep and at worst to bury a body, and we were supposed to believe that this molar-deficient individual, whose dental hygiene was matched only by the state of his clothes, owned more land than the King of Luxembourg. Besides, we knew the real owners of the estancia. To agree with him seemed tantamount to mocking him, but to voice disagreement seemed only to invite our quick execution.

So Fredrico merely nodded, 'Sí,' and we sped off.

By the time we reached Trelew, the sun had risen, it was a glorious day and it felt especially good to be alive. Dee continued on to the port town of Puerto Madryn where, among other things, she reported the 'strangers in the night'.

The rest of us were left with a few hours to kill, as it were, in Trelew. It is a strange place. Founded by Welsh colonialists, some people in Trelew still speak Welsh (Trelew literally comes from the Welsh for 'Lewis's House'). It is a decidedly seedy city with a shopping area that might be barely adequate for a town of five thousand, but which is pitiful for a city of one hundred thousand. The diminutive and rundown state of the commercial district spoke volumes about the prosperity of this area, and the hordes of hovels — shabby houses no bigger than an outhouse — echoed this.

The one bright spot is the central square with its park. A statue of José San Martin, the liberator of Argentina, and large leafy trees provide some respite from the noise and exhaust fumes of vehicles that have never seen a tune-up. Alongside the park is the one modern shop in all of Trelew — a café called Sugar — to which we repaired eagerly.

A peculiar thing I have noticed about South Americans is that they seem to thumb their noses at all the health warnings coming out of the West: they smoke like trains, drink like fish and regard sugar as the foundation of a good diet. Dulce de leche, a sort of very sweet caramelised condensed milk, is eaten with everything. I suspect that some of them even wash with it.

To call a restaurant Sugar in the health-conscious areas where I come from would be tantamount to filing for bankruptcy: you might as well call it Coronary By-Pass Café or Adipose Heaven. But when we went in, Sugar was packed. Most tables were full of gorgeous young girls smoking and giggling. We took the only remaining booth. On a serviette in the centre of the table someone had crudely scrawled, 'Trolos'. It is local slang for 'Poofters'.

We ordered cappuccinos, which, though none of us had requested it, came sweetened with enough sugar to form a thousand cavities. As I sipped my way through the sweet froth, I couldn't help but contemplate the incredible beauty that surrounded us.

Three, and sometimes as many as five, young girls sat around each table. They all looked the same to me: that is to say, perfect. They were slim and tall with their long dark hair pulled back in ponytails. Their complexions were clear and apricot in colour. Their trousers were so tight you'd swear that they must have been painted on. They couldn't have been much more than sixteen.

At one table I noticed there was a boy squeezed into a booth with five of these nubile beauties. He had impossibly thick hair tied in a long ponytail. His features were exquisitely hewn, as if he'd been made by Michelangelo. In fact, were it not for his sideburns and his jeans being way too baggy, he could easily have passed as one of his female companions.

At a certain point, he stood up and kissed each girl at his table in turn. He then moved across to the table next to us and kissed all the girls there. He didn't so much kiss them as present himself, head thrust forward like a peacock in full train, and the girls stood up and one-by-one anointed his cheeks with kisses of such gentleness and affection that he could have been a god.

Darwin himself noted that in some species of animals certain individual males did extremely well when it came to getting the attention of the females. The male elephant seals that commandeered parts of the beaches up and down the Patagonian coast enjoyed conjugal pleasures that the vast majority of the lesser big-nosed male seals could only dream about. Although Darwin could not have known the stats then — that five per cent of the males get to do ninety-five per cent of the mating — he could see with his own eyes that the spoils of love, just like those of war, were not evenly distributed. Thus, it occurred to him, there must be extreme competition amongst males to get access to the females and, if one male is getting 'a whole lotta love', as Led Zeppelin may have put it had they written *On the Origin of Species*, it means that a whole lotta males must be missing out. And this is where Darwin's genius kicked in, because he recognised that this would create strong selection for those characteristics of males that either allowed them to out-compete their male brethren or made them more attractive to the opposite sex. The Michelangelo Effect I might have been tempted to call it, had I been sitting in Sugar and writing *On the Origin of Species* myself that day.

It occurred to me then, that despite the apparent poverty of the city, that to be a sixteen-year-old halfway good-looking male in Trelew must be as close to Heaven as you can get. But I tell you, to be on the wrong side of forty, unable to even glimpse the halfway line, and to be sitting in Sugar at a table reserved for 'poofters' was an unbearable Hell. So we left.

• • • •

If I could find the willpower to drag myself away from the sweet young things in Sugar, it proved much harder to do the same for Argentina. Not only was Argentina populated seemingly by women who all resembled super-models, it had a character in its desolate open spaces and hardened animals that seduced me even more assuredly. I was as smitten with South America as Darwin had been and so the leaving was never going to be easy.

Aerolineas Argentinas has most of the trappings of an international airline — that is to say, they can lose your bags as well as the best of them. Consequently, when we boarded our aircraft for the two-hour flight from Trelew to Buenos Aires, they neglected to give us any of the necessary documentation we would need subsequently to retrieve our bags at the other end.

On the other hand, the flight attendants were Elle Macpherson and Claudia Schiffer, which did much to assuage my indifference to what Aerolineas Argentinas considers an in-flight meal: a packet of Ritz crackers and a glass of wine so cheap that it had the hour at which it was bottled on the label. But, to be honest, Elle and Claudia could have served me sheep shit and dog urine and I would still have said, 'Gracias.'

– 15 –

Argentina's Fossils and Evidence for the Modification of Species

I determined that for safety reasons — mine if no one else's — I should only return to South America with my wife. Yet even she was taken aback by the beauty of the females the first time we touched down at Buenos Aires airport when, eventually, we returned. As my wife noted, the young woman serving behind the duty-free counter would be a shoo-in for Miss New Zealand — even on a bad hair day — such was her poise and exquisite beauty. Where my wife and I disagreed was on the number of times I needed to return to purchase duty-free items: and while the pisco has long gone, it is true that our cupboards are full of jars of dulche de leche that never have been, and probably never will be, opened.

But lest I be accused of being a dulche de lecherer: remember that Darwin too was enamoured with Buenos Aires and its feminine charms. As he wrote, 'Our chief amusement was riding about and admiring the Spanish ladies. After watching one of these angels gliding down the streets, involuntarily we groaned...' I couldn't have put it better myself. You don't get to father ten children, I suppose, unless there is a wee bit of bull male elephant seal in you, and Darwin once likened his own nose to being the size of a fist. In fact, FitzRoy nearly did not take Darwin with him because he did not like the shape of Darwin's nose upon their first meeting: seemingly trivial perhaps, but inasmuch as it nearly meant no voyage in the *Beagle* for Darwin, his elephant seal-like proboscis almost meant no

On the Origin of the Species either. FitzRoy, himself, would marry twice and have five children; his second marriage, like Darwin's marriage, to a very close cousin (she was related to him on both her mother's and father's side). Compared to the morality of such incest, then, a few jars of unwanted caramelised milk hardly seemed worth getting exercised about.

I wanted to return to Trelew. My motivations I told myself were pure. For, after leaving city life behind, Darwin had found himself down on the start of the Patagonian coast at a place called Punta Alta where he unearthed a great deal of large fossil bones, the discovery of which was to prove instrumental in shaping his thoughts. In Trelew, a museum that was a repository for the types of skeletons that Darwin dug up had recently been opened. I wanted to be able to see what Darwin saw, without literally doing the dirty work.

Our flight arrived into Trelew late at night. A woman from Avis was there to meet us and after making me sign an inordinate number of papers, she handed over the keys to a small but remarkably well-tuned car. Had she not been so kind as to drive ahead of us through the dark to downtown Trelew, we would have made Darwin's five-year circumnavigation of the globe seem like a Sunday afternoon outing: there was every chance we would have been lost for decades, our tail lights last being seen disappearing across the Patagonian pampas.

We booked into the Touring Club — a hotel of decayed grandeur with the musty air of a place that had shut its doors seventy years ago with all the clients and workers locked inside, and who had gone on ageing together with the furniture and bottles behind the bar. An ancient bus boy showed us up a spiral marble staircase to a room that had last received a paint job in another geologic age. In the expansive bar an ancient waiter served us a meal where the bread would surely have been stale even seventy years ago. I loved it! The Touring Club is in its own way a living museum where every table and chair is a preserved artefact, and its customers and custodians living fossils.

Trelew, however, had changed. It seemed that many of the hovels, so evident on my last visit, had gone, bulldozed into oblivion. I didn't want to appear too anxious, but it wasn't long before we found ourselves down at Sugar; at least *it* was still there beside Independence Square. To my relief, there were the same semi-circular booths, the same sweet fare: cakes dripping dulche de leche and the like. But it was nine-thirty p.m. and all the schoolgirls were gone, replaced by very ordinary families and swarthy men discussing business over a dish of pasta.

We made our way to an ice-cream parlour just around the corner from the Touring Club. Ice-cream parlours have become the Argentine equivalent of McDonald's. It was eleven p.m. and this one was packed. Three motorcycles out front were in constant use making deliveries. In Trelew, if one gets the munchies, one doesn't call up for two large pizzas: it's a kilogram of ice-cream — dulche de leche flavoured of course. I couldn't help but notice that the jeans, while just as tight, were stretched noticeably wider than I remembered. Evolution was taking place before my very eyes.

The Museo Paleontológico Egidio Feruglio was just a block or so along from the Touring Club, a smart modern building with the entrance way protected by a mustard-yellow veranda supported by sea-green pillars. While the modern architecture was continued inside, the contents were anything but modern to anyone other than the patrons of the Touring Club. Here evolution really was set out before your eyes. Just past the check-in there was a large circular pillar with a picture of Charles Darwin wrapped around it and a long blurb that began, 'Naturalista británico fundador de la Teoría Evolutiva…' I had come to the right place.

In Punta Alta, Darwin, too, had found the right place. The *Beagle* had sailed about six hundred and fifty kilometres south of Montevideo to Bahía Blanca, and going around the low headland of Punta Alta in September of 1832, FitzRoy asked Darwin whether the bones they could see sticking out of the gravel at the foot of the reddish cliffs might be fossils. They had hit upon the motherlode:

the death beds of animals from another time, if not another place. Working around the clock, Darwin retrieved bones, many of them of 'great size'. He recognised the bones of *Megatherium*, a giant sloth first found in Argentina about half a century earlier. But there were others that he did not recognise and which would be formally described only with the help of the infamous Richard Owen — a man destined to become one of Darwin's staunchest critics — after the *Beagle* had finished its reconnoitring of the globe. There was *Scelidotherium*, a giant armadillo, and *Macrauchenia*, a giant guanaco that stood as big as a camel. There were bones from another huge sloth, *Glyptodon*, and *Toxodon*, an enormous version of the capybara.

It was not that these were extinct fossils that captured Darwin's imagination, nor even their immense size. More than anything it was that given both those features, these fossils should all be so clearly similar to existing animals — albeit smaller — that still roamed the South American landscape. If the Great Flood had come, as the devout FitzRoy insisted, and these fossilised animals had been simply too big or too slow to get aboard Noah's Ark: that might explain their being extinct, but it couldn't explain why there should be modern forms of those same animals still around. Could it be that the large extinct forms had begat the small modern ones?

In the Museo Paleontológico Egidio Feruglio there were also the fossilised bones from the surrounding area that Darwin did not discover. There was *Amargasaurus* a (five-tonne, ten-metre-long) plant-eating dinosaur in the same family as *Diplodocus*, which lived over one hundred and twenty-five million years ago in Argentina but which had to wait until 1991 to get a name. There was the much larger *Epachthosaurus*, at up to a whopping twenty metres long; while somewhat more recent, living ninety-five million years ago, it was first described only one year earlier than *Amargasaurus*. In contrast to the two huge plant-eaters, there was the skeleton of the smaller, meat-eating *Carnotaurus*: at only seven and a half meters long and weighing in at one tonne, it was a ferocious-looking beast that must have scared the living hell out of the likes of *Epachthosaurus* — which lived at the same time — despite the differences in body size. The one skeleton of *Carnotaurus* ever found, albeit remarkably complete, was discovered near Trelew, becoming known to science only in 1985. There is a reconstruction of a much older meat-eater with a name designed to foil even the most rabid of dinosaur-loving children, *Pianitzkysaurus*, which is known to have lived in Argentina over one hundred and sixty million years ago from fossil fragments described in 1979. What, oh what, would Darwin have made of these?

Actually, I think he may have been more taken by a couple of non-dinosaurs. There was *Achlysictis*, a ferocious marsupial with more in common with Thylacines (or Tasmanian tigers) than the present-day South American animals. And, most impressively, there was the skeleton of a remarkable flightless bird, a Fororraco: about two metres high, thick-set and with a skull that resembled nothing so much as the pincers of a crane used to crush cars. This bird could have delivered one serious bite, just as capable of crushing a Ford, it would seem, as any animal unfortunate enough to get in its way. But in these two specimens there were vital clues.

New Zealand had the moa, some specimens of which were taller than Fororracos, but none with anything like its head. Yet, the conditions under which a big bird like the moa could afford to be flightless, and therefore potentially vulnerable to predators, were supposedly those conditions that characterised New Zealand: it was isolated and free of mammalian predators. Could it be that South America was at one time nothing more than a huge isolated island, free from the mammalian predators that were evolving in North America? And if large landmasses could, over geologic time, lose their connections with other landmasses in that fashion, could they also gain connections? Might South America at one time have been connected to Australia, thereby accounting for the presence of similar marsupials on two continents that are so isolated now?

Indeed, just based on the large fossils he unearthed from around

Punta Alta, Darwin guessed that at one time the Panama isthmus, that thin strip of land that joins North and South America, must have at one time been under water. That way, he reasoned, the large sloths, guanacos, armadillos and capybaras could have existed happily until a land bridge allowed predators from the north to invade and wipe them out. It was audacious reasoning by FitzRoy's standards. These fossils were not the victims of some biblical flood, Darwin reasoned, but of the slow changes wrought by a changing Earth, a changing geology. But even had Darwin found a fossil *Achlysictis*, it is doubtful he would have come to the right conclusions. It is one thing to suppose the level of the seas could go up and down, but quite another to suggest that continents could drift about on the crust of the Earth like bumper boats at Disneyland, at times banging into each other and forming land bridges, at others opening up and forming great seas. Even I cannot grasp it in these modern times: just as with the concept of infinity, though I'm told it's true, that doesn't make it any easier to get my head around it.

The best I could do was to put my lips around a cappuccino in the smart café of the museum before we headed off in our tiny car for the Peninsula Valdes. The big animals may have gone from the land, but there were some left that had found refuge in the sea. I wanted to see in the flesh what Darwin had seen in the fossils.

– 16 –

From Feet to Flippers
at Peninsula Valdes

The drive to Puerto Madryn was straight forward, literally, as the flat boring pampas afforded no real reason for steering corrections. I settled down somewhere near the speed limit and let my mind wander.

The armadillo I had seen at Punta Tombo with Dee had been a delightfully small creature, no bigger than a small cat. The guanacos that wandered through the bushes of the penguin colony stood no higher than small ponies and were thin like the newborn foals of a race horse. What should I think of an armadillo-like creature 'as large as a rhinoceros' according to Darwin, or a guanaco built like a camel? I knew, too, that there had been fossil penguins found that stand as tall as a man, certainly taller than my wife: but could I presume that they had necessarily given rise to the knee-high little jobs that now called Punta Tombo their home? Perhaps big and slow were just recipes for failure. The dinosaurs, the big flightless birds like moas, fororracos and human-sized penguins, the elephantine guanacos, sloths, capybaras and armadillos: maybe they were just life's failures? That they once lived was indisputable; that they evolved into the smaller, faster forms that abound today seemed much too big a jump to make without other evidence.

Peninsula Valdes is famous for one thing: its wildlife. And, with David Attenborough's help, it has become especially famous for the beaches on the northern tip where killer whales have learnt — and continue to teach the skill to new generations — to drive themselves up the pebbly beach and grab sea lions. While that would have been intriguing to see, it was more an example of cultural evolution (like the monkeys in Japan that have learnt to wash potatoes in hot pools and pass this tradition onto their progeny). It wasn't hard-wired, and therefore, not something that really had much bearing on actual evolution, the change of one form of animal into another. Like my wife teaching me to cook, it might make me a better person, but it didn't change the beast underneath — as she would be the first to admit. Although it was the wrong time of year to see the killer whales, it was the right time to see what we had really come to see: right whales. Southern right whales to be specific. They come into the calm waters of Golfo Nuevo around the peninsula to calve.

We stopped at Puerto Madryn for lunch, a modern bright seaside port town, before detouring onto an unpaved road that hugged the coastline on the peninsula proper. To say the road was corrugated is to give no real sense of the bone-jarring ride and, when conditions did not improve after a few kilometres, I was ready to turn back. But then we noticed a lighthouse, pulled over, and as we did so, I could see the black tail fluke of a whale being waved tantalisingly close to shore. Further investigation showed a half dozen or so whales, some with calves, were in the bay, the closest a mere twenty metres from the shore (I know this because I could read the focusing distance off my digital camera). We stood on the sandy beach and watched spellbound as these giant creatures — at sixteen metres long, they were more than four times the length of our rental car — blew, and every now and then, slapped a flipper or a tail fluke on the water.

Before investigating the whales more closely, however, we had to keep an assignation with another large sea creature. We headed for the eco-tourism village of Puerto Pirámides, where we found excellent accommodation at the Hosteria Paradise. After the Touring Club it was like undergoing time travel and finding ourselves two centuries into the future. Whereas the Touring Club still lived on the faded glory of its yesteryear, the Hosteria Paradise was modern in a ranch-style kind of way. What it lacked in spiral marble staircases it made up for with its superb seafood fare. As is true of much of the wine from Chile and Argentina: the reds are to die for but the whites are likely to kill you. Nevertheless, we found a passable chardonnay and then made the mistake of ordering the chowder before the main course. Half the contents of the San Diego Seaworld aquarium could be found in the chowder and, by the time we had made even a partial impression upon it, we were full. It was only with a superhuman effort and the lubrication provided by another bottle of the by then 'excellente' chardonnay that we managed to eat even a little of the marvellously fresh fish that formed the supposed main course.

The next morning we set out along the road to Punta Delgado: the surface was muddy and soft, and the car scythed from side to side. For the second time in as many days, I considered turning back. But turning around seemed like it would be as difficult as continuing on, and so, with our hearts in our mouths at times, we used the momentum of the little Chevrolet to carry us through thick pools of mud as deep as the tiny wheels on the car.

With half of Peninsula Valdes caked to the outsides of our car, we eventually pulled into the long driveway that leads up to the lighthouse that marks Punta Delgado. An impressive structure as a lighthouse, it had an even more impressive restaurant associated with it. To be sure it was windy, but it seemed like the whole population of Punta Delgado (about two busloads) was not down on the beaches looking at the elephant seals but up to their elbows in starched linen serviettes. It is a curious thing that we would note at several Argentine tourist spots: they seem to be used more as venues for eating than as opportunities to commune with nature. Buses transport people considerable distances into areas of spectacular beauty only for the customers to pour out of the bus and spend at least three-quarters of their time at the location eating. As a way of dining I suppose it works, but for me, I'd rather commune with the seals. Except, as it turned out, we could not do that there.

I'd made vague, very vague, plans to meet up with a colleague, Claudio Campagna — Argentina's elephant seal expert — at Punta Delagdo.

'If you are ever up there, pop in to see me. You are always welcome.'

'Okay, I will.'

Hardly precise, I know, but I have attempted to go on dates on the strength of much less enthusiastic and precise invitations. And it was not like Claudio had stood me up, it was just that he had used 'Punta Delgado' as the designation for the general area, rather than the landmark it denotes. Fortunately, one of the chefs at the lighthouse knew Claudio and gave us directions for how to get to an estancia several kilometres away.

The road changed from muddy road to muddy track, and with every obstacle we negotiated, I started to get more worried about what we were letting ourselves in for. Was there anything in those myriad papers that Avis had made me sign that said I would be responsible for cleaning? It was impossible to say what damage we had sustained with any of the bumps and chunks the car endured, so caked in mud was it. But, just when it seemed it would be foolhardy to go any farther, a low ranch-style palace with a huge veranda came into view. Knocking on the door I discovered what a place looks like that can cost several thousand dollars a night to stay in: despite the mud, the house was immaculate, every piece of the furnishings decorated in a chic white. Muttering something about seals and keeping a close eye on two large Alsatian dogs that seemed to regard me as foe if not food, I was directed to a small place at the rear.

No Claudio. Jumping back into the car with the dogs barking fiercely at me now, a green four-wheel-drive vehicle appeared with the unmistakable face of Claudio. Claudio is handsome in a Latin kind of way, with his hair kept casually long and swept back, and a smile that could wilt the willpower of a thousand virgins. After a brief period of hugs Claudio insisted we follow him in our car as he set off in his four-wheel-drive down a track that made all that had gone before seem like pavement. I gunned the engine and followed through muddy ford after muddy ford, not with any conviction that we could make it — the Fernando Alonso in me by now replaced by the Frank Spencer in me — but with the knowledge that Claudio could, and almost certainly would have to at some point, tow me out. We headed for the cliffs.

The cliffs around Punta Delgado are typically higher than those Darwin saw a little farther north at Punta Alta, yet they had the same reddish hue and it was possible to make out millions of fossils sticking from them: in this case mainly large oyster-like shells that Claudio said were about ten thousand years old. We picked our way down the cliff face, and at one stage my wife and I inadvertently put our arms into the nest of some 'fire ants' and found ourselves dancing wildly on the sides of the cliff while we frantically removed them from our clothes and each other like two monkeys engaging in speed-grooming. The tide was a long way out, exposing a strip of perhaps one hundred metres or more of rocky tidal pools, but on the twenty-metre-wide swathe of brown pebbly beach at the base of the cliffs lay scores of logs. Except that every now and then some of the logs would move: we were about to enter the breeding domain of the elephant seal.

There were svelte females, some nursing dark pups (svelte is a comparative term in the elephant seal world, but as a full grown male can weigh up to ten times heavier than the female, watching them mate is what I imagine it would be like if Pavorotti ever got together with Kate Moss). The ones that interested me most were the craggy males with their bulbous noses. One in particular reared its head up and then with a deft flick of its right front flipper, tossed sand over itself. Whether to ward off insects or help with thermoregulation did not concern me at the time — it was only later that I remembered seeing similar behaviours in sea lions. What struck me was the instant when the fore flipper, which had looked for all the world like the fin of a fish, had been bent backwards and caught the afternoon light, highlighting the underlying musculature and bone structure with the shadows on the hide: the flipper looked like nothing less than the forelimb of a bear or that of a cow; more elephant than seal, certainly more elephant than fish.

Darwin must have seen something similar too, because when it came time to write *On the Origin of Species*, he reflected on the seal's flipper, believing that the animal that gave rise to seals must have had 'not a flipper but a foot with five toes fitted for walking or grasping'. And suddenly I was in Antarctica being chased by a leopard seal as I danced from ice floe to ice floe, its head and half its body rearing out of the water, first one side of me and then the other.

Bidding Claudio adios, as we drove away we spotted an odd pair of ground-dwelling owls with speckled brown wings, white faces and big yellow eyes. Odd because here was a type of bird that I'd only ever seen before associated with trees. Let's hope that the logging companies in Oregon don't hear that some owls can exist without trees or the Little Spotted Owl is a goner. But the reality is that these owls really can exist without trees. Why? Had some prehistoric logger come and cut down the forest? It reinforced an impression that the elephant and leopard seals had already given me: that, given enough time, animals seemed infinitely adaptable. If you could have a bear that lives like a fish, why not an owl that lives like a rabbit?

There were still more surprises in store for us. Farther up the road we saw a pair of animals that looked like a cross between a sheep and a rabbit. They were in fact large rodents called mara. Not quite as big as a capybara, the largest of all living rodents, they were nevertheless the size of a small to medium size family dog, with a heavy head and legs that seemed much too skinny to support their broad bodies. Their strangest attributes, however, were the white and black horizontal lines they appeared to have painted on their bums. These stood out like road signs in the low evening light that was giving the grasslands a golden hue.

In some ways mara are more like Adelie penguins than other rodents, and I'm not just referring to their black and white underwear. They are monogamous and apparently mate for life — well, until death do them part. The young are born in communal burrows that, in the seabird world, would qualify as a colony, and they form crèches for the first four months of their lives.

On the long deserted drive back to Puerto Pirámides, I saw what I thought was an orange skunk-like creature heading across the pampas. Instinctively I pulled the car over to the shoulder of the road to stop. Big mistake. After affirming that it really was a skunk, I discovered that the shoulder was very soft and that we were very stuck and already it was starting to get very dark. The more I tried to get the car out, the deeper we became mired. Then, for reasons that defied the physics of the situation, in one reversing manoeuvre the car twisted against the joint forces of shingle and gravity and lurched up the bank. In the hour's trip back to the hotel we saw not a single other car going in either direction. We had come within a skunk's breath of spending the night cramped and cold inside the smallest car Avis had in South America — and the dirtiest. Argentine white wine never tasted so good as we had another bottle of the chardonnay with dinner.

• • • •

The beach at Puerto Pirámides is sandy, low and flat: with a greenish coating of some sort of algae below the high tide mark the only thing that would prevent it scoring high as a travel destination in its own right. To the right, the side of the beach is flanked by slabs of low, pitted rock and it is possible to walk out quite a way to where the water nearby is deep enough for shags to fish and, as we discovered, not so shallow that a mother southern right whale would not take her calf. Set into some concrete was a cast of *Titanosaurus* bones like those we had seen back at the Museo Paleontológico Egidio Feruglio in Trelew — a huge dinosaur similar to the *Epachthosaurus* and almost as big. And you couldn't help but draw the comparisons. Here was essentially the gravestone to an eighteen metre long monster that had roamed the Earth, while waving its flipper fluke at us in the waters was an eighteen metre long monster of the sea, alive and well and clearly capable of breeding successfully. Why should one live and the other die? What made the whales the successful dinosaurs of our seas? If the survival of the fittest was anything other than a lottery, what made the whales better? Where was the unseen hand of selection? Why could it not be just God's crap game: you snooze, you lose? Dinosaurs may not have seen the coming of the North American mammalian predators that accompanied the joining of the northern and southern Americas as the sea levels lowered, and that might have made them 'unfit' — or unsuited to the new environmental conditions — but that didn't mean they evolved into anything else. You live. You get unfit. You die. End of story. Or was it?

Most of the whale watching boats operating out of Puerto Pirámides appeared to be large white double-decked catamarans. We opted for a much more expensive but relatively tiny Zodiac that took only a dozen of us: a great decision as it turned out. Using survival techniques developed from too many days being pushed around in rugby scrums, I managed to position myself, my wife and, most importantly, my camera gear at the front of the Zodiac.

Initially we sped out to look at a mother and calf where the mother was almost an albino: a creamy white, spotted with black, so that you suspected her own mother must have been crossed with a Dalmatian: except that this was like having one hundred and one Dalmatians in the same body. She rolled over slowly revealing a huge expanse of oddly textured blanched skin that looked like chocolate-chip ice-cream and I began to wonder whether it got sunburned. This was one female's back I'd rather not rub sunscreen on: it would take you all day.

Apart from the water's level view of the whales, the value of the Zodiac quickly became obvious. Our driver could spot a whale breaching miles away, quickly alter course and speed over to get near it. There are, of course, rules about how close boats can approach the whales and the drivers adhere strictly to them. But these are large-brained curious creatures, used to going where they please, and it was one thing to stop at a distance from the whales, quite another to stop the whales coming to us. A large male, the largest whale we would see all morning, headed towards us and in the clear waters we watched it slide gently under the Zodiac like a slow-moving train, its head visible on one side while its tail region still had to pass underneath. Mesmerised, we stared into the water as its huge tail flukes eased under us and beneath the boat. We were still staring over the side, entranced by what we had just seen, when there was the smallest of splashes and the sky turned black. The huge barnacle-encrusted head of the male whale reared out of the water to within thirty centimetres of my wife's face. It was too close, I was too startled, and it happened too fast for me to take a photograph, but somewhere in my brain a shutter clicked. Forevermore I will have the frozen image of my wife's face caught in that half moment between terror and wonderment.

Darwin certainly saw whales on his voyage. In one particular reference in his journal he comments on seeing them 'jumping upright quite out of the water' near Tierra del Fuego. But I get the impression that Darwin would have been more excited seeing an unusual cockroach, and definitely, a new beetle. By comparison, I have always been into the big stuff — the charismatic megavertebrates — and in that value system, things don't come much bigger than whales. Yet it wasn't just the fascination of a naïve animal lover: in the whales I saw evidence for Darwin's evolution that frankly I had difficulty getting excited about in beetles. Even though Darwin all but ignores whales in *On the Origin of Species*, he makes the point that we should not be seduced by external similarities between a whale and a fish, because these are not characters derived from a common ancestor but the result of analogous changes occurring in very different animals to make them suited to the same environment. He points to the observation that black bears swim for hours with their mouths wide open fishing for insects. Darwin comments that he could imagine 'a race of bears being rendered, by natural selection, more and more aquatic in their structure and habits, with larger and larger mouths, till a creature was produced as monstrous as a whale'.

Whales probably evolved from creatures more like hippos than bears, but that's beside the point. In some ways I look at the same evidence yet judge it differently to Darwin. I see the whale as evidence for evolution precisely because of the analogous changes wrought upon its hippo-like ancestors to turn it back into something that resembled a fish (rather than whales arising, say, from the modification of an eating habit). In the same way that the breeding behaviour of a bird and a rodent can come to resemble each other given certain conditions — and nobody would pretend it is because those behaviours have descended from a common ancestor — the process whereby those changes arise is surely evolution. In this regard whales can be at least as informative as beetles.

Beetles and their kin are no less prone to misinterpretation, either. When I first started my undergraduate degree in zoology, a professor in my department was a leading expert on collembola, tiny primitive wingless insects, from the southern regions of the world. During a prestigious career stretching over decades he had described many new species — often on the basis of differences in the colour and patterning found on their carapaces or shells. About the time I was completing my bachelor's degree one of the professor's own students discovered that the colour and pattern on the shells of these beasts was determined by their diet and not their genes. Way to see a lifetime's work go down the drain. While I do not pretend that anything I discover will necessarily stand the test of time any better, if I am to observe nature, then I'll take whales and penguins and monkeys any day of the week, thank you.

As we drove into Trelew airport and handed over our car to the same Avis lady (who said not a word about the five centimetre coating of mud that had by now set like a concrete carapace over the entire car, as if it were some sort of giant collembola that had dramatically changed its diet), I couldn't help but think that maybe Darwin had missed the point about the whales. It wasn't that we shouldn't be fooled into thinking that they and fish had a close common ancestor; it was rather, that something must have turned a lump of a creature like a hippo into a giant fish-*like* creature, and that sure as hell wasn't what it was eating.

– 17 –

Tierra del Fuego and the 'Bottom' of the World

Tierra del Fuego sits at the very bottom of South America, a large jigsaw piece of an island, separated from the mainland by a thin strip of waterway called the Magellan Straits. It promotes itself — at least in all the tourist literature — as 'the end of the world'. Captain Stokes, FitzRoy's hapless predecessor, and even FitzRoy himself, would no doubt have been more inclined to call it 'the arse-end of the world'. In December 1832, a year after leaving England, the *Beagle*, with its religious but acknowledged masterly captain, found itself, even in midsummer, battling huge seas for a month as it tried to get around the notorious Cape Horn — eventually finding safe harbour in the entrance to the channel in Tierra del Fuego discovered by FitzRoy on his previous expedition and named after the little ship.

Sitting beside the Beagle Channel is Ushuaia, the capital of Tierra del Fuego — at least on the Argentine side. Tierra del Fuego is actually shared between Argentina and Chile. Flying into Ushuaia was definitely easier than the boat journey Darwin had taken to get there. But it did not seem like the end of the world — at least not yet — there was still a horizon and Ushuaia itself is nestled at the base of snow-capped mountains with the white-capped waters of the Beagle Channel clearly visible just beyond its harbour. Far from being 'uncivilised' the airport at Ushuaia was thoroughly modern. The centre of Ushuaia, however, was more reminiscent of a Canadian frontier town: its streets dirty and mushy with snow, even in September, and an approach to town planning that suggested there was little of a plan. Surprisingly, given its isolated location, the main street of Ushuaia, San Martin, consists of little else other than restaurants, banks and internet shops. Ushuaia has become the stepping-stone for cruises to the Antarctic Peninsula.

My wife and I got a ride to our accommodation at the Posada del Fin de Monde. The woman in charge of the place turned out to be a charming nutcase. But our room was more than adequate and you couldn't complain about the breakfasts: lovely little sticky croissants and decent coffee. It's one of the bugbears of being a coffee drinker travelling through South America that in most places it is impossible to get anything other than Nescafé, despite the fact that the world's best coffee beans are grown on the continent.

Throughout my travels in Argentina and Chile, I would try in vain to ask for a bowl of latte: and each time it would be a lottery as to what I did get. Then one day, in a hotel in the Chilean town of Pucón, my wife noticed that the sign in the toilet giving instructions not to dispose of paper down the toilet bowl because of the frightful state of the plumbing, was also translated into English: it was then that she also realised that with my infinitesimally small grasp of Spanish, I had all this time been asking every café and restaurant worker I met for a 'toilet bowl of coffee'. Quite honestly, given some of the stuff I was served up, I suspect that is where they got it from.

FitzRoy, it has to be said, probably did not give a toss what the coffee was like. There was an ulterior motive for such a God-fearing man to be in such a God-forsaken hole: at one stage when he had been mapping the coast of Tierra del Fuego on his previous visit, the native Fuegians had stolen a whaleboat from the *Beagle*. As part of his reaction to this, FitzRoy took eleven of the locals hostage to trade for the return of the boat and to act as interpreters. But while he was out looking for the whaleboat in the *Beagle*'s other whale-boat, all but three children escaped from the *Beagle* by swimming ashore during the night. He subsequently handed over two of the children, but kept the third, a little girl about eight years old or so, whom he intended to educate. The sailors named her Fuegia Basket.

Later, FitzRoy kidnapped a young man they named York Minister after a local landmark previously christened by Captain Cook. On one encounter with those who had taken the whaleboat, he caught up with a fleeing canoe and fished a young man from the water who was given the moniker, Boat Memory. Finally, FitzRoy traded a pearl button for a boy, called thereafter Jemmy Button.

By then all prospects of getting the whaleboat back had vanished, but FitzRoy hatched a new plan to take the native Fuegians back to England and to try to civilise them — to Christianise them, teach them English and then bring them back to do God's work and bring decency to Tierra del Fuego. Boat Memory would die of smallpox in England, but when the *Beagle* eventually set out from Plymouth, Darwin was not the only special passenger on board: there were York Minister, Fuegia Basket and Jemmy Button, by now decked out in the clothes of Londoners and with a smattering of the Queen's English and the Queen's manners. They'd even had an audience with — or rather, been exhibited before — King William and Queen Adelaide, who had given Fuegia Basket a bonnet. While a bonnet may not seem like the most useful piece of equipment to send with someone returning to the arse-end of the earth to set up a mission, it paled into comparison with what was sent by the Church Missionary Society of the Anglican Church, which included, among other things, such useful items as wine glasses, soup tureens, white linen, tea trays and chamber pots.

Darwin was taken aback by the native Fuegians when he encountered them: 'Their appearance was so strange, that it was scarcely like that of earthly inhabitants.' They seemed wild, with matted hair, copper skin and they went completely naked. Now you might argue that to live at nearly 55°S you either had to be a nutcase, like the proprietor of our lodgings, or the conditions would eventually make you into one. But even so, what kind of person goes buck-naked in temperatures that would make castrati out of brass monkeys? I can understand going in the altogether if you evolve in the heat of the African plains — and there has long been a scientific theory that humans evolved to be the 'hairless apes' in just such a climate so that we can dissipate heat more easily. But Tierra del Fuego is practically the Antarctic for Christ's sake: it's the sort of environment that woolly mammoths evolved in. Note: they were not called the 'nude mammoths' or the 'hairless mammoths'. If Natural Selection really was at work, then surely native Fuegians should have been born with the equivalent of half a sheep wrapped around them. And if they didn't have it naturally, surely they should have the wherewithal to knit a jersey or something. But no, they cultivated nothing — let alone sheep — lived in crude skin huts, through which the rain poured, and ate what they could of fish, birds, shellfish and seals.

A woman, completely naked was amongst those in a canoe that came out to the *Beagle*, and she sat there with her equally naked baby in the tossing waves while the sleet alighted on her breasts and melted.

My wife and I took a day-trip up the Beagle Channel in a boat. The wind threw long trails of spume every time the boat hit the crest of a wave. On the rocky shores, seals and shags hunkered down against the cold. And just when you might have thought it couldn't get any worse, as if in testimony to the fortitude of that woman, it started to snow: at first sleeting, then snowing heavily. Even the odd Gentoo penguin brave enough to walk along the beach looked miserable. I couldn't imagine being outside, let alone being outside with a baby — but being outside and naked, well, all I could think was that they must build 'em tough in Tierra del Fuego.

The attempts to set up a mission were a complete failure. York Minister and Fuegia Basket became a couple and reverted to their old ways almost immediately. The young Anglican missionary, Matthews, was run off and had to be taken back on board by

FitzRoy after only a few weeks. Jemmy Button was the only one to show any tenacity, but a year later, when the *Beagle* returned, he was naked but for a loincloth; skinny, and eking out an existence there as his forefathers had done. Darwin would wrestle with the notion of 'savages' when he came to write *The Descent of Man*, but for all their wildness, he never considered the Fuegians anything other than members of our own species.

For me, the most interesting thing about Tierra del Fuego was its proximity to Antarctica and its forests, which looked very much like the beech forests I knew from New Zealand. The forests in Chile are the same: when my wife and I had finally stopped laughing after reading the sign in the hotel toilet in Pucón, we went hiking in the nearby national park through a beech forest that could have been in New Zealand or Australia were it not for the odd woodpecker and monkey-puzzle tree.

The bottom of South America sticks down at exactly the same point that the Antarctic Peninsula sticks up. If the seas around the Panama Isthmus could rise and fall, creating land bridges at times, might not South America have once been joined to Antarctica, providing a route for the trees to get to New Zealand and Australia? It seemed like an obvious point with one obvious flaw: while South America and the Antarctic were suitably close, Australia and New Zealand were frigging miles away, with nothing but the deep blue sea between them. I once sailed to New Zealand in a boat from Antarctica travelling at five knots and the trip took over two-and-half weeks: as well as an incredibly long time to be seasick, it seemed like it'd be way too far to build any bridge: a land bridge or otherwise.

There was another thing that interested me about Tierra del Fuego, and that concerned its penguins — but to find the ones I wanted, I would need to travel to Punta Arenas on the Chilean side of the island.

• • • •

I love Chile and I love driving, but if Chile has one fault it is its drivers. At first, it seems incredible that Chile should never have produced a Formula One World Champion. They all drive like maniacs. To use less than fifth gear around town is to be a sissy and it seems that oncoming trucks or blind corners should never be an impediment to passing the vehicle in front of you. I drove a little, but for the most part we hired taxis. We asked one taxi driver in particular to take us out to a colony of Magellanic penguins breeding at Otway Bay, about sixty kilometres from Punta Arenas. He spoke no English, though we gathered his name was Christian, and the one hope we had that he would not be like all the rest was that he had a brand new car. It proved to be a forlorn hope. Midway through the journey over dirt and shingle tracks, Christian turned to me (I was sitting braced with both hands clutching the dashboard), pointed to himself, then raised a finger in the air and said 'Uno rally'. I was unsure whether he meant that he was the number one rally driver in all of Punta Arenas or that this was his first rally. When he hit the next raised cattle-gate at one hundred and forty kilometres per hour and we veered off wildly in a spray of stones to the sound of the muffler parting company with the car, I had my answer. It did not help my composure that every few kilometres or so Christian would cross himself — like it was a bloody miracle that we had survived thus far — which, of course, it was. When we finally limped back onto the sealed roads of Punta Arenas — the car vibrating violently because the alignment had been completely shot, the muffler protesting loudly — it became obvious why Chileans never feature in Formula One: neither they nor their cars could survive.

But their penguins do. The black and white striped Magellanic penguins at Otway Bay (the same species that Dee and I had been researching in Punta Tombo) survive by adopting a different feeding strategy to others of its species breeding nearby.

The bay was windswept and barren, yet was set below the impossibly pointed peaks of Torres del Paine, which provided a

stunning backdrop. Although, I had been so shaken by the ride —
and the thought that it had to be repeated on the return journey —
the Iraqi desert would have looked attractive to me at that moment
as long as I was out of the car and still breathing.

Without much food nearby, the Magellanic penguins of Otway
Bay must travel farther to find food than penguins breeding at other
places. Yet — and this was the curious, the instructive thing — they
were able to alter their nest attendance patterns to cope. Whereas
if you had looked at other Magellanic penguins you might have
supposed that the duration of the shifts they took on the nest and
off it were roughly a fixed amount, a characteristic of the species, it
was clearly not the case. This flexibility, this plasticity of behaviour,
did not seem to sit so well with the hard wiring that we take to
accompany heritable characteristics. Surely evolution can only work
on what is coded in the genes? If the same animals can have two
different outcomes when placed in different environments — be the
outcomes the feeding patterns of penguins or the living conditions
of humans — what does that tell us about Natural Selection?

Maybe I was approaching all this from the wrong angle. Maybe
the time scale I was using was too immediate, too me, too now. If
Tierra del Fuego and the Fuegians taught Darwin something about
the human condition, it was the Andes that taught him about time.
And maybe, just maybe, the Andes could help me understand how
species might change over a time scale I couldn't comprehend.

– 18 –

The Andes and the Power of Nature

When Darwin left England, Professor Henslow gave him a copy of the first volume of Charles Lyell's *Geology* and sent him the second, which caught up with the *Beagle* in Buenos Aires. Darwin's interest in geology had already been ignited in the summer of 1831, when, at the behest of Henslow, he had accompanied Professor Adam Sedgwick on a trip to fossick among the rocks and formations of northern Wales. Darwin's passion for geology continued to develop throughout the voyage on the *Beagle,* and afterwards, he would go on to write several books about geology. In South America it was the Cordillera, the range of mountains we know as the Andes, that Darwin most wanted to see, to touch, and to examine. If the Earth really was older than the Bible said, surely the answer to the question of just how old the earth might be lay in those hunks of rock.

After leaving Tierra del Fuego, the *Beagle* popped over to the Falkland Islands. There they managed to bang the bottom of the *Beagle* — I suspect that FitzRoy, an expert sailor, cannot have been on board that day and that they had instead a Chilean taxi driver called Christian at the helm. At any rate, they headed back to Argentina and the mouth of the Rio Santa Cruz, where, in a fashion similar to the killer whales of Peninsula Valdes, they beached the *Beagle* on a high tide. Taking three weeks' provisions and three boats, FitzRoy, Darwin and a group of twenty-three men not needed for the repairs, headed inland up the unexplored Santa

Cruz with the hopes of reaching the Cordillera. But it was harder going than they realised and for much of it they had to take turns pulling the boats. Eventually, after some two hundred and twenty-five kilometres, they had to stop while still fifty kilometres from the Andes, the white-capped peaks tantalisingly close but unreachable. Just as Shackleton had done after turning back when within a few days' march of the South Pole, Darwin returned to his base, the *Beagle*, with a heavy heart.

Personally, I do not go much for pulling sleds (which I tried on one of my own Antarctic expeditions), and the notion of pulling boats seemed even less appealing: consequently, my wife and I flew into El Calafate. In one sixty minute flight we managed to cover all the ground and more that Darwin had made in three weeks.

The palette of colours visible from the air was limited. Writhing across the brown plain like a blue snake, the Rio Santa Cruz poured from Lago Argentino on its downward journey to the mouth where the *Beagle* had lain propped on its side while the carpenters fixed it. Small ponds dotted the plain, reflecting as gold in the evening light. Higher up, clouds shrouded the mountains, hiding what secrets they held like a table draped with a grey cloth. The tops of the clouds were tinged with orange by the setting sun while, higher still, the evening sky was a surprisingly light blue.

Some thirty years after Darwin had been forced to turn back, Francisco Moreno, having read Darwin's account, travelled up the Santa Cruz and reached the huge lake that he was to christen Lago Argentino. But the real treasures were what fed that lake and Lago Viedma to the north: giant glaciers. These glaciers were what we had come to see, and in particular, the largest one that bore the explorer's name. Perito Moreno Glacier is a fine sounding name, but with my limited grasp of Spanish, for the longest while I thought it translated as Puppy Moreno Glacier. Puppy is actually perrito and perito is actually expert. Either way, it didn't make much sense to me.

On the way up to the glacier from El Calafate, we stopped our bus so that I could take photos of a pair of condors circling high in the sky. Darwin had seen condors on the journey up the Santa Cruz and commented that apart from when taking off, he had not seen one 'flap their wings'. Indeed, these birds with their expansive wings (Darwin shot one that had nearly a two-and-a-half-metre wingspan) seemed ideally built to exploit any updraughts — and, when it came to finding updraughts, it was hard to imagine a better place than the Andes. As our bus approached our destination, the clouds occasionally parted, revealing mountains that I could only describe as standing with authority. They were like my old headmaster in that way, only better-looking.

If the mountains were big, we were not prepared for the scale of the glacier. Its tongue was so big it seemed like it must straddle a couple of time zones. Well, maybe not that big, but big enough that one company ran boat tours across the Lago Argentino to the left side, while another company ran tours to its right side, and it was surely many kilometres between their respective departure points. At the end of the road in Los Glaciares National Park, we all decamped from the bus, and while the Argentines went to have a three-course meal in the restaurant, my wife and I took first a boat trip to the face of the glacier and then a hike along as much of the walkway in front of the glacier as we could manage in the three-hour stopover. Every vantage point was different. From the water it was the sheer face that intrigued, stretching some sixty metres above the water level. From the high points of the land, it was the crumpled top, like a sheet of frozen popcorn five kilometres wide, that fascinated. From every which way, the size of the glacier was enormous. And from everywhere, the glacier could be heard creaking and groaning, as if to remind us it was a living thing. Every now and then there would be a bang like a hundred cannons firing, and bits of the glacier would tumble into the lake or onto the ground. The loudness of the bang never seemed terribly correlated with the size of the pieces falling down.

This was nature at its most mind-boggling. This was a force that didn't just shape rocks: it broke them. And if Darwin had seen what it could do to rocks, would it have been too much of a stretch to ask whether it could move mountains too?

– 19 –

The Pacific Side of the Andes and How the Earth Moved for Darwin (and me)

To get to the Cordillera, Darwin had to wait until the *Beagle* reached the Pacific side of South America: a rough trip through the Straits of Magellan that took them a month battling huge seas — and, even then, the storms did not abate, following them up the Chilean coast until they eventually disembarked at the port city of Valparaiso on 22 July 1834. The third volume of Lyell's *Geology* was waiting for Darwin, having been sent on by Henslow.

In the nineteenth century, Valparaiso was an important stop-over for ships travelling between the Atlantic and Pacific Oceans by way of the Straits of Magellan or around Cape Horn. A Chilean friend escorted my wife and I there but the grandeur of the place has largely deserted Valparaiso in the twenty-first century. It is still very much a port city and we spent a lot of time down at the fish market watching pelicans and sea lions compete for morsels brought in by a rag-tag selection of boats. Chilean grandeur has now slipped a little farther up the coast to Viña del Mar, a sort of Chilean version of Monaco, where the rich and not-so-famous hang out and the not-so-rich come to see how the other half lives.

My personal favourite Chilean coastal spot lies just south of Valparaiso. Algarrobo is a quaint fishing village nestled on a beautiful beach. It is a place where the Chileans with any sense, as opposed to lots of pesos, holiday. Colourful fishing boats not much bigger than canoes lie pulled up on the sand or moored in the bay, where they form a perch for the pelicans and gulls. On shore, doughty fishermen sit in the shade mending nets. At the southern end of the beach, a marvellous headland ends in a small island reserve. And, if all that were not picturesque enough (speaking on my own behalf, and not for my wife) I swear that the chief attraction of Algarrobo lay on the beaches. Gorgeous women lay sunbathing everywhere in groups of four or five; all of them had olive complexions, long dark hair, and legs that stretched forever — or at least until meeting the confines of bikinis so brief you had to wonder why they bothered.

There was something wondrous about having all this beauty concentrated in the one spot, but puzzling too: because the Chilean men associating with these women were, from my perspective, most undeserving of the task. I was reminded of birds of paradise, where one sex is elaborate and the other dull. But as Darwin noted, it is typically the males that look like *Priscilla Queen of the Desert* and the females of the species that are the drab ones. (He didn't put it like that exactly, but no doubt he would have if he'd seen the film.) A big tail, a bright breast, a sultry dance: there are many tricks that males use to attract females. Darwin recognised the phenomenon existed in the animal world, but he did not understand why it should be males that put on the make-up. Yet, had he hung around Valparaiso and Algarobbo a little longer, he might have.

Nowhere in either his journals or *On the Origin of Species* does he mention phalaropes. While it is true that these birds breed in the northern parts of North America, well away from the path of the *Beagle*, they winter over in the south and can be seen from vessels putting out from Valparaiso, often in their hundreds. The curious thing about phalaropes is that the females are larger than the males and more brightly coloured. And this is where the exception proves the rule, because remarkably, phalaropes practise polyandry: which is another way of saying that the females get it on with more than one guy, leaving the guys to look after the kids and do the housework. Sound familiar but back-to-front?

So what is the rule? The rule is that the sex that invests least in rearing the offspring should make itself as sexually attractive as possible to the sex that does most of the work: in Darwin's world, a male that can attract many females will have relatively more offspring than other males, and those offspring will carry the genes that made the male attractive to the females in the first place, thereby perpetuating the big tail, the red breast or whatever. However, when the stiletto is on the other foot, so to speak, as it is in phalaropes, it is the females that get rewarded, in an evolutionary sense, for making themselves attractive. One can only presume that in Algarrobo, when the Chilean males are not down at the beach rubbing oil onto the backs of their sleeping partners, they are at home barefoot in the kitchen and up to their eyeballs in diapers?

• • • •

As glad as Darwin was to get ashore, it seems to have been not the women that caught his eye, but the mountains. Not long after, he headed into them on mules. There he made an amazing discovery: at over three thousand metres, he found fossil shells, and a little farther down, fossilised trees in marine sediment. FitzRoy's reaction was, 'So what' — the mountains had always been there, the fossils were the result of the great flood. But to Darwin they said that, as difficult as this may be to accept, the crust of the Earth was a changing beast that could rise and fall. What was forest could end up in the seas, and what were oysters clinging to an underwater life could end up on the tops of mountains — given enough time.

Fortuitously for Darwin's developing ideas, but not so fortuitously for the Chilean people, the earth itself would talk to Darwin. Take a drive down the side of the Chilean Cordillera, as my wife and I did, and every now and then, there'll be a snow-covered perfectly formed cone like a mountain out of Dr Suess or a model from some mathematical class. Such was the shape of Volcan Villarrica, which we saw near Pucón, but there were many others, and if the bulk of the Andes had a weathered, sheer-faced jagged look, like they had been there since the beginnings of time itself, these cone-like mountains seemed to shout 'volcano' — by mountain standards, they seemed like teenagers, young and easily excitable.

So it was that one night in January 1835, while at anchor at San Carlos on the island of Chiloe after the *Beagle* had moved back south along the Chilean coast, Darwin and the others witnessed the volcano Osorno erupting. A spectacular event that underscored for Darwin the notion that the earth was not solid and immovable, but a crust sitting atop some molten interior that every now and then would burst forth through vents such as those at Osorno and Villarrica.

The most momentous event occurred a month later, on 20 February 1835, by which time the *Beagle* was farther north and at anchor in Valdivia. Darwin went ashore with his servant, Covington, and lay down to rest under some trees when the earth moved. The earthquake lasted, according to Darwin, 'two minutes (but appeared much longer)'. Its epicentre was close to the nearby city of Concepción. FitzRoy and Darwin rode to Concepción to find it completely levelled.

When my wife and I rode into Concepción ourselves — in a car, not on mules — my first reaction was that there were few places on Earth to my mind more deserving of being levelled. It is I believe what is euphemistically called a 'coal town', as if that tag somehow gives it the excuse to abandon any pretext of the sort of beauty we had left behind on Algorrobo — and I am not talking feminine beauty but a combination of natural beauty and man-made structures in harmony with the environment.

On the day he arrived in Concepción, Darwin had found no evidence for any harmony between nature and man-made structures either. He was taken aback at the brutality and devastation wrought by a few seconds of the earth shaking: 'it is quite impossible to convey the mingled feelings with which one beholds this spectacle'. Apart from the devastation, the most significant thing Darwin noticed was that the land around Concepción's harbour appeared to have risen. Spending several days making measurements, Darwin concluded finally that the earthquake had raised the land over two metres. And, if it could rise two metres, why not two kilometres — or more? Why couldn't the Andes have arisen from the sea, taking with them the seashells and the likes of the marine creatures that he now observed around Concepción and which had been lifted to early graves above the high tide mark?

'To my mind since leaving England we have scarcely beheld any one other sight so deeply interesting. The Earthquake & Volcano are parts of one of the greatest phenomena to which this world is subject,' wrote Darwin in his diary. He was starting to accept Lyell's vision of geology, which was that the Earth was fluid, flexible. Over time, even continents could change. If continents could change, then why not the animals and plants on them? Even as such thoughts began to trouble Darwin, he withheld them from the religious FitzRoy.

– 20 –

Paraguay, *The Mission*, and the Jesuits

Our hotel in Concepción was supposedly its finest, but whereas the Touring Club in Trelew had worn its faded glory with an admirable panache in the face of a world that had advanced all around it, this hotel had simply faded, it had never had any glory days. The one good restaurant in Concepción seemed out of context with the rest of the city until halfway through the meal everyone in the restaurant started to play housie: *haute cuisine* had been transformed into a bingo hall. Actually, the proclivity of the Chileans for this particular pastime stunned us: even on the bus journey from Concepción back to Santiago, they played bingo.

The overnight bus trip had left my wife and I surprisingly refreshed. Normally an attempt to sleep in any type of moving vehicle would have led instantly to my sharing the contents of my dinner with my fellow passengers. But the seats in Chilean buses are ridiculously comfortable: they lie right back like some sort of giant La-Z-boy. I've been in hotels — the one in Concepción being a prime example — with beds much less generous with space and comfort. Once the bingo had stopped, and mercifully, the credits had started to roll on *Speed*, which had been playing on the onboard video player (there is something about Sandra Bullock and the South American sense of beauty that means one is hardly able to go anywhere without seeing persistent reruns of otherwise tiresome movies starring the dark-haired actress), I settled down to the best sleep I've ever had in a bus or car. In fact, the only sleep I've ever had in a bus or car.

Later in the day we flew from Santiago airport to Asunción, the capital of Paraguay. I know that Darwin did not get to Paraguay, but I had two reasons for this apparent diversion. First, I wanted to go to the Foz de Iguazu, the falls on the Iguazu River at the confluence of Paraguay, Argentina and Brazil that featured famously in the film *The Mission*, starring Jeremy Irons and Robert De Niro. Second, and most particularly, I wanted to visit the Jesuit missions. It haunted me how the conversion of an entire continent to Christianity and a belief in God the Creator should ironically occur in the very same continent that would provide the food for Darwin's contradictory ideas.

Paraguay is as I had imagined the whole of South America to be: warm, simple, poor. I had been brought up with the notion that South America was the 'Third World' and I had not been prepared for the sophistication of Buenos Aires or the European feel of Santiago when I first saw them. But in Paraguay, life exists without Perrier and Prada.

Although it was getting dark, instead of finding a hotel we opted to try another night bus to take us to the other side of Paraguay, to Ciudad del Este. The bus was considerably poorer than its Chilean cousin — it didn't have windows for one thing (well, not windows with glass in them, anyway) — but it did have the same reclining seats, and with the warm night air washing over us, we enjoyed a pleasant enough trip to Ciudad del Este, arriving some time after midnight. We drove past people in singlets sitting outside around tables and fires, eating and drinking, content with what they had because they knew of nothing else. Paint peeled. Dogs roamed. It felt like driving through an Ernest Hemingway novel.

In Ciudad del Este, we caught a taxi to a German hotel, which was one of two especially recommended in our *Lonely Planet* guidebook. Unfortunately, it was full, so we went to the other. A courtyard full of luxuriant plants appeared to suggest a small oasis, but the attitude of the night watchman was anything but welcoming. The heat was stifling even at this late hour and we hurried to our room with the promise of air conditioning. Except, as we discovered, the air conditioning did not work. Another room, another air conditioning unit — and that too would not work. Eventually, after more complaints and encouragement, the reluctant worker led us to, as far as we know, the only room in the whole complex that had a working air conditioner. By now it was after one a.m., and dog-tired, we tried to settle down. Impossible. Every cycle or two, the air conditioning unit would make loud shuddering noises.

I am, regrettably, one of those cursed with being a light sleeper: the slightest noise and I awake. My children still tell the story of the night we were in a motel in Twin Falls, Idaho, when in a frustrated rage I jumped out of bed and kicked a noisy air conditioning unit. Of course, it was an entirely stupid thing to do: my cries of agony were far louder than the rattling vibrations of the unit — which continued to vibrate — and I broke a toe that would hurt me for months to come.

Not wishing to risk another toe, resignedly, I turned the unit off and we drifted into a sticky fitful sleep, lying side by side, without any sheets. Unable to stay asleep for long in the heat, I got up to use the bathroom. Turning on the bathroom light, I discovered cockroaches that seemed as large as my feet crawling across the floor. Realising that one encounter with these and my wife would be on the next plane home, I dealt them a quick death with my Tevas, and despite the ungodly hour, walked around to the German hotel where I sought, and received, an assurance that we could move in first thing in the morning.

Ciudad del Este is like one big market. Stalls with every kind of imaginable junk line the streets. Leather goods. Electronic goods. You name it, you can buy it: well, at least a reasonable approximation of it. The only part of copyright they seemed to understand was the first four letters. A bridge, with a deliciously curved concrete arch supporting it, separates Paraguay from Brazil. We crossed the Paraná River and, after some bargaining, found a taxi driver who would take us to the Brazilian side of the falls.

I had seen the film *The Mission* so I thought I knew what to expect, but even a large cinema screen cannot begin to capture the scale of these falls. It is the aquatic equivalent of the Grand Canyon. It is not one vista, it is a thousand. Turn your head in any direction and there is another view, another perspective of the falls. Coatis, racoon-like creatures with long, banded tails, came up to us expecting food handouts.

The next day we went to the Argentine side of the falls. My wife delights in telling people that I am so generous that I once took her to three countries in one day. Then she will add the killer punchline that it cost me the princely sum of one dollar. And indeed it did. The bus started in Paraguay, passed briefly through Brazil and then ending up at Puerto Iguazu on the Argentinean side of the Foz de Iguazu. But, hey, I paid for the return trip too.

By then I had given up doing my Jeremy Irons impersonations — for the longest while my wife thought I was doing The Hunchback of Notre Dame — but as we were able to stand on the lip of the falls on the Argentine side, we decided to re-enact the iconic image from the film. This is the one where, Robert De Niro, strapped to a large wooden cross, is flung upside-down, down the face of the falls. I wasn't about to leap over the edge strapped to a board, but having discovered that in our haste to evacuate the nasty hotel in Ciudad del Este we had taken all their keys with us, we had a small ceremony where we tossed the keys over the falls and imagined they were De Niro. It gave us no end of satisfaction.

In the film, a Jesuit mission is set around the Foz de Iguazu. The Society of Jesus, or the Jesuits, established the province of Paraguay and there they set up small communities, reducciones, for the local Guarani Indians, which were built around missions. These were very successful, but then in 1767, less than seventy years before Darwin arrived in South America, the King of Spain ordered them out. In a deal with the Portuguese, the missions were simply abandoned. They fell into disuse, the Guarani were abused, traded for slaves and by the time Darwin got there, their numbers were down to only eight thousand or so.

On the way back from Ciudad del Este, we took a detour on a bus heading to Encarnación because I wanted to stop at La Santisima Trinidad de Paraná, the site of a Jesuit Mission and a UNESCO World Heritage site. Passing through flat country, much of it cultivated in sugar cane, the bus eventually set us down, it seemed literally in the middle of nowhere. There were no houses, no shops, and certainly no mission — although we understood from the driver that the mission was only about three kilometres away. It might just as well have been three hundred kilometres away given our luggage: while I normally travel with a backpack, for reasons that would take too long to explain but which, suffice to say, did not involve much forethought, we were travelling with two large Samsonite cases.

As the bus pulled away and we were pondering just what to do about this, a Toyota of sorts pulled up. I have seen some wrecks of cars, but this was the winner by a country mile, although a mile looked like it would stretch its capabilities. There were more holes from rust than there were body panels. A rough-looking driver got out, pronounced that he was a taxi driver (well, he said the word 'taxi') and offered to transport us to the ruins. If Paris Hilton had stepped out of the car, she would have made a more convincing taxi driver, but at that particular point in time we did not have too many options. I negotiated a price, and then he took out a screwdriver and proceeded to try to pry open the boot. Even with the lack of options, one glance at my wife told me that she was not certain about proceeding with this arrangement. Still, she wedged herself in the back, next to a stack of meat — or perhaps it was the remains of the previous passenger? I placed my feet strategically on the floorboards to avoid them going through the holes and watched the muddy track flick past under them as we bounced the three kilometres to the entrance to the ruins.

This presented us with another problem: what to do with our

bags while we looked around the ruins and how to get back to the bus stop? If it had been fortuitous that this opportunistic 'taxi' had shown up at the bus stop, it would take a freakin' miracle for one to turn up down the not-so beaten track to the Trinidad ruins. I managed to communicate to the taxi driver that he should return at three p.m. to pick us up. He started to head off, intent on keeping our bags, but while I was prepared to entrust our future movements to him, I was not about to leave all our possessions with him. The ticket collector in the small entrance pavilion agreed that we could leave the bags in there. There were no luggage lockers, security, or anything, but as far as we could tell we were the only visitors there that day and — anyway — who would be stupid enough to try to walk around Paraguay with two bloody great Samsonite bags on wheels?

The ruins were quite spectacular in every way. Their scale was unexpectedly huge. This was not a church; it was a village. The craftsmanship, the stonework, were all excellent. You could say what you like about the Church, at least the one brought by the Jesuits, but you could not deny that they had brought a measure of prosperity to the area that it had not found before or since. The Guarani learned to read and write, and to grow crops like mate (tea) and sugar cane. But then, when it all ended, they dispersed and with it their communities and wealth disappeared. The Church had also battled the slave trade, which Darwin would encounter later in Brazil.

So in a sense, it was easy for me to see why the Guarani should have embraced the Church. It may have been foreign but its intentions, as opposed to those of the Spanish conquerors themselves, were noble, and in many cases, the outcomes for the people were not so bad. If you've been conquered, then you might as well at least focus on the good bits.

Our driver had duly shown up exactly at three. We had loaded up the Samsonites, squeezed in by the meat, and been delivered back to the bus stop, where a bus intended for the locals took us on a ridiculously cheap, horrendously cramped, but altogether intriguing ride to the bus station in the city of Encarnación. As we sat on the bus from Encarnación back to Asunción, with bloody *Speed* being played again on the television overhead, I began to ponder what the beliefs of the locals must have been like before God arrived in the form of Jeremy Irons or whoever. I thought to myself, who was conquered by the Spanish? Wasn't it the Incas? And what do I know about the Incas? They sacrificed virgins. They worshipped the sun. Oh, and they built a trail.

That was it really. It wasn't like it was terribly deep or terribly complicated. I was seeking the truth, not Darwin *per se*, and in South America it seemed that, at least as far as the locals were concerned, the truth came largely in one flavour: we were all part of a world created by the father of a guy who died on a cross as surely as De Niro had apparently perished on his. Yet all my training as a scientist up to that point said that the religious story of creation should be impossible. The Earth, the Andes, far too old. Seals and penguins, more obviously derived than contrived. If given the choice, why would someone worship the Son over the sun?

And that is how the Foz de Iguazu and a mission in Paraguay should be linked to my search for meaning and Darwin, and why, eventually, my wife and I would find ourselves on a plane flying into Lima, intent on walking the Inca Trail.

In the interim, however, I had to complete the last leg of Charles Darwin's South American sojourn.

– 21 –

Copiapo and God's Quarry

I had made a pact with myself that I should travel through South
America only with my wife, but as she was unable to join me for
the leg to examine Darwin's last great sortie on the South American continent, I found myself sitting on a beach in the northern
Chilean town of Coquimbo with a hirsute red-head who answered
to Dave, sometimes. We sat in an outdoor restaurant on the sand,
pisco sours in hand, watching a giant red ball of a sun gradually
edge itself into the Pacific Ocean, as romantic as any moment could
have been apart from the company.

On 27 April 1835, Darwin, four horses, a couple of mules, and
some Chilean guasos (guides) had left Valparaiso and headed up to
Coquimbo. From there they travelled a rather circuitous route to
the mining town of Copiapo, taking in parts of the Cordillera as
they went. Dave and I both had a few days to kill, so we hired a car
and headed, as Darwin had headed, for Copiapo.

We drove northwards through a desert, but one that screamed
of life not death. Carpeted across its dry surface were spectacular
wild flowers and cacti. At one point we reached a peninsula and
turned off towards a town that our maps suggested was by the sea
and where we envisaged spending another night looking at the sun
going down slowly to the accompaniment of pisco sours going
down quickly. The road became rougher, the landscape now more
deserted than desert. No flowers. No people.

As dusk was gathering, we found ourselves in a town by the sea, a ghost town by the sea. None of the buildings were occupied as far as we could tell. Many of the windows were boarded up. Gates creaked. It wasn't just uninviting, it was unsettling. We opted to drive on through the dark to Copiapo, from where, the next morning, we would head into the mountains.

Dave has worked in extreme environments most of his life and I have led more than a dozen expeditions to the Antarctic: so in many ways it is as inexplicable as it is inexcusable that we should head off into such an unknown realm without any water or food of any kind. While naïvely we had expected to find a town, that just did not happen. The roads changed from tarseal to shingle, the hills from bare and rounded to bare and rugged; molehills became mountains. And save for the first hour or so, we saw no one. It was a deserted place of rock, God's Quarry. There was really not a plant or animal in sight. If one played the game 'I Spy' in this environment, there would be no need to ask whether it was 'animal, vegetable or mineral'. As Darwin himself said of the area, 'I am tired of repeating the epithets barren and sterile'.

We came across Indian ruins — perhaps the same ones Darwin did — small square mud huts, no longer supporting roofs. We were staggered, not so much because they had been abandoned, but because someone should have chosen to live there in the first place. As Darwin noted, 'the land produces absolutely nothing, and what is still more extraordinary … there is no water'. Which was something we were just beginning to appreciate.

Dave had an altimeter — no food but a frigging altimeter — and at a certain point we realised we were over the three thousand seven hundred and fifty-four metre height of New Zealand's highest peak, Mount Cook. We were getting anxious now. The road had got rougher. We had seen nobody for four hours. Then the road simply petered out — or rather — I could get our car to go no farther forwards. We were at four thousand metres on the side of a mountain on a steep, skinny, rocky track with nowhere to turn. I backed down the mountain until we felt it safe enough to turn the car around. Ostensibly, we had been heading to some salt-pans, and some time earlier we had come to a fork in the road and made an educated guess. Not only did we have no food or drink, we had no map. Retracing our steps we took the other road at the unsigned fork. We got to the salt-pans, but if they contained flamingos, our goal, then they were too far away to tell. What we could tell was that it had started snowing. And no, we were not prepared for that either. However, what we really were not prepared for was that we had somehow, unbeknownst to us, passed into Argentina. We now found ourselves approaching a border crossing to get back into Chile, which might just have been okay if we had had any of the necessary documentation.

The border crossing seemed to be closed. We walked around the deserted building trying to figure out what to do, as the way forward, for us and our car, was obstructed by a big white metal barricade. Eventually an armed border guard showed up. He seemed unsurprised to see us. The missing documentation was excused. We could go on. Which should have been a relief, but by now we were extremely low on petrol and there seemed no way to find out where the next opportunity for gas — hell, the first opportunity we would see all day — might come from. With darkness approaching, we made our way through a series of switchbacks to an untidy town of hovels with open-air carts that functioned as restaurants but which could just as easily have functioned as cattle trucks and been no less clean. It did not matter. I have never been so grateful for food, drink or gas.

If there was some consolation in our stupidity, it was that Darwin had been caught out too by the sheer lack of the basic necessities for life to be found in this landscape where the word 'barren' was perhaps the only thing it had spawned:

> [...] it was most disagreeable to hear, whilst eating our own suppers, our horses gnawing the posts to which they were tied, and to have no means of relieving their hunger ... they had eaten nothing for the last fifty-five hours.

It is a world where rocks rule, a community in which its citizens are all called schist and granite and the like. And yet, despite its solidity, Darwin discovered irrefutable evidence around Copiapo that these great hunks of the South American continent had risen over time.

One other benefit Darwin derived from being up in the Cordillera was that it seemed, mercifully, unfit for fleas. In Coquimbo he had complained bitterly of the fleas: 'The rooms in Coquimbo swarm with them'. Yet he was obliged to go down to sea level again to meet up with FitzRoy and the *Beagle* before heading off to Peru. In the dark we drove down to the coast too, having been from sea level to four thousand metres and back again in less than twenty-four hours. Unfortunately, the hotel we stopped in was literally a fleapit. I awoke the next morning covered in bites, itching to get out of Chile and to follow Darwin to Peru.

– 22 –

Lima and Last Suppers

It was dark and late as the Lan Peru aircraft descended into Lima. Normally I travel on a budget that makes the term 'budget traveller' seem impossibly extravagant. The first time my wife and I had gone to India, we had started out staying in hotels that cost thirty dollars per night and ended up in those costing two dollars. Admittedly, we had not lasted long in the latter. A rat that jumped out of the bedding had not helped, but when the toilet overflowed when it was flushed, well, my wife had insisted that I take her to Delhi airport and put her on the next flight home. The midnight hour of our arrival in Lima, the fact that I did not wish to have a repeat of our New Delhi experience and, mostly, because it was our wedding anniversary, I had made an advance booking with a five-star hotel. One of the bonuses of this was that we were to be met by a limousine, and sure enough, as we came out of immigration, there was an immaculately groomed man in a suit with keys to a Mercedes and a board with my name.

For nine months of the year, Lima is enveloped in a *garúa*, which is essentially a cloud of moisture or coastal mist. Given the high humidity, at night — when the temperature drops — it seems like rain, but it is really just air laden with so much moisture you can touch it. The areas from the Aeropuerto Internaçional Jorge Chávez to the city centre are rundown and I couldn't help but notice that our driver never changed speeds at traffic lights, no matter what their colour. He explained, in impeccable English, that it was too dangerous to stop at red lights as bandits would likely rob us, or worse. I felt my wife grasp me and, while under the circumstances I might have been forgiven for thinking it was a preliminary of more to come, I knew her well enough to know that it was fear that held her tightly to me.

• • • •

Out on the streets of Lima, tanks and armed policemen abounded, but the square with the yellow and white church of the Monasterio de San Francisco was left to the pigeons and the people, exuding the same colonial air it had projected for more than three centuries. At the centre of the monastery is a large courtyard, flanked by covered walkways completely lined with intricate patterns of tiles in blues, yellows and whites, so that the impression was that some giant shiny quilt had been pasted to the walls. It was easy to get lost and I almost lost my wife, our guide and the rest of our tour party as I lingered in one large room. But I couldn't help myself. For at one end was an enormous painting of the Last Supper, on a scale to rival the famous fresco by Da Vinci that graces the dining room wall in the convent of Santa Maria delle Grazie in Milan. But this was the thing, the mind-boggling, fascinating thing from my perspective: for his last meal, Christ and his disciples are depicted as eating guinea pig, the local Peruvian delicacy. Now what believer in their right mind would contemplate for a moment that Christ should, like a condemned man requesting his favourite food, demand guinea pig for his final repast? It would be like me painting the Last Supper and showing them all tucking into a Domino's pizza because I happen to like them. I don't even know if they had guinea pigs in Jerusalem. If the food Christ ate could be depicted in such a patently incorrect way, what is to say that the other parts of the Christ story were not also wrong? And let me just say, that were I Jesus, and were I offered guinea pig, I think I would have gone for the loaves and fishes or whatever every time.

I base this assertion on actual research: to my wife's disgust, I opted to eat guinea pig at a restaurant some nights later. There's not much on them and while the taste might be reminiscent of rabbit, it is a lot harder to eat. My wife could not stand the crunching of the bones. I guess I did not make it any better for her by pronouncing that I preferred alpaca. She hated me for eating alpaca too.

The most interesting part of the monastery, however, was its catacombs. Up to seventy-thousand souls were interred there in what was effectively Lima's first cemetery. The practice stopped a little after Darwin visited Lima, and according to our guide, in the nineteen fifties, after a century of disuse, the catacombs were cleaned out and what remained of the bodies was taken up and put in piles in the courtyard. Pretty much the only bones able to withstand the process of decay and the process of such handling were the heavy ones: the skulls and the femurs. Rather than keep the bones of individuals together, they were stacked according to kind: the head bones went with all the other head bones, the leg bones with all the other leg bones. Consequently, after re-interment, the catacombs have become largely collections of bone types rather than the final resting place of individuals. In fact, with this type of assortment, an individual was bound to have several final resting places. Most bizarrely, though, when laying out the skulls and femurs, the conservationists (and one has to use this term loosely) decided to get creative and make patterns out of the bones: consequently the femurs are often arranged in herring-bone patterns, like the fabric of some Harris Tweed jacket, and the skulls often alternate with the femurs, sometimes in rows, sometimes in concentric circles.

And why not, I thought? It mattered not what I found culturally insensitive: this wasn't my culture. If you are comfortable with Jesus eating guinea pig, maybe you're not going to be concerned with someone making jigsaw puzzles with the bones of the dead? Going into the vaulted interior of the church proper with its Moorish-style plaster walls and ceilings, I couldn't help but notice in one alcove an icon of the Virgin Mary shown in the 'gaucho clothes' of the South

American. And surely that is the point. Religious beliefs have to be relevant to the people. A Christ eating chateaubriand and a Mary dressed in Yves St Laurent may not work in Peru, but it might in Paris, say.

Was that the difference between faith and fact? Religious beliefs depend on faith, so I could hold similar religious beliefs as someone else, even if the foundations of my faith were different. Science, on the other hand, depends upon facts and they are not open to local interpretation. Either Christ ate chateaubriand, guinea pig or bread: he cannot have eaten all three except in the imagination. Yet that does not stop the Peruvian or the Parisian believing in the same God, with the same Son, who had the same Mother and the same Last Supper. But if I as a scientist say that guinea pigs evolved after fish and another says it is the other way round, we cannot both be right, and the evidence will prove one of us wrong.

If religion can be so malleable, so adaptive, what is to say that the pre-Christian religions were any less correct? That was the thought I would carry with me later, as we descended through the cloud, dodging snow-capped mountains, to land at Cuzco.

First, however, we walked a block and a half from the monastery to the Plaza de Armas. Once the heart of Lima, it has a timeless air that is more contrived than real: nothing of the original buildings remains after a couple of devastating earthquakes had levelled them. On one side there are the mustard-coloured colonial arches of the Municipalidad, the residence of the city's mayor (hence, the name, Mayor Plaza), in front of which two horses with elaborate white carriages stood motionless. To the right, another side of the plaza is taken up with the Presidential palace, Palacio de Gobierno, which despite its geriatric appearance was built in only 1937. Armed guards tried to usher us away, but perplexingly, allowed us to return just as the President himself came out onto the steps of the palace, flanked by some of the most outrageously dressed armed guards this side of the Vatican or Buckingham Palace. An armoured vehicle, like a small tank, sat at one side, its long gun trained somewhere else, but menacing nevertheless. These were not the sort of police you would ask for directions or the time; not unless you fancied the prospects of having so many holes put in you that you could be used to drain pasta afterwards.

Moving farther around the square, and opposite the mayor's digs, was the object of our search: La Catedral de Lima. Originally built in 1555, the cathedral needed to be reconstructed after receiving a one-two punch from earthquakes in 1687 and 1746. Like the nearby monastery, the cathedral projects a colonial air, enhanced by the square itself, which is filled with flowers, palm trees and a delightfully elaborate fountain. There was not much to see — or at least not much we wanted to see — except that just to the right of the main door is a chapel festooned in mosaics and housing a coffin. The elaborate coffin, topped by a bronze lion, contains the remains of Francisco Pizarro, the founder of Lima but also the conqueror of the Incas: as controversial a figure now as he was nearly five hundred years ago.

A statue of Pizarro on horseback was originally erected in the plaza in front of the cathedral, but church authorities objected to having the rear end of the horse facing the cathedral and it was moved to the other side of the square near the mayor's residence and the presidential palace where, some argued, something that produced a little horseshit should go largely unnoticed amongst such prodigious producers of bullshit. Except that in 2002, at the request of an architect and the then mayor, the statue was removed from the square altogether. It wasn't so much the horse's bum that they found offensive, but the bum on its back.

Pizarro, based in Panama, had heard stories of Indian civilisations in South America with incalculable riches. In two expeditions in the 1520s he sailed south, enduring much hardship, but eventually he discovered the Incas, who at that time controlled the area from southern Columbia to central Chile. In 1531 he set sail for Peru again, this time with about one hundred and sixty men, sixty-five horses, some bows, spears, swords and guns. The Inca leader,

Atahualpa, controlled an army of more than thirty-thousand men. Pizarro and his small group pushed inland to the Andes and set up camp in a square at Cajamarca, inviting Atahualpa to a meeting. Atahualpa, believing he was divine, arrived for the meeting with a few thousand guards armed with slingshots and adzes. But there was to be no meeting. Pizarro and his men attacked with their cannons and superior weapons. The Incas were trapped inside the square, and having never encountered guns or horses or swords, they panicked. In the end, Pizarro and his one hundred and sixty men captured Atahualpa and slaughtered six thousand or so Incan guards. A ransom was requested for Atahualpa and, over the following months, the Incas brought to Pizarro gold and silver ornaments that when melted down would yield six thousand kilograms of gold and twelve thousand kilograms of silver. Instead of freeing Atahualpa, however, Pizarro executed him. The Incan empire had as good as lost its power, and by November 1533, Pizarro was able to ride into the Inca capital of Cuzco unopposed.

– 23 –

The Inca Trail and Worshipping the Sun

Cuzco has a magic, almost medieval, appeal. Alpine, the air is as clean and crisp as a newly picked apple. Many of the locals wear traditional garb, with brilliantly coloured shawls — which they employ as ingeniously versatile backpacks for carrying anything from food, to clothes, to babies — and, most incongruously, with hats that resemble the bowler hats of some London banker. And they are just as sharp as any banker.

While I was waiting for our bags to come off the carousel, a man came up to me and said, 'Señor Davis?' 'Sí', I replied, glad that the driver from our pre-booked hotel had actually turned up. The man insisted on picking up the bags from the carousel and hoisting them onto the cart, even though I was considerably bigger than him and had already grasped one. My wife and I followed him in a procession outside the terminal, where we found a man with a sign with my name on it. And then it sunk in: this chap wheeling our bags had simply read my name on the board in the official waiting area then gone around the passengers at the carousel until he had located me, whereupon he pretended to be our driver. Clearly he expected a tip for transporting our bags the thirty metres or so — and, indeed, I felt obliged to reward such ingenuity, rather than the trivial amount of effort he had saved me.

Like most South American towns and cities, life in Cuzco is centred around a square, in this case the Plaza de Armas. Our hotel, the unimaginatively named Cusco Plaza II, was on a side street off the main square. Calle Saphi is narrow, cobbled and lined with an eclectic range of buildings at various departures from the perpendicular that made you realise that this is a part of the world that has never heard of a building inspector, let alone seen one. The ubiquitous shops selling alpaca jerseys and jewellery are outnumbered in this bustling street by the many tiny restaurants and travel agencies. It was to the latter that I headed immediately after checking in, and it was at the latter that our troubles began.

One of my graduate students, who had travelled extensively in South America, had advised me to wait until we were in Cuzco before booking to walk the Inca Trail as that way we would get a much better price. My usually eager-to-book travel agent had, in an uncharacteristic fit of apparent altruism, agreed. The only problem with this advice was that it was sorely out of date. The Inca Trail, a four-day trek that winds its way over mountain passes to Machu Picchu, has become such a popular tourist activity that in order to protect the trail, the Peruvian government has stepped in and placed strict limits on the numbers allowed on the trail each day. Furthermore, people are now required to register for these guided hikes a *minimum of one month* beforehand. Registration involves providing passport details, photographs, and in the event of cancellations, bookings are strictly non-transferable and non-refundable. Like the Inca soldiers in Cajamarca, I began to panic, running from agency to agency only to get the same response: yes, they could book us on the Inca Trail, but, sorry, the earliest they could possibly take us would be in one month. I was as gutted in a mental sense just as surely as Atahualpa's soldiers had been gutted in a literal one.

We went to bed that night in the Cusco Plaza II feeling utterly miserable: walking the Inca Trail was the major reason for our trip. We had no Plan B.

Around eight-thirty in the morning I was showering, if indeed standing under such a trickle of water can be construed as showering, when the phone rang in our room. It was a woman I had spoken to at one of the agencies the night before. I think she had been particularly concerned that I was going to break down, I had been so upset. Naked but barely wet, I yelped into the phone when she asked whether I could meet her at the agency right away. There had been a cancellation on the hike leaving that morning and, although it was most out of order and somewhat risky, for them as well as us, they were going to attempt to substitute us. We would need to be packed and ready to go by ten a.m., but first I would need to see her with our passports. Throwing clothes on as I went, I leapt out of the door and down Calle Saphi, leaving my wife to pack hastily.

Cuzco is at over three thousand metres elevation and altitude sickness can be a problem for some people. It seems that when the bus had gone to pick up two of the passengers from their hotel earlier that morning, the woman had been too sick to contemplate getting out of bed, not to mention a four-day hike that would take them even higher. The attraction to the travel agency of the scam we were about to attempt was obvious: that couple had forfeited their fees and, even though it was extremely risky to substitute my wife and I, if the agency could get away with it, they would be paid twice. My ethics in such a situation, I discovered, were nowhere to be seen and I forked out the money gladly. I was less pleased about handing over our passports but as we had no other options, no Plan B, I decided to trust them. I returned to the hotel to help complete the packing.

When we heaved ourselves and our disturbingly heavy packs into the agency an hour later, we were each presented with a re-markably accurate counterfeit British driver's licence with our pho-to on it and a photocopy of the main page from a British passport, also with our photo on it, except that our names were now Simon and Anita. Because the bus had long since left to take the day's party to the start of the trail, we needed to travel by taxi to join up with them. A tiny red and grey Daewoo (the ubiquitous and as far as I could tell, perhaps the only car type in Cuzco) pulled up in front of the agency. What it lacked in room (my pack had to be strapped to the roof), it potentially made up for by being much newer than any other car in Cuzco and a four-wheel-drive version to boot. However, as it would transpire, whatever they were paying the driver was not enough. The costs to fix the damage the little car would sustain would have been much higher.

Two women ran the agency and it was the other one who travelled with us. She was clearly not as comfortable with attempting this ruse as the one who had taken pity on me had been. As she explained, they would lose their licence to operate if they were found out and she constantly asked me whether I thought we could carry off impersonating Simon and Anita. 'Hell yes,' I reassured her, just pleased that the couple who had cancelled had not been Chinese.

North of Cuzco is a fertile valley, nearly six hundred metres lower than Cuzco itself and known as El Valle Sagrado or the Sacred Valley of the Incas. It was here that the Incas took advantage of the microclimate to plant crops and establish several centres along its length. We drove along an unexpectedly modern tarsealed road, passing parched fields where locals in their bright clothes worked with donkeys in tow, or with ox with them in tow. The women — and they seemed to be mainly women — were especially noticeable in their billowing skirts and strange hats. Ridiculously steep snow-coated mountains bordered the valley on all sides. In places, terraced fields extended as high up the mountains as they dared. The sky was an electric blue, punctuated with puffy, promising clouds. 'Anita' and I sat in the back of the Daewoo pinching each other.

There was no time for sightseeing; we needed to catch up with a party that had left Cuzco four hours before us. At the head of the Sacred Valley, we came to the village of Ollantaytambo. We drove by a colourful couple with a pair of llamas, one white the other brown, pulling an even more colourful and elaborately attired carriage. But what caught our eyes most of all was a huge terraced fortress that sat above the village. When Francisco Pizarro had arrived in Cuzco unopposed in 1533, he brought with him Manco Capac II, half-brother of the assassinated Atahualpa, who was installed as a puppet

Inca leader. However, after being mistreated and imprisoned, Manco Capac retaliated and lead a siege against Cuzco in 1536, when up to fifty thousand Incas surrounded Cuzco and set fire to it. Unable to deal with the superior weapons of the Spanish conquistadors, Manco retreated to the fortress at Ollantaytambo. Pizarro's younger half-brother, Hernando, lead an attack using cavalry and foot soldiers on Ollantaytambo, but was repelled by Manco and his men, especially after they flooded the plains below the fortress, making it difficult for the horses to manoeuvre. Hernando would return later with a much larger force and the Incas retreated farther, to a place called Vilcabamba, from where Manco and his successors put up resistance to the Spanish for nearly forty years.

Almost etched into the mountainside itself, the fortress at Ollantaytambo consisted of a cascading series of stone terraces built by the Incas with stones carried from a quarry about five kilometres away. Even from a distance, even from the window of a moving car, you could tell that this was a piece of high quality handiwork. Huge pieces of stone fitted intricately and exactly into each other; it was solid in a way that had withstood earthquakes as easily as it had Hernando's weapons. These were no ordinary people. It struck me, then, that this place we were heading towards, Machu Picchu, had been made by a people that knew heaps about building even if they knew nothing about God or evolution. If they were ingenious enough to figure out how to move huge stones over great distances and to devise canal systems for water, perhaps they could work out why we were here, too. I wanted to know more about their religious views.

After Ollantaytambo, things did not go well for our driver. We left the sealed road and followed a track beside a river. Between hitting large rocks and falling into large holes, the car took a beating. My wife and I exchanged worried glances. Had we got so far only to be thwarted by the lack of a road, or, as it quickly turned out, the lack of a bridge? The driver stopped the car and contemplated the rushing stream that crossed the track before us. He got out, he got back in, he put the car in four-wheel-drive and he gunned the engine. The water must have been over the top of the wheel arches by then and I was convinced we would be wading not walking for four days as planned. But the little Daewoo somehow managed to skid and clatter up the other side of the stream and we bounced along the track, occasionally passing the odd cow, occasionally encountering a stuck bus, until at last we arrived at the start of the Inca Trail.

Five hundred people per day are allowed on the track, including guides and porters, and it seemed that a good proportion of that five hundred were amassed there, having a final meal and making final preparations before setting out. Our agency was contracted to supply people for a company taking a party of ten other souls. I have always thought that I would make a good James Bond, or at least a John Le Carré character draped in intrigue and nubile young ladies. I approached our group with the words from the agency woman still ringing in my ears, 'Can you carry off impersonating these people?' A Peruvian Indian with a round face and big smile stood up, extended a hand and said, 'I'm Al.' By reflex, I shook his hand and replied, 'I'm Lloyd.' Quickly realising my mistake, I added, '…er … Simon'. If they noticed, no one sitting in our group showed any hint. Our guides and fellow walkers were not in on the scam, and Al asked my wife how she was feeling, evidently concerned that 'Anita' should be attempting such a gruelling hike when suffering altitude sickness.

Even if we had been able to choose our walking companions, we could scarcely have done any better. The rest of our party consisted of five young English women — recent graduates out to experience the world — a young professional Peruvian couple, two Brazilian lads with all the good looks and bravado that one might expect of a country that had given the world Ayrton Senna and Felipe Massa, and a youngish Canadian woman who worked in a bank.

The Inca Trail begins by crossing a narrow swing bridge over the Urubamba River. Before the entrance to the bridge is a thatched roof checkpoint with two guards: this would be our first real test. Whatever the outcome, I wanted to get it over with quickly, so, with cap pulled down low to cover my grey locks and with sunglasses on, I marched with 'Anita' to the head of the queue. It is supposedly mandatory to carry a passport on the trail but, given the speed with which the agency had to fabricate our documents, producing a complete counterfeit British passport had been out of the question. Hence, we had been coached to say that we had left our passports in our hotel safe and brought with us a copy of the main page from our passports along with our drivers' licences for verification. This part of the plan seemed to work: although not happy with the arrangement, the guard accepted our explanation. He checked that our passport numbers, names and details matched those registered. I reached behind the grill to retrieve my driver's licence as quickly as I could, but the guard stopped me. He then spent what seemed like an hour but was probably no more than thirty seconds, examining the photo of 'Simon' on the licence and the photo of 'Simon' on the passport copy and occasionally shooting a glance at me. Both photos had been lifted from my own passport, so it was hard to discern what discrepancy he may have noticed. Eventually, he sighed, stamped my permit and, without a word, waved me on with a perfunctory flick of his hand. 'Anita' followed soon after.

It was all we could do to stop leaping up and shouting when we stepped off the bridge and onto the trail proper. Yet I am sure, had we done so, the guards and whoever else would have excused it as simply the exuberance of youth. You see, while we had been extremely fortunate that there had been two people who had cancelled, extremely fortunate that they had been a couple, extremely fortunate that they were English-speaking Caucasians, my wife — even though a few years younger than I — was more than double 'Anita's' sprightly twenty-two, while I had just had to impersonate a twenty-eight-year-old when there was so little daylight left between me and fifty that it did not matter.

One of the downsides of our sudden appearance on the Inca

Trail was that the three days we had planned to stay in Cuzco, to ac-
climatise to the altitude before attempting the trek, had disappeared
along with our usual identities. But the twenty-two-year-old Anita
and twenty-eight-year-old Simon found no problems, leading the
way as we marched along a comparatively easy track as it followed
the Kusichaca River. The hilltops were bare and rocky, the vegetation sparse and scrub-like. We passed a small hamlet of stone buildings, thatched roofs and roaming chickens. Behind us, the pointed
Mount Veronica watched over us as we climbed gentle valleys while
the other mountains seemed to close in around us: we were being
sucked into a vertical world, where the lie of the land was always
up, the horizon something you leaned back to see. At one point we
overlooked Llaqtapata, the remains of an Incan town that seemed
to be folded into the base of the Kusichaca Valley. Even from our
vantage point, because we had climbed steadily since leaving the
Kusichaca River, the intricacies of the Inca stonework were obvious.
Most obvious were the series of terraces, where they had created
microclimates for growing their crops. There was science of sorts
being practised by these people, even if it was trial and error — and
if they could figure out the best regime of sunlight and temperature
to grow maize, maybe they could figure out where all these animals
and plants in the natural world had come from?

Just as our legs were starting to tire and the air was starting to
chill in the shade created by the squeeze of mountains, we came to
an open valley floor, complete with stream and tents: our stop for
the night. Anita and I retired, congratulating ourselves on how well
the old-young legs and lungs had handled the hike without much
preparation or acclimatisation.

The moment I put my pack on in the morning, I realised how
premature we had been in our congratulations: it seemed that my
pack was hiding a couple of elephants. The rest of our group had
hired porters to carry their bags but there had been no time to ar-
range that with our hurried entrance to the trail even if we would
have considered it. The two Brazilians (Roberto and Nathan) also

carried their own gear, but as they seemed to wear the same clothes and take only a few photographs on a pocket-sized camera, their packs were light. We, on the other hand, were carrying extra clothes, extreme weather gear, toiletries, sleeping bags, snack foods, bottled water, and enough photographic gear to set up a studio at Machu Picchu. Anita had even brought along a book that made *War and Peace* look like the *Reader's Digest.* At least the tour company looked after portage of the tents and food for the main meals.

As we edged our way to the next checkpoint, each step I took required much more effort than I supposed it should. While we waited for the rest of the party to get checked — I had made no attempt to hide my age, but as everyone at this stage was looking shagged, it didn't seem to be a problem — a slightly built Quecha man in sandals with a yellow baseball cap and a brown dog approached me. He wore trousers, a long-sleeved check shirt and a cream-coloured woollen vest. He looked at least my age when I wasn't being Simon. He looked as if he would be at home in a supermarket somewhere, not turning up in the middle of nowhere. He asked me in sparse English reinforced with Spanish if I wanted a porter to go to the top of the pass. I was about to tell him to go away in sparse Spanish reinforced with a few English words all starting with F, when Anita intervened. 'Sí' she said, and we negotiated a price. Later she would say that it was the best fifteen dollars we ever spent.

Our porter wore my pack, I wore Anita's comparatively modest-sized pack, and dog loping along beside us, we set out on the rest of day two of the Inca Trail. First, I want to say that I have no idea why it should be called the Inca Trail; it should be called the Inca Steps. As you walk up all of them — and there are literally thousands of them — it is amazing to think that the Incas carried in each one of the many stones making up each one of the many steps. Not even halfway up to the pass, Anita's small pack had turned into the weight of the world. I had become Atlas, except that I felt more like Charles Atlas when he was a ninety-pound weakling getting sand kicked in his face. Anita offered to take the pack for a bit, but after a few metres realised the folly of her suggestion. I was putting her pack back on when our porter produced a rope: he motioned that he would tie the smaller pack to the larger one and carry both. He was the one that physically looked like a ninety-pound weakling, but I was feeling too feeble to resist his offer with more than a few grunts of protest.

The pass is at four thousand two hundred metres and the last few hundred metres really take it out of you. Along the way we trudged past many of the other trekkers on the trail that day sitting down having a breather, or prostrate in agony. Every thirty steps or so we would pause and catch our breath. The porter, too, was wheezing heavily now. The pass is called Abra de Warmiwanusca (Huarmiwañusqa) or Dead Woman's Pass — and for good reason. The steps twisted around rocky outcrops through snow and tussock. I pushed myself to forge ahead so that I could photograph Anita's triumphant arrival at the top. Exhausted, I sat down, focused and waited. And waited. And waited. Eventually, when I was preparing to go back down, my wife came into view, the exertion needed for every forward movement of her feet etched onto her face. She clutched her water bottle, from which she seemed to have poured the contents over her hair, or maybe it was just the sweat that kept it lank and plastered to her face. She leant heavily on her Leki walking pole. Cruel bugger that I am, I took the photograph anyway, then leapt down to help her. She was shivering, dizzy, and nauseous: she was suffering symptoms of altitude sickness.

I paid our porter, this time throwing both packs on my back, and, arm in arm, we quickly descended a hundred or so metres down the other side. This made all the difference. We were able to stop, let our lungs recuperate, and then march on to the campsite.

You had to wonder why the Incas would have done this to themselves. Why hump all those stones to make steps that are themselves more a trial than a trail? For all the effort, however, the Inca Trail was worth it: a life-affirming moment if not a life-changing one too. The next day we passed more Inca ruins, trudged over a couple of passes (one at four thousand metres), stepped down through a tunnel scraped out of the rock in what must have been an interminably slow process. And there was not a single moment on the walk when I did not consider it fantastic. Yet all that cannot prepare you for the final morning. Even though you may have seen photographs of Machu Picchu clinging improbably to its shark-tooth-like mountain ridge, no photo can capture the magic of that view at dawn from Intipunku (the Sun Gate), where the sun first rises through a notch in the hillside and lights up the stone buildings that make up Machu Picchu.

In 1911, an archaeologist and climber from Yale University, Hiram Bingham, came across Machu Picchu after scrambling through forest above the Urubamba River and being told about 'ruins' by a local farmer. He came to 'a magnificent flight of stone agricultural terraces, rising 1,000 feet up the mountainside'. Although much of Machu Picchu was overgrown, he could see enough of the huge granite blocks and buildings to experience the same feelings that Anita and I experienced from the Sun Gate. As Bingham so accurately described it, we were all 'spellbound'.

Bingham thought that he had found the legendary 'lost city of the Incas,' Vilcabamba, the place where Inca Manco and his successors put up resistance to the Spanish conquistadors until finally crushed in 1572. But that makes little sense: while Machu Picchu's site makes it easily defensible, it is certain that it was built and abandoned even before Pizarro and his band of not so merry men rode into Cuzco. Besides, archaeologists are now agreed that the real site of Vilcabamba lies about thirty-five kilometres south-west of Machu Picchu.

Whatever its purpose, Machu Picchu is exquisitely sited: clasped onto a steep-sided mountain saddle, with canyon walls on three sides that drop precipitously to the partially encircling Urubamba River far below. Machu Picchu is shrouded as much in mystery about its origins as it is by the cloud cover that often lingers over it. Dating of artefacts, the building style, and carbon-14 dating all suggest that it was built during the era of Inca Pachacutec, the great Inca statesman who expanded the Incan empire beyond the Cuzco valley and governed from 1438 to 1471. But its function, and why it was abandoned, and apparently lost for three centuries, are still the subject of conjecture. Some have suggested that it was an administrative centre or 'llacta' for the Incas, but I don't buy into that as it was sited nowhere near other such centres, which were all built along Capac Ñan — the royal road of the Incas that ran two thousand four hundred kilometres from Cuzco to Quito in Ecuador. It is also far more elaborate than any llacta, and it seems that ordinary citizens were not allowed there. Another theory suggests that Machu Picchu was a fortress: but that doesn't wash either. It was too out of the way, too awkward to get to, as my legs and lungs would attest. Sure, it was magnificently defensible, but what in God's name was there to defend by the time you got there? Another, recent theory, suggested that it was a summer retreat for the Inca emperor and his royal retinue from Cuzco.

In a sense, none of that conjecture matters regarding its ancillary uses. What is indisputable is that it was a site of religious significance. How could it not be, put there atop the mountains by a people whose gods were the sun and the stars? This was a place where you didn't just pray to the gods, you were close enough to whisper in their ears. Forget the satisfaction of walking to the site, forget the grandeur of the scenery and historical sites encountered along the way, it is reward enough for the exertion just to view Machu Picchu at sunrise — before the crowds of tourists are bussed up from the train station at Agua Calientes, turning the whole place into a people-packed museum — and to see it as the Incas must have seen it, as a monument to the Sun God.

The view from afar is of a small village maybe — certainly not a city, lost or otherwise — set against a backdrop of Huayna Picchu, the serrated shark's tooth of a mountain that overlooks Machu Picchu. From some angles it looks like a stone maze, as if a hurricane has ripped the roofs off rows of terraced housing, like those in *Coronation Street*, leaving only the stone walls and pointed end walls, and no doubt, a three hundred-year-old Ken Barlow looking as unchanged as ever. Walking down amongst them, it's like a maze too, with various interconnecting pathways linking stone houses, stone temples, stone baths, and stone terraces; some separated by open green areas but all bound together and bonded, it seems, with the earth.

My favourite, The Temple of the Condor, incorporated a natural rock formation resembling the outspread wings of a condor in flight. On the floor of the temple was a grey slab of rock that formed the bird's head. Looking at it, I could see where it had been carved to represent the bill, and where yet more carved rock, this time in a light grey, had been added to represent the ruff of feathers around the condor's neck. That grey slab, that head of the condor, it turns out was nothing less than a sacrificial altar. Under the temple, in a small cave, Hiram Bingham found a mummy. In all, of the one hundred and thirty-five mummified corpses recovered from Machu Picchu by Bingham and his colleagues, one hundred and nine were females. In some ways Machu Picchu was just like the All Saints Church I had been brought up attending, except that instead of taking along a few cents to put in a collection plate as an offering, these guys made real sacrifices. Virgins. The bodies were mummified and placed in a crouching position in the clefts of walls. And I had to think that had I been a virgin, I would have found Christianity somewhat more attractive.

The Church revered virgins too — well, one virgin, and even she had a baby (so make of that what you will) — and they certainly did not make you die for the gods or a harvest. They did the opposite, in fact, and got God's son to die for you. How good that must have seemed ... I began to wonder how the Incas would have reacted to Christianity when it was first put to them by the Jesuits and the like. If the Inca religion and Catholicism had been cars at an exclusive car sales yard, say, then the Inca version must have seemed like a Hummer; except one of the type used in Iraq, not like the one

Arnie Schwarzenegger drives around LA. It would have appeared functional, but not comfortable, and there would be no denying that it was associated with death and destruction. By comparison, Christianity must have seemed like a Cadillac stretch limo with air-conditioning and bar service. While the Incas may not have cared too much for the drinks served — and let's face it, who markets a wine by calling it 'The Blood of Christ'? — it must surely have seemed better than supplying their own blood. Surely it wouldn't just be virgins that would feel this way. People that grow virgins (i.e. parents), people that virgins become when they grow up (i.e. women) and people that sleep with virgins (i.e. guys), surely they would see the advantages of the stretch limo over the Hummer?[4]

Despite the inherent logic of this argument, which should have seen all the Incas trading up to God, they continued to resist the Spanish from Vilcabamba until 1544, when Manco Capac was stabbed to death by some treacherous Spaniards he had been protecting from Pizarro. Manco's son, Sayri Tupac, followed his father's philosophy but, eventually, after thirteen years, decided that it was better to be in Cuzco and a Christian than in Vilcabamba and an outlaw. One small clue that his conversion had not been as complete as it might have been was that he insisted on marrying his sister, as is Inca custom, to maintain the direct line of descent from the Sun God. Displaying an enormous amount of pragmatism, if not good genetic practice, Pope Julius III provided a papal dispensation to have the marriage consecrated. Poor Sayri did not get too long to enjoy whispering sweet nothings into his sister's ear: within four years he was poisoned. His place as head Inca was taken by another of Manco Capac's sons, Titu Cusi, who set himself the task of doing the Christians as much harm as possible, until he, too, decided to seek accommodation with the Spanish. He had his own

---

[4] While it seems there was a preponderance of females sacrificed at Machu Picchu, discoveries elsewhere indicate the Incas were also prone to sacrificing young boys.

son baptised, no doubt in part because the King of Spain intervened to get a papal dispensation, this time for Titu Cusi's son to marry Sayri Tupac's daughter.

Just when it seemed like the Inca and Christians could agree to get along if they ignored a bit of incest, Titu Cusi (who was living at Vilcabamba) was poisoned too. It was 1570 and although Friar Diego Ortiz — a close companion of Titu — was very unlikely to have killed him, the Indians killed the priest after a protracted period of torture that lasted days and which, to Friar Ortiz, must have seemed like he had been condemned to Hell for eternity. Yet another of Manco Capac's sons, Tupac Amaru, succeeded as the Sapa Inca (God Emperor).

By now the new Viceroy of Peru, Francisco de Toledo, had recognised the danger the Inca posed and ordered that Vilcabamba be taken and the Incas stopped for good. On 21 September 1572, Tupac Amaru was captured and led, by a gold chain about his neck, into Cuzco's plaza before a crowd of up to fifteen thousand Indians. It was announced to the wailing crowd that he had converted to Christianity, and then, on Toledo's orders, he was beheaded. According to Friar Gabriel de Oviedo, Prior of the Dominicans at Cuzco, the last words of the last Inca emperor were 'Mother Earth, witness how my enemies shed my blood'. Now call me cynical, but that doesn't sound to me like the sentiments of someone who had taken on the mantle of Christianity all that seriously.

Back in Cuzco, Anita and I sat in the Café Bagdad overlooking the plaza. Three blocks away, Tupac Amaru's two bits had been buried in the Church of Santo Domingo, which ironically was constructed upon the remains of the Coricancha, the Incan monument to the sun that had housed the mummies of Tupac's ancestors. The Son of God triumphant over the Sun God. Earlier, I had walked by Santo Domingo, but could not bring myself to go in. By night, the plaza was lit up. Beside the restaurant was the huge cathedral built on the site of the Inca Viracocha's palace; on the left side of the plaza, as we sat looking down from the balcony, the lights picked out the beautifully ornate baroque facade of the Church of La Compañía, built on the foundations of the palace of yet another Inca, Huayna Capac. It all looked far too pretty, the people in the plaza far too happy, when you thought for even an instant about the history of the square and the blood it had seen spilled in the name of God or gods and, always, supposedly, for enlightenment.

We went back to the Cuzco Plaza II and I enjoyed for the last time sleeping with a twenty-two-year-old: in the morning my wife and I would get back our true identities as we hopped on a train that would take us away from this battleground that pitted men of God against sun worshippers. Before going to sleep, I drank several cups of tea made with cocoa leaves, the plant from which cocaine is derived. It is supposed to help with the altitude, but in this case, it was me that got high. I lay in bed hallucinating, convinced that someone had come into our room. Was it Friar Ortiz crying for mercy or was it the unholy Toledo carrying Inca Tupac's head? I don't know. All I know is that I was frightened. If this was Christianity then give me evolution. Nature may be red in tooth and claw, but it's got nothing on the Church.

The Galapagos and Other Islands

– 24 –

Discovering the
Galapagos Islands

The Galapagos Islands are really the heart of Darwin's theory of evolution, the spiritual if not the actual beginnings of his realisation that species are not immutable but have evolved from one to the other. Given its importance to the development of Darwin's theory of evolution by Natural Selection, it comes as a surprise that Darwin spent only a month there out of a journey of nearly five years.

To get to the islands I would need to go via Ecuador, which annexed the islands in 1832, just three years before FitzRoy pointed the *Beagle*'s prow north-west from Lima's port of Callao and headed towards them. Onboard, Darwin waited with excitement. As he wrote to his cousin, 'I look forward to the Galapagos with more interest than any other part of the voyage.' If this seems like some sort of prescience that somehow in the Galapagos he would find the biological equivalent of the Holy Grail — a means of making sense of life on Earth — it was not. Darwin was simply interested in the islands' geology. He knew they were volcanic and recently formed and he was keen to see the new earth after the old earth of the Andes.

The trouble for me was that getting to the Galapagos required first flying to Ecuador, which meant flying into Quito, the capital. Quito was founded in 1534 by the Spanish and was built on the site of an Indian city, which had been razed to the ground the year before by the Incas when it was apparent the Spanish were coming and there was not much they could do about it. It sits at a breath-sapping two thousand eight hundred or so metres above sea level. Flying into Quito you get a sense that Ecuador was never meant to catch up with the twenty-first century, that the sixteenth century would have continued to suit it just fine: the mountains seem too impossibly steep for planes to land there. Looking out the window as forested mountain sides whizzed by much too close for my liking, I was reminded of the Incan road, the Capac Ñan, which was made of stones and ran the two thousand four hundred kilometres from Cuzco to Quito at a uniform width just shy of eight metres. It struck me then that the Incas had got it right: Quito was one of those places best left to approach on foot.

I was travelling with four other blokes — big, strong, hairy creatures who looked as out of place in Quito as a yeti would be in Times Square. The small, dark-haired Indian locals seemed minuscule by comparison. Two were underwater cameramen, from whom one could accept a certain diffidence given the long periods they had spent without much oxygen; one was, in the parlance of the documentary maker, a topside cameraman (which meant simply that he liked breathing air and didn't like getting his feet wet); and the other was a soundman. Me? I was at once the most dispensable and the most crucial member of the team: I was the director. This meant that I didn't actually do anything physically important in securing the footage, but I was the one who determined the type of footage that was taken and, therefore, the type of story that could be told. Theoretically, it should have meant that I was treated with respect and called Sir or Director or anything vaguely like Lord, but from these hirsute mountains of testosterone it was usually something like, 'What do you want now you little bastard?'

Quito, like many South American cities, has a grand Spanish-influenced heart, surrounded by poverty, street merchants, colour and corruption. We walked to the central plaza for a meeting with our 'fixer' — a person paid to leaven the way through the bureaucracy that accompanies anyone going to the Galapagos and which is magnified a hundred-fold for film crews.

Adrian, the soundman, is colossal: built from the same mould as New Zealand's famous rugby player, Colin Meads, he has a chin that could dent a thousand ships and a physique that only the blind or the foolish would consider taking on. As we walked through the jostle of people selling alpaca wool jerseys and balsa wood toucans, a small dark-haired man with an ice-cream banged into him. Adrian reacted as we all would: startled, he stepped back and removed his hand from his pocket, where it had been resting on his wallet, and wiped the ice-cream off his shirt. In the second it took him to put his hand back in his pocket, his wallet had gone.

Several hundred dollars lighter, we met up with our fixer in a bar that was all colonial plush and could have by itself justified Quito's listing as a UNESCO World Heritage Site. The good news, the fixer relayed, was that the Ecuadorian authorities would permit us to film in the Galapagos; the bad news was that they wanted an extra one thousand American dollars from us for the privilege of doing so.

We had charted a yacht, a two-masted schooner, to travel about the islands. First, however, Robert (the topside cameraman) and I would fly to the island of Santa Cruz to film giant tortoises in the hinterland. The others would remain in Quito for a couple of days to sort out the last of the permits and payments, since the two were inextricably linked, before joining us on the yacht.

Tame Airlines is actually operated by the Ecuadorian military, which means that there is some excuse for the appalling service. We touched down in Guayaquil — a sultry tropical coastal city — before leaving the mainland of South America behind us and flying the best part of one thousand kilometres to Baltra in the Galapagos. Robert and I were picked up by a driver, taken across to the island of Santa Cruz and, then, up a rough road that took us surprisingly high through surprisingly cool, lush, forested areas. The cold waters of the Humboldt Current, which travel up the western side of South America from the Antarctic before diverting across the Pacific and upwelling around the Galapagos, help create a microclimate that is not always as tropical as one might expect from these islands that straddle the equator.

We stopped the vehicle and, after a short hike, came to an open area in the forest. Here, we didn't just step back in time, we jumped back. As in a scene out of *Jurassic Park*, creatures of another geologic age were incongruously dotted through the grassy clearing. They were big, they were slow — but mostly, the impression that they gave, is they were ancient. Their necks moved like elephant trunks, extending and retracting as needed to bring their horny mouths in contact with the grass they were eating. Everything about the way they moved was deliberate, slow, almost drugged. This was the ultimate in conserving energy.

It felt such a privilege. Like we had been invited to a very special party — even if all the guests seemed to be up to their eyeballs on Prozac and we had arrived a couple of a hundred million years too late. The tortoises didn't seem to mind our presence as long as we moved liked they did. The shell of one had green moss hanging from its slightly upturned edges as if to underline just how little they moved: if a tortoise could gather moss, it was a fair bet that it didn't roll about too much.

Darwin's reaction to the giant tortoises when he first saw them was not dissimilar to my own. He described them as 'old-fashioned antediluvian animals' and 'inhabitants of some other planet.' He even climbed aboard one and calculated that on a good day — with the wind behind it, I suspect — it might cover a distance of four miles (six-and-a-half kilometres).

The great size and slowness of the tortoises of the Galapagos would bring them unwanted attention. The Galapagos Islands were only discovered by humans in 1535: just as the Spanish were establishing Quito, the Bishop of Panama, Fray Tomás de Berlanga, was taken offshore by currents when en route to Peru at the behest of the King of Spain to sort out the problems that had arisen from Pizarro and his mates' brutal conquest of the Incas in Cuzco and elsewhere. Bishop Berlanga reported on the islands he encountered and their notable inhabitants, thereby sealing the fate of the very creatures for which the islands would be named. The islands started to appear on maps from the late sixteenth century and were called 'Insulae de los Galopegos' (Islands of the Tortoises). Pirates and, more particularly, whalers, would treat the Galapagos Islands subsequently as a place to replenish supplies. And it was not like they stocked up on sides of mutton. They took tortoises. Killed them in their thousands. The tortoises were slow and easy to catch. They were huge: providing meat for a ravenous crew. Best of all, they came with their own freshening device. Upside down, they could be kept alive onboard ships, where they could survive for months without food, providing crews with fresh meat. The big whales of the area certainly suffered: the blues, the sperm, the humpbacks — a veritable litany of endangered names — but the Galapagos tortoises were the innocent collateral damage, the harmless bystanders all but exterminated too in the war on whales.

– 25 –

The Galapagos Islands and the Crux of a Good Idea

The *Encantada* is a twenty-one metre long schooner. The brochures described it as 'charming' and it really was. Had it been a house, a real-estate agent would have marketed it with the term 'character.' For the five of us, our two guides, and the three-man crew, it was ample. I felt a little like one of the pirates who stopped by the islands to pick up water and tortoises. But really, I felt most like Darwin himself. Because, from a distance, when you looked down on the *Encantada* with its twin masts and sails backlit by the setting sun so that its red hull became a silhouette, it took hardly any imagination at all to see it as the *Beagle* (certainly less than a cup of tea made from cocoa leaves). And if you could see that as the *Beagle*, well, it didn't take too much more to put yourself in the place of Darwin and see the islands as he might have seen them.

Initially, however, I couldn't stop myself from seeing the islands as *not* being how I had imagined them. I suppose for most biologists, the Galapagos are a sort of Mecca. I don't face east five times a day and offer a little prayer, but I do think of them as Natural Selection's holy site. Perhaps because of that, my expectations were that this was to be some type of animal Shangri-La with weird and wonderful beasts dripping from every cornice and corner: an archipelago of zoos where the intervening seas were simply moats that kept their animals packed in and all we had to do was sail by and marvel at how clever evolution had been.

But the Galapagos Islands are not at all like that. They are largely barren, infertile. Sure, there are patches of greenery, like the forested high country of Santa Cruz and the mangrove swamps of Isabela, but much of the Galapagos wears its volcanic origins on its sleeve. Bare swathes of brown rock or treacle-like ripples of blackened lava make up much of the land. Darwin described it in his diary as being 'what we might imagine the cultivated parts of the Infernal regions to be'. The best parts of Hell indeed. Or maybe the worst parts of Earth. When he went ashore at Isla San Cristobal he added, 'Nothing could be less inviting than the first appearance'. The animals are there, and in places they may even be dense, but the Galapagos are really small isolated pockets of biology set in a landscape that is otherwise all geology.

In that sense, Darwin got it right. The crucial starting point of interest in the Galapagos Islands is their geology. Initially we sailed from Baltra to Bartolome and moored off the aptly-named Pinnacle Rock. We took a Zodiac to the shore, leaping onto jagged volcanic lava, watched over by a marine iguana of a similar shade to the black-grey rock. It nodded its head, but I knew enough behaviour to know that this was not a welcome but a warning. We had entered its home. We hiked up the bare reddish-brown volcanic soil until we reached the six-hundred metre top of the island. Looking to our right we could make out two perfectly formed dome craters. Volcanoes in miniature. Bonsai volcanoes. Although there was no smoke or plume coming from them, the area all around was so desolate, so devoid of living things, that it seemed that these volcanoes and this ground upon which we stood had only stopped erupting relatively recently. In fact, it didn't feel as if they had stopped erupting so much as if they had just stopped mid-sentence, to take a pause for breath or whatever volcanoes do between blasts. This was more moonscape than it was the earthscape I knew, or anything else that Darwin would have experienced from Shrewsbury to South America.

Looking to our left, with the equally barren Santiago on the horizon, we could see the silhouette of the *Encantada* moored beside Pinnacle Rock.[5] And from this distance, no imagination was required at all. That was the *Beagle* — and if the *Encantada* could be the *Beagle*, then I could surely be a new-age Darwin. And I started to realise that, as such, it would be the formation of these islands that would interest me more than a couple of slow-moving monoliths or an ugly head-bobbing lizard.

We returned to the *Encantada* and sailed to an area where the divers could go down deep. When we reviewed the rushes captured from a small video camera, I saw great fumeroles spitting bubbles like an electric jug that wouldn't stop boiling. The volcanic cones on Bartolome may be silent, but the crust of earth from which the Galapagos Islands have arisen is still very much alive. The best estimates are that the Galapagos rose out of the ocean no more than five million years ago. A blink of the eye in geologic time, these islands were so young they should have been in diapers.

So if the Galapagos Islands are new, where did all the animals and plants that populate them, sparsely or otherwise, come from? It didn't seem likely that the Creator could have woken up on the five-billionth day or the six-thousandth day (or whatever your take on the age of the Earth may be) and decided, as an afterthought, to add the giant tortoise, the marine iguana and the Galapagos flamingo to the list of animals He had created on days five and six. This is where all Darwin and FitzRoy's mucking around in South America over the previous four years paid dividends. If someone were organising a trip around the world now with the express purpose of discovering evidence for Natural Selection, they might be tempted to high-tail it to the Galapagos and set up camp, but it was really Darwin's intimate familiarity with the South American flora and fauna that allowed him to see links that other detectives would have missed.

---

[5] The names Darwin used for the islands are not the present ones: hence he called Santiago: *James Island*, Isla San Cristobal: *Chatam*, Isla Espanola: *Hood*, Isla Santa Cruz: *Indefatigable*, Isla Isabela: *Albermarle* and so forth.

After initial examination of the scene, Detective Inspector Darwin reviewed the evidence. The islands were undeniably young. Yet, this was the puzzling thing: although sparingly inhabited, most of the animals and plants were new species, peculiar only to the Galapagos. Of the twenty-six species of land birds he collected, twenty-five were found nowhere else on the globe. Of the nearly two hundred species of flowering plants he found on the islands, Darwin estimated that one hundred existed only in the Galapagos. But it got curiouser and curiouser. Darwin realised that despite having so many species peculiar to it, the creatures and plants on the Galapagos had similar counterparts on the South American mainland: 'all show a marked relationship with those of America, though separated from that continent by an open space of ocean, between 500 and 600 miles in width'.

One relationship you could pass off as coincidence, but not *all* of them. Darwin realised that the most likely scenario was that representatives of the South American flora and fauna had somehow been transported to the newly emerged islands — by wind, sea, storm, or driftwood — and once there had become modified to the new forms. But *how* and *why*? As Darwin himself put it, 'both in space and time, we seem to be brought somewhat near to that great fact — that mystery of mysteries — the first appearance of new beings on this earth'. The clue to solving this mystery would actually come, not from examining the origins of the animals and plants that arrived in the Galapagos, but their fate once they got there.

As we made landfall around the Galapagos, we saw finches with big thick bills crushing berries on the ground at one location, while in other places there were finches with very fine bills — but really, why would you notice the difference any more than you would a couple of different birds in your garden? More striking perhaps were the marine iguanas, because they sat at the margin of the sea and, when they weren't sunning themselves, they moved down to the water's edge where they ate seaweed off the rocks as the tide went out. When we followed them into the water, we discovered they fed underwater, clinging to the rocky substrate with their claws while the rest of their bodies swayed in the currents, as they tore off great chunks of the seaweed they favoured with their mouths. Darwin did not have a snorkel, but he did dissect some marine iguanas and also ascertained that they were eating seaweed. Furthermore, some of the *Beagle*'s sailors determined, through a cruel experiment, that marine iguanas could survive long periods under water: they weighted one, threw it overboard, then retrieved it an hour or so later when it was still kicking and breathing. The iguanas, which are about a metre or so long and have a row of white spines down their backs that lend them a dinosaur-like appearance, show other adaptations for the water that Darwin noted too. Their tails are flattened and they use these to propel themselves through the water with the sinusoidal movements of a sea snake. They have webbing between their toes. But the really remarkable thing was that when we moved inland a bit, we came across a similar iguana, except this one was an orange-brown, had no webbed toes, a rounded tail, and it ate cactus fruit. Go figure.

We took the *Encantada* around the top of Isabela, sailing hard up against rocky cliffs in the morning mist. The water there was a dark slate-blue, a depth of colour that interior decorators could only dream about. Taking the Zodiac, we ran into a sea cave and there, roosting on ledges at head height, was a line of blue feet and nothing else. As our eyes adjusted to the dim light in the cave, we saw that the feet were attached to a line of blue-footed boobies. They looked like gannets given a new paint job, as if some interior decorator, in a creative moment, had removed all the yellow bits from the head, thrown together a concoction of blue and violet pigment, then sprayed the resulting bright pastel blue paint onto the birds' legs and webbed feet. Yet elsewhere in the Galapagos you could find boobies that were the same to all intents and purposes, except that their feet had been sprayed a bright red.

It is not hard to imagine the young Darwin puzzling over why an all-wise Creator would bother to plant similar species of iguanas or boobies within the confines of relatively isolated, tiny and obscure islands. But there had to be more to it than that, more to it than simply a proliferation of new species with similarities to the continental species a thousand kilometres away. Sure, one might imagine that some immigrants arrived from South America and, finding themselves in the newly-formed and uninhabited space of the Galapagos, became modified to conditions there. That would be evolution, but it tells us nothing of the process.

We had one advantage over Darwin. We had aqualungs. We could see a side of the Galapagos that he could not. We took the *Encantada* out to a stack of rock too small to be called an island like the rest. On the way we saw humpback whales breaching, propelling their gigantic bodies from the water and splashing down with large belly flops.

This was to be a deep dive: we were trying to film hammerhead sharks in an area where — we were assured by our guides — they would be congregating for breeding. The divers, Andrew and Ed, disappeared overboard. To fill the time while we waited, I donned a snorkel and mask and jumped into the water, intent on exploring the sea life by the rock stack.

I was pretty close to the stack when a large brown submarine passed under me. At least, that is what I thought it was. In the water it seemed at least three times my size and it cruised just a metre or two below me, looking up at me with one large eye. It was a bull male sea lion. It looked as invincible as I felt vulnerable. I retreated — more like flew — to the *Encantada* and, soon after, a large shark approached the yacht. By now the unnatural movements of the anchored boat were making me ill and the thought that I could have been shark bait if not sea lion bait only added to my queasiness.

To say that I don't like sharks is not the same as saying that I don't like country and western music. I'm absolutely petrified of sharks. And while the thought of listening to *Achy Breaky Heart* can be scary, I figure that an evening of Billy Ray Cyrus is not likely to kill me. Actually, that's not a good example because it probably would: but at least I wouldn't bleed to death and the act of throwing myself out of a window would arguably be a means of relieving suffering as opposed to meeting it in the form of a bite.

The shark that came up to the boat was not a hammerhead, nor was it like the white-tipped shark that I had seen earlier when snorkelling around Bartolome. On that occasion, while my first reaction had been one of panic, the second had been one of fascination, and, as I sucked air a lot faster than I needed to through the snorkel, I found conflicting parts of me fighting for control. The big yellow bit wanted to get the fuck out of there, while the biologist in me wanted to follow the shark, impressed by how its body moved so effortlessly through the water. If there were ever a design competition for animals, the shark would win hands down. It is the E-type Jaguar of machines powered by the Krebs Cycle. Even if you didn't want to go riding in one — and I didn't — you had to admire its lines.

The more I snorkelled around the Galapagos, the more I realised that while the shark lines may be the prettiest, the shape itself wasn't peculiar to them. The sea lions, when in the water, had the same spindle shape as the shark, as did most of the other fish, including a large school of barracuda. The breaching whales had it. Even the tiny Galapagos penguins had it. A large green sea turtle had swum by, its forefeet more like the fins of the shark, the flippers of the whale and the seal, than the legs of its supposed near-relative, the giant tortoise. It didn't take much insight to realise that what was occurring below the Galapagos seemed to be the opposite of what was occurring on top. That on the land something was causing species to proliferate into a myriad different forms, whereas in the water, most creatures adopted a fish shape — even if they were reptiles, birds, or mammals. Why would evolution operate in such seemingly conflicting ways? Difference above. Conformity below.

Darwin noticed the difference even without an aqualung. He referred to the 'law of aquatic forms' and that they were 'whether marine or fresh water, being less peculiar at any given point of the earth's surface than the terrestrial forms of the same classes'. The common aspect of aquatic environments is, of course water — and one might suppose, for whatever reason, that water exerts some constraints on design. So to understand how designs could proliferate unfettered — that is, for evolution to occur — it would pay any budding detective to look to the land for suspects.

This is where the Galapagos Islands really came up trumps and why they are so crucial to Darwin's view of the world. For Darwin's great stroke of fortune was to realise — eventually — that within the Galapagos archipelago, each island had a different suite of animals and plants, even though they existed under roughly the same conditions and circumstances:

> I never dreamed that islands, about 50 or 60 miles apart, and most of them in sight of each other, formed of precisely the same rocks, placed under a quite similar climate, rising to a nearly equal height, would have been differently tenanted.

Darwin was initially clued into this fact by the Vice-Governor of the Colony, Mr Nicholas Lawson, who told Darwin that he could tell what island a tortoise had come from just by looking at its shell. In hindsight it seems that this should have been a '*Eureka!*' moment for Darwin, but Lawson's remark fell like water off a tortoise's back and it was only later, when onboard the *Beagle* after they had set sail from the Galapagos, that Darwin recalled the remark and recognised its significance. To make use of the hours en route to Tahiti, Darwin was sorting through the specimens of the 'mocking-thrush' that he and others onboard had shot and he realised to his astonishment that of the three species, all those shot from Isla Santa Maria belonged to one species, all those from Isla Isabela to another and, while the remaining specimens had come from two islands, these had neighbouring islands between them to provide a connecting link.

The penny dropped. He started to think about his collection of finches, of which he had many species and which he had already considered noteworthy for the marvellous variety and gradation in their bill sizes and shapes. Unfortunately, he had not twigged to the importance of identifying the island on which each specimen was collected soon enough and much of his collection of finches had been mixed up without noting the specific island from which they had been procured. Even so, from the pattern he observed where he did know something of the island source, he concluded that he had 'strong reasons to suspect' that at least some species of the finches 'are confined to separate islands'.

And so, catching the same train of thought as Darwin, we might suppose that immigrants from the South American continent somehow arrived in the Galapagos archipelago and, as they occupied each island, over time became modified. Hence, for evolution to occur it seems that a necessary prerequisite must involve some form of isolation — at least reproductive isolation, a separate breeding group as it were — and then some process that alters the design of the animals to fit the peculiarities of the specific environment.

Darwin would later write of his time in the Galapagos:

> It is the fate of most voyagers, no sooner to discover what is most interesting in any locality, than they are hurried from it; but I ought, perhaps, to be thankful that I obtained sufficient materials to establish this most remarkable fact in the distribution of organic beings.

Our time was up too. We would have to leave the *Encantada* so that it could pick up a group of those tourists who flock to the islands for the same reason I had: that somehow through the experience they hope it will bring them closer to that mystery of mysteries. But on our last evening, as I sat with the others on the stern of the *Encantada*, raising a glass or two of rum to the setting sun, I looked across at the spiny silhouette of a marine iguana watching us from the nearby rocks and I thought that it was pretty much still a mystery to me. Still a mystery how that process of change could work. I could accept the ancestor, the immigrant from South America. I could accept it had changed, evolved. But I did not understand how.

I didn't snap out of this reverie until after our plane had touched down at Quito. Some official in the cargo department of Tame Airlines — who at a quarter of the age of the giant tortoises we had just filmed, still managed to move twice as slowly — was telling us in an extremely arrogant fashion that if we were patient, and if all went well, we might possibly expect to see our gear before the end of the next bloody millennium. At that moment, I happened to put my hand-carry bag down and must have, in the process, inadvertently squashed a mouse. I noticed it twitching, and I pointed to its little white body kicking with the last spasms of life leaving it. The hitherto macho and immobile administrator transformed abruptly into a slobbering, wailing maniac: he shouted at me between tears that I had killed his pet mouse. Our quick-thinking cameraman averted potential disaster. Rob jumped in front of the man and said, 'This time it's just the mouse. Now get our gear!' I don't know whether he understood Rob and respected this brazen counter-machismo, or whether he did not understand and was simply too distressed to contemplate the rest of the paperwork, but for whatever reason, suddenly all thirty of our bags and boxes appeared.

As Rob and the Tame man squared off against each other, I was suddenly back in the Galapagos looking at two male marine iguanas facing off, bobbing their heads, their skin flushed, the spines on their backs menacing, like a row of very odd teeth. 'Imps of darkness', Darwin had called them, and who could disagree? Was it really possible that all this posturing I saw in the world around me, all these differences between animals and plants — from the booby's blue feet to the Tame man's bushy moustache — could all be explained by a theory founded on procreation as opposed to creation? Was it really love — well, sex — that made the world go round? Because wasn't that the lesson that the Galapagos had taught Darwin, and had taught me too, that the fountain of diversity — the production of new forms — was fed from our loins? We may be what we eat, but to evolve we must beget.

'Survival of the fittest' is meaningless without sex. It is sex that drives us, and drives evolution too. That sudden insight, however, vaporised as soon as we left the airport: we passed a high wall festooned with graffiti in huge black letters. Our driver translated. 'The ugly women of the world have a right to live — but why all of them in Quito?'

What was I to think of a world where men loved mice more than women?

– 26 –

New Zealand and Missed Opportunities

After the Galapagos Islands, the *Beagle* headed to Tahiti. I touched down in Tahiti just long enough to realise, like Darwin, that it looked like a paradise and that its locals were physically attractive. But Darwin and FitzRoy were chiefly concerned with the role of the missionaries there and the natural history of the islands seems to have played little part in their thoughts. Eleven days later they set sail again.

On 21 December 1835, the *Beagle* anchored in New Zealand's Bay of Islands. The three-and-a-half week journey to New Zealand had been a source of more seasickness and, by the time Darwin reached New Zealand, homesickness too. At this stage of the journey they were all looking forward to getting back to England. Perhaps because of this, Darwin paid the biota of New Zealand as little heed as he had that of Tahiti. He did note, however, that in New Zealand the place of mammals had largely been taken by flightless birds (moa), just as on the Galapagos, reptiles had occupied the ecological spaces that were normally the province of mammals elsewhere. While this was a seemingly innocuous comment, almost a throw-away line, it would later have immense relevance to the development of his theory. When it came to writing *On the Origin of Species*, Darwin would dwell upon just this point. If animals placed into an open, uninhabited environment could evolve into a variety of different forms and take up a variety of different lifestyles, the corollary of that was that in normal situations where the environment was not new, where species already occupied most conceivable lifestyles, there must be a competition, a constraint, that prevented new forms of animals from moving in on the territories of established animals. This notion of competition would become central to the development of Natural Selection. But in December 1835, Darwin was as far from that point intellectually as New Zealand was geographically from his homeland: he merely noted that where there were no mammals, reptiles and birds could fill those lifestyles.

Like those about Tahiti, most of his ruminations about New Zealand concerned the state of the natives and the role of the missionaries. But where he had liked the Tahitians, he was not impressed by the New Zealand Māori:

> their persons and houses are filthily dirty and offensive: the idea of washing either their bodies or their clothes never seems to enter their heads. I saw a chief, who was wearing a shirt black and matted with filth, and when asked how it came to be so dirty, he replied, with surprise, 'Do not you see it is an old one?'

In Kororāreka (the site of present-day Russell), which at the time was the largest New Zealand settlement, they found the English settlers to be living in conditions no better than the natives. 'There are many spirit shops, & the whole population is addicted to drunkenness & all kinds of vice,' Darwin recorded in his diary. As luck would have it, Kororāreka would prove to be an even more troubling place for FitzRoy.

Less than five years after Darwin and FitzRoy's visit, New Zealand became a British colony in 1840 with the signing of the Treaty of Waitangi, whereby a group of Māori chiefs ceded sovereignty to Britain in exchange for full rights and privileges as British subjects. After the *Beagle* arrived back in England, FitzRoy would first be elected to parliament and then, in 1843, would become only the second Governor of the new colony of New Zealand. Not all Māori remained enamoured of the new arrangements that the treaty brought and in 1844 the Māori chief Hōne Heke, who ironically had been the first Māori chief to sign the treaty, cut down a flagpole at Kororāreka that displayed the Union Jack. FitzRoy had the flagpole restored but in January of the next year, Hōne cut it down again. FitzRoy reacted by having the flagpole rebuilt again, this time sheathed in iron, and he had a permanent guard stationed there to protect it. But two months later, Hōne Heke arrived in town with two hundred men, cut the flagpole down for a third time and then razed and looted Kororāreka. While most of the Māori chiefs were sympathetic and friendly to FitzRoy, his inability to deal with Hōne Heke — even after getting reinforcements from the colony in Australia — would prove a pivotal moment in New Zealand's history, with dissent from a faction of Māori with the Crown continuing to the present day. Later that year, FitzRoy's appointment as Governor was terminated and he was recalled to London; whether at the behest of dissatisfied settlers or a concerned British government is a matter of debate, but incompetence in dealing with the natives at Kororāreka cannot have helped either way.

The *Beagle* lifted anchor and left the Bay of Islands and New Zealand a mere nine days after arriving. Darwin's parting words were: 'I believe we were all glad to leave New Zealand. It is not a pleasant place'.

But as New Zealand is my home and I profess a certain love for the place, I determined that I should see what Darwin could have found to assist him in the development of his theory had he lingered longer. It would have been easy for me to have stayed in Northland, to recount what might have happened had Darwin caught a kiwi or found the bones of a moa; but he had found similar such beasts in South America. They might have affirmed for him that the world was full of weird creatures and that some of them had died out in the past, but I don't think they would have added substantially to the view of the world that he had gained already from the *Beagle*.

I began to wonder what would have happened had Darwin visited the South Island of New Zealand and gone into its interior, as he had in Argentina and Chile. As I had not yet walked the Routeburn Track — supposedly one of the great treks of the world — I decided that this should be my task: to walk the Routeburn and to experience it as Darwin might have experienced it.

– 27 –

The Routeburn Track and Nature's Progression: From Simple to Complex

I enlisted the company of my obliging if mystified wife, and as we set out from Dunedin on the drive to Queenstown, the omens did not look too good: cement skies and continuous rain accompanied us the whole way. We did stop at a cute schist-covered café along the way for a latte and scone. Well, it said 'scone' on the menu, but it turned out to be half a scone with a gigantic mound of cream on top to disguise the fact that half of it was missing.

One problem with walking the Routeburn is that the track crosses a mountain range so that the entrance point to the track is nowhere near its exit point. Our plan was to leave the car in Queenstown, catch a bus up to the start of the track and, four days later, be picked up by another bus that would eventually return us to Queenstown. That semi-scone ended up costing us more than the outrageous amount on the bill had suggested: by the time we got to Queenstown, the last bus had already left. We decided to drive to the track entrance and figure out how to collect our car after the trek.

We drove at speed down the western side of Lake Wakatipu, New Zealand's longest lake, and miraculously the rain cleared by the time we reached Glenorchy. Another half hour drive and we were in the trees of Mount Aspiring National Park. Leaving our car, we began our walk through a forest right out of a Disney set. The ground was covered in moss too thick to be real. Mist filled the void between gnarled trees and the recent torrential rain had made even the smallest creek a cataract of Niagra proportions.

After two hours we reached a small clearing and then began a slow trudge up to Routeburn Falls Hut. I could feel the weight of each peanut in my pack as I contemplated the uncanny likeness of the forest to those we had walked through near Ushuaia in Argentina and Pucon in Chile. How could it be that trees half a world away could so resemble each other? It's not like trees can walk or fly, so surely, had Darwin or anyone else wandered through the South American forests and then the New Zealand ones, they would be likely to conclude that the distribution of these trees pointed more to a Creator that could plonk life forms down where He wished, uninhibited by great oceans or mountain ranges?

The Falls Hut is superbly sited and I slept spectacularly well as the three cups of wine I had consumed counteracted the two cups of coffee. The morning was glorious, not a cloud in the sky, as we headed above the bushline. The sun soon heated the wet forest below us, causing steam to rise as misty clouds that followed us up a large open valley to the Harris Saddle. The valley was covered in tussock, but most noticeably, was dotted with flowers: Mount Cook Lilies and mountain daisies. But compared to the alpine flowers I had seen in Mount Rainier National Park in Washington, when we were there to visit Dee, these were not colourful. Gone were the reds, oranges and blues of North American or European meadows: these were white with yellow centres. The New Zealand alpine flora is unusual in that it evolved isolated from the rest of the world. The mountains are only five to seven million years old and the flowers maybe only two million. Of the five hundred species in New Zealand confined solely to the alpine regions, ninety-three per cent are found only in New Zealand. And nearly all of them are white.

I attempted to photograph one of the mountain daisies and fell into a bog, burying my calf and wounding my knee. These flowers were white it seemed because of the paucity of pollinators in this high zone. The butterflies too were all white. White flowers attract generalists, whereas coloured flowers have been selected over time to attract specific pollinators. So there on the Routeburn, Darwin could have seen evidence that Natural Selection takes time to fashion specific forms; that it works from simplicity to complexity. Surely this was a sign of evolution and not creation? Surely a Creator could make a plant or animal as complex as He wished the first time around? There'd be no need to work up to it like a swimmer taking the first tentative steps into a cold pool. Surely it was a prediction of evolution, that complexity should be greatest in those environments that had persisted the longest?

We climbed Conical Hill, which seemed more Mount Everest than hill, but were rewarded with views along the whole length of the Darren Mountains to the sea and Martin's Bay. From there it was another three hours to the next hut, looking down on the Hollyford Valley with just the occasional plane overhead to remind us that these were not Darwin's times.

The MacKenzie Hut nestled beside a small green lake with an indented shoreline. The bunkroom held eight large mattresses, each of which was intended to sleep four. We claimed our half mattress and settled down to sleep — but nights do not get much worse than that one. Across the way from us lay the world's most obnoxious snorer: Herschell. After hiking all day he had donned Asics and shorts and gone for a run around the lake. Had he worn a sign that said 'plonker,' people could not have got the message any sooner. Near Herschell lay a couple, including a woman of ample proportions who snored like a kākāpō[6] booming: deep, echoing sounds that started somewhere below my hearing range so that initially I

---

[6] A kākāpō is a large flightless parrot native to New Zealand. Males mate by creating an arena where they make booming sounds. Perhaps not the most successful pick up line: at one stage in the late twentieth century there were only forty-two kākāpō left in the world.

felt the exhalations as a small earthquake before they washed over me, fog horn-like.

With the snoring in stereo, I pushed tissues into my ears and wondered what it must have been like in the bowels of the *Beagle* with all those men swinging in their hammocks. Did some fucking nineteenth-century Herschell disturb the rest of them for nearly five years?

At around one a.m., a couple of English girls with their two attendants came in giggling, knocking over pots in the dark and talking like they were at a convention for the deaf. Grabbing our sleeping bags, my wife and I retreated to the kitchen where we tried forlornly to sleep on benches that were as hard as they were narrow. The quiet made it just about worth it until two keas, New Zealand's native mountain parrots, decided to play a game that involved pushing a wooden box backwards and forwards inside my skull, but which in reality turned out to be on the veranda just beyond my head. Then the first of the early risers came in to prepare breakfast, so we repaired once again to the bunkroom where, miraculously, Herschell was still snoring: he hadn't missed a breath — unfortunately.

An even more lamentable moment awaited us at the end of the whole trek. I was driving a rental car while my wife drove behind me in our car, which we had just retrieved from the start of the track. At a certain point, I noticed that she was no longer following. I turned back only to find our car parked on a very steep slope. As I got out my wife said, 'I've got two punctures, I may have hit a rock.' Walking around the other side of our car, I discovered both tyres were pancake flat. The wheel rims that had been holding them were buckled severely, with huge indentations as if some car-eating creature had taken big bites from them.

In my defence, I just want to say that I tried to keep my response measured, although I will concede that it may have come out somewhat louder than was useful under the circumstances. 'WHAT DO YOU MEAN YOU *MAY* HAVE HIT A ROCK?!' My wife said that the rock was on the road and, looking around, I could see that technically she was correct if you included the two metres of the shoulder outside the white line.

Darwin, too, seems to have hit a rock of sorts when he landed in New Zealand. He did not make the most of his opportunities and his normally enquiring mind seems to have been parked as surely as my wife's car was on that road out of Glenorchy. Had he been to the mountains, had he seen the white flowers and their similarly bland-coloured pollinators, he might have realised aspects about the progress of evolution more quickly than he otherwise did. He might even have got to appreciate New Zealand. Admittedly, this last point seems doubtful given his back-handed compliment when he came across a party of children preparing to celebrate Christmas: 'I never saw a nicer or more merry group; and to think that this was in the centre of the land of cannibalism, murder, and all atrocious crimes!'

– 28 –

Australia and a
Different Creator

Darwin's reaction to Australia was quite the opposite of his one to New Zealand: he loved the place. Landing first in Sydney and later in Hobart, he professed a preference for Tasmania. In Sydney he took a trip inland to the Blue Mountains. When I first visited Sydney, I did the same thing in a car. I remember my delight when a kangaroo hopped across the road in front of the car. Darwin apparently saw relatively little in the way of wildlife on his trip, although he did catch and skin a platypus.

If there is one animal that I cannot imagine killing, let alone skinning, it is a platypus. I first saw one at Sydney's Taronga Park Zoo and I fell in love with it as fully as I have fallen in love with anything in my life. It is like a mix-up at an animal factory, where the enlarged bill of a duck somehow got affixed to the body of a cute and furry mammal like an otter. It was so industrious, skimming down to the bottom of its tank and fossicking along the bottom before gliding up to the surface to take a breath of air. I watched it transfixed, literally for hours. Later I would encounter platypus in the forests of Mount Field National Park near Hobart as I continued to retrace Darwin's steps. They did the same thing in the little streambeds there, but it was that first encounter at the zoo, my first love, that stayed with me.

Another wonderful thing happened to me at the zoo. I had been feeling rather depressed and I stood in the nocturnal house leaning against the wall, indulging myself in my misery in the darkness of the exhibit. Suddenly a small bear came up to me and nuzzled my hands. I had not realised there was no glass on the front of this particular exhibit, and it took a moment to realise that it was not a small bear, but a wombat that had nudged me. I fell in love with that wombat almost as much as I did with the platypus.

On the way down to Hobart I spent time in eucalyptus forests near Philip Island, and there, clinging to the high branches of the trees, were wild koalas. Again, I watched transfixed as they slept, scratched, and occasionally ate the eucalyptus leaves. This is surely the only animal that looks like a stuffed toy, not the other way around.

And so by the time I arrived in Hobart, I was inclined to agree with Darwin's observations in his diary as he sat looking out at the eucalyptus forests of the Blue Mountains, that it was as if this country, Australia, had been made by a different Creator to the one that made the rest of the world: 'Surely two distinct creators must have been at work.' And there were aspects of this second Creator that I would really take issue with: okay, I could forgive him for bunging a bird's bill onto an otter, but I really didn't care too much for the flies, the leeches or the snakes.

We had encountered all three when I had determined that I should take my family up Mount Warning in northern New South Wales, through its World Heritage-designated forests, to get a perspective on how Australia would have looked to Darwin in his time. Australia doesn't really possess mountains — more like hills that they accord the title 'mountain' in the absence of anything larger to claim that accolade. Mount Warning, at least when seen from some angles, sticks up from the surrounding landscape as a dark-green swathed hill with what looks for all the world like a 'W' forming its top. The prospect of climbing a monogrammed hill seemed much more inviting than climbing a mountain.

As we set out, a local assured us not to worry about snakes as there were only carpet snakes around the area and they were harmless.

A short way through the astonishingly lush forest, I noticed blood streaming from my daughter's ankles: leeches were dropping from the trees and gorging themselves on our blood as they hitched a ride. Rounding a corner in the path we encountered a large, two-metre long snake, thicker than my closed fist — and I have large hands — lying directly across the path and, apparently, asleep. I assured my daughter there was nothing to worry about, put her on my back piggie-back style, and then calmly stepped over the snake. The snake woke up during this procedure and slithered quickly into the nearby vegetation. Congratulating myself on my bravado did not last for long: farther up the track we encountered a second snake, but this one was smaller and of a completely different kind. I still don't know which one was the carpet snake.

Darwin had a similar experience when in Hobart: he caught a snake, thinking it to be a non-venomous, egg-laying one similar to snakes he had been familiar with at home. But when he caught it, its abdomen burst open and a small snake emerged from a developed egg. It seems that this snake, which bore live young, had to have been either a black tiger snake or a copperhead, both of which are highly venomous.

Our time at the top of Mount Warning was extremely limited, as the flies there bit mercilessly, we were all bleeding profusely from our ankles from the leeches (which use an anticoagulant to encourage the blood to flow), and we were feeling uneasy about the snakes. My son wanted to leave quickly and I gave him instructions that he must wait for the rest of us at a halfway point where there was a seat. Unfortunately, the mosquitoes were as rapacious there as the flies had been at the top and, when we eventually got to my son, we found him distressed and extensively bitten but, nevertheless, determined to do as he was told and wait for us. All in all, it had been one of those memorable family outings that nobody wanted to ever repeat again, but in some masochistic way I was thankful for having experienced it. It had given me an insight into Australia as Darwin must have surely found it: different maybe; dangerous and uncomfortable, definitely.

Somewhat north of Mount Warning we visited the World Heritage Lamington National Park, an area of rainforest growing on what are the remains of an eruption from Mount Warning twenty-two million years ago. It seemed strange to be within a slip-slop of sunscreen from the heat of the Gold Coast beaches, and to be faced with such a luxurious forest, in what is to all intents and purposes a drought area.

On the day we visited, the temperature was at near record levels, hovering around 40°C. Brilliantly coloured parrots greeted the visitor, looking for hand-outs of seeds and as likely to land on your head as on the branch of any tree. A tree-top walk took us through the canopy of the forest, but for me, the major attraction of the trees was at ground level. In this forest, the dominant tree is known as a boyoong tree. As the nutrients in tropical forests tend to be on the surface, it has to have a very shallow root system even though it is a very tall tree. Ordinarily, this would be a combination likely to lead to disaster, but the trees have developed an ingenious system of buttresses: their roots are tall and wedge like, creating something akin to an umbrella stand that supports the tree.

I guess you could look at this two ways. One: isn't the Creator marvellous — even the number two Creator given responsibility for Australia — in the way He fashions the perfect solution for each animal or plant? Two: isn't evolution marvellous the way it can create the perfect solution? And that was really the problem with Darwin's scenic trip through the animal and plant kingdoms as he toured the world aboard the *Beagle*: the perfect fit of animals and plants with their environment could be taken as evidence for God or evolution. *Surely*, I thought, as we drove down from the forest to the coast for a much needed swim, *the answers can be more readily found in imperfection*?

Once in Tasmania and at the Mount Field National Park, I discovered that instead of boyoong trees and eucalyptus, I was back amongst a forest of beech trees, just like those I had walked through on the Routeburn, in Chile, and in Argentina. It was something that did not escape Darwin either. When writing *On the Origin of Species*, he commented on the similarity of the flora between New Zealand, Australia and South America and noted that this apparent anomaly could be explained if they were 'stocked' from the Antarctic islands. He could not have imagined that continents drift, but he was on the right track. He did not even attempt to explain the similarity of plants in south-western Australia with those in southern Africa, merely noting that it 'will, I do not doubt, be some day explained'. And indeed, south-western Australia was at one time joined to southern Africa in the same way that South America, Antarctica and Australia once formed a whole too.

I had had the concept of continental drift shoved down my throat pretty much ever since I was a student, pretty much ever since the theory of plate tectonics gained credence in the 1960s. I could spell 'Gondwanaland' before I could even spell 'New Zealand'. But knowing about something is not the same thing as believing it — this journey was testimony to that — and there is nothing quite like walking through the beech forests of southern Australia, New Zealand and South America to tip you from the hypothetical to the heretical: to see the distribution of life forms on this planet as a product of science not God. Or, as Darwin did, the product of science as yet unknown.

– 29 –

The Great Barrier Reef and the Story of Coral

After bidding farewell to Hobart, FitzRoy, Darwin and co. had travelled around the bottom of Australia, stopped for eight days in King George's Sound in western Australia, and then headed to the Keeling Islands in the Indian Ocean. The chief reason for this was to look at coral reefs as — surprisingly, really, given that he had passed through the Pacific where coral reefs are virtually synonymous with Pacific Islands — Darwin had not had a close look at one save for a brief glimpse of the surf crashing around an atoll in Tahiti.

Darwin's reason for examining coral reefs so closely was not from a desire to have a holiday or to see the pretty colours and myriad fish that we associate with such reefs: but because they held the key to understanding something fundamental about the Earth and its crust.

It was known that such reefs were formed by polyps, and that these polyps could not survive below certain depths; hence, all the lower parts of coral reefs were made up of the calciferous deposits of long dead and long gone polyps. But the question remained, how did the polyps get to such depths in the first place? Presumably, at one time, the bottom parts of the coral reefs had to have been at shallower depths. This was one instance where Darwin really did prove himself to be a superman of deductive reasoning. When in the Andes, without ever having seen a coral reef in his life, he hit upon a possible answer. The earthquake at Concepción and the marine fossils at high altitude all helped convince Darwin that those parts of the Earth had risen up from the seabed. So, he deduced, if parts of the crust could rise, maybe — in fact, maybe it was necessary — other parts could subside? And where better to expect subsidence than on the sea floor? Maybe coral reefs were in areas where the sea floor was sinking slowly and, as it did so, generations of polyps were building their homes upon the abandoned homes of past generations. If so, it could explain why coral reefs were often in a circle around islands, because Darwin did not buy Lyell's explanation that they were built on the rim of underwater volcanoes.

As much as I would have liked to go to the Keeling Islands, getting to them was beyond my meagre means. As the purpose was really to examine a coral reef, surely, I reasoned, any such reef would do. Or, in fact, not just any reef, but the world's biggest: the Great Barrier Reef. So that was where we prepared to go.

We flew to Brisbane, hired a car, and drove to Gladstone. From Gladstone we took a ferry out to Heron Island, a small palm-fringed hump of sand that sits within the Great Barrier Reef itself. There, my family and I took a glass-bottomed submarine ride across the reef. Like Darwin before us, we were astounded by the beauty and diversity of fish life we observed on the reef.

Afterwards, I donned a snorkel and mask and set out to swim to the edge of the reef. Naïvely I had expected the water to be warm, but this was July, mid-winter, and I was about to be taught a lesson — a lesson already learnt by penguins, seals and whales — that the open ocean is no place for a warm-blooded animal to be for long periods without a layer of blubber, insulating feathers, or a wetsuit. It seemed to take an age to reach the edge of the reef as I skimmed across the jagged branches of coral, barely managing to avoid their steak-knife-sharp edges on the outgoing tide. It was overcast and late in the afternoon and, by the time I reached the edge of the reef, where the coral below me simply dropped away, the visibility was as gloomy as I was chilled. I could certainly make out some coral that was broken, blanched and, seemingly, dead. Whether this was due to the depth or damage from storms and surf, I could not tell, and, quite frankly, by then I did not care. I needed to get warm. I needed to get back.

At Keeling Island, Darwin and FitzRoy had similarly gone out to the edge of the reef but they had difficulty controlling their boat in the surf and had to abandon the exercise as too dangerous; but not before they procured enough samples from soundings on the deep, seaward side of the reef to establish that its lower parts really were dead.

From the Keeling Islands it was on to the island of Mauritius. Darwin wrote to his sister Caroline:

> I am just now beginning to discover the difficulty of expressing one's ideas on paper. As long as it consists solely of description it is pretty easy; but where reasoning comes into play, to make a proper connection, a clearness & a moderate fluency, is to me, as I have said, a difficulty of which I had no idea.

Darwin spent some time looking at the geology of Mauritius, but by now his thoughts were fixed firmly on home and the journey's end. As he expressed it to Caroline, 'Now one glimpse of my dear home would be better than the united kingdoms of all the glorious Tropics'.

The *Beagle* pressed on farther westwards towards the coast of Africa, catching a glimpse of Madagascar, before anchoring in Simon's Bay, just south of Cape Town on 31 May 1836. Whereas I loved Cape Town with its backdrop of Table Top Mountain, Darwin, who stayed in a boarding house there, was not much impressed. Perhaps the most notable event that occurred there was that Darwin and FitzRoy met the astronomer, John Herschel, who had gone to the Cape of Good Hope with his six metre long telescope to observe the return of Halley's Comet in 1835. In May 1836, just before Charles Darwin arrived at the Cape, he would make the last sighting of the comet by anyone on Earth until 1909. Charles would write of Herschel, 'He never talked much, but every word he uttered was worth listening to'. When Darwin met Herschel again, he would talk even less: it was Herschel next to whom Darwin was laid to rest in Westminster Abbey.

The last part of the *Beagle*'s voyage would take Darwin via St Helena, the island on which Napoleon was incarcerated and eventually buried. Darwin noted that St Helena, plopped in the Atlantic so far from any continent (presumably why it was chosen as a jail for ol' Bony), possessed some unique plants and insects but no birds or mammals of its own other than those that had been introduced. Did the alarm bells go off? Evolution on new environments like the Galapagos and St Helena depended on the happenstance of which life forms could get there. Life small enough to be borne by currents of air or sea, such as seeds and insects, might travel great distances, but those that must get there under their own power had more limited ranges.

From St Helena it was on to Ascension Island, another volcanic island like the others (Cape Verde Islands, Mauritius and St Helena) that Darwin determined had been raised from the sea. It was about this time that Darwin was writing up and reviewing his collections made in the Galapagos. When reviewing the birds, he noted that some appeared to have different 'varieties' associated with each island. He compared them to the supposed differences between the fox on the East and West Falkland Islands. 'If there is the slightest foundation for these remarks the zoology of the Archipelagos will be well worth examining; for such facts would undermine the stability of Species.'

FitzRoy commanded that the *Beagle* return to Bahia on the coast of South America to check his original measurements of the meridian distance. Then they travelled via Cape Verde Islands, once again, and Terceira in the Azores, before finally making it back to England, anchoring in Falmouth on 2 October 1836. After four years, ten months and six days, the voyage of the *Beagle*, which Darwin would later describe in his autobiography as 'by far the most important event in my life', was over.

It had taken me even longer to retrace Darwin's journey as best I could. Was I changed because of the experience? You betcha. I had seen Darwin's finches on the Galapagos. On an earlier journey (the same one where I had been moved by the Argentine cemetery at Goose Green), I had even seen his Falkland Island foxes. I had seen the Andes and, from that sight alone, I had gained an appreciation of the antiquity of the Earth and, more than that, an inkling of how labile its surface could be. From the glaciers near El Calafate to the reefs around Heron Island, it was possible to understand that, over time, the face of the Earth had changed as surely as my own. An isthmus here, a mountain range there: they were nothing less than the wrinkles in my mirror that marked the passage of time. Mostly, however, I think I was simply overwhelmed by the great variety of life forms that peppered the planet and the many, minute and often bizarre ways they seemed so perfectly fitted to their individual lifestyles. Was I more enlightened because of this experience? Like Darwin, I would need a period to try to make sense of it all, a period to reflect on my journey.

Reflections

– 30 –

Back in England and the Essence of an Idea

Darwin arrived back in England a happy and changed man, but it would be a mistake to presume that he was a rabid evolutionist at this time. True, he no longer wished for a career in the clergy and hoped that he could make a worthwhile contribution to science. However, he had not renounced God and, despite all that has been written about philosophical disagreements between himself and the God-fearing FitzRoy, the truth is that FitzRoy and Darwin got along remarkably well (allowing for the bouts of depression that occasionally overtook FitzRoy) and that there is really no evidence for substantial disagreement between them.

While the voyage of the *Beagle* undoubtedly altered Darwin, there was no single 'Eureka' moment, no single event that unequivocally shouted at Darwin that he should replace God with evolution.

As for myself: I had invested a great deal of time and money re-tracing the pertinent parts of Darwin's journey as best I could, and I felt less close to the truth than I presumed I might when setting out on this course. Certainly, I had been apprised of the great variety of nature, its intricacies and interdependencies. And while there were relationships between the plants and animals that clearly suggested evolution — or a change from one species to another — what I lacked was also what Darwin had lacked: a mechanism that could make sense of it all.

Back in England, Darwin busied himself with the task of having his collections described, rather than with the lofty questions that they inspired. In this regard he was extremely fortunate in the advice he received and the people he chose for each task. Charles Lyell, whose volumes on geology Darwin had relied upon so heavily during his travels, met Darwin and befriended him in the same month that those travels ended. At dinner, Lyell introduced Darwin to Richard Owen, an up-and-coming anatomist, who offered to look at his fossils. Owen was only five years older than Darwin and was then the Hunterian Professor at the Museum of the Royal College of Surgeons in London. Eventually Owen would become both director of what is now known as the Natural History Museum and a bitter opponent of Darwin's ideas on the transmutation — evolution, as we would call it — of species. But in the immediate aftermath of the *Beagle*'s return, Owen was all sweetness and light, and he advised Darwin to present his collections of animals to the Zoological Society of London. The taxonomist John Gould agreed to classify the birds — and the various collections of plants, reptiles, mammals and insects were passed to other notable experts.

Gould reported back, rather quickly, that the finches from the Galapagos were an entirely new grouping, found nowhere else. Furthermore, like the mocking birds, it seemed that different species of finches may be restricted to particular islands, although the inadequate labelling of some individual specimens did not allow this point to be established definitively.

Some time in 1837, just months after the *Beagle*'s return, Darwin began to think seriously of the transmutation of species and in July of that year he began his first private notebook on the subject. There is a perception among the public, and indeed biologists too, that Darwin arrived back from his voyage and then dilly-dallied for over twenty years before being spurred into writing about the origin of species by Russell Wallace independently deriving the concept of Natural Selection. The impression given is that Darwin was something of a lazy bastard, living off his father's wealth, not required to earn a living, and free to potter about somewhat aimlessly on topics that took his fancy.

Charles Darwin, however, was nothing if not prolific as a scientist and a writer. In 1839 he published his account of the voyage as the third volume of a three-volume set (the others being written by Captain P.P. King — FitzRoy's senior officer on the first *Beagle* voyage — and FitzRoy himself). Darwin's volume quickly outsold the other two, was subsequently reprinted as a separate volume, revised in 1845, and has remained in print ever since. Darwin arranged and oversaw the publication, under his joint editorship, of *The Zoology of the Voyage of* HMS *Beagle,* consisting of five parts and published between 1838-1843, in which hundreds of new species were described. Owen did the fossil mammals (Part I) and, notably, the fish (Part IV) were described by Leonard Jenyns, the man originally offered Darwin's post aboard the *Beagle* and with whom Darwin had competitively hunted beetles while at Cambridge.

In 1842, Darwin published his book on coral reefs, which was followed a couple of years later by one on the geology of volcanic islands visited by the *Beagle* and, a couple more years after that, by one on the geology of South America. During this period, he also kept notebooks in which he wrote copiously. In one, he noted that in October 1838 he 'happened to read for amusement' the work by Thomas Malthus, *An Essay on the Principle of Population.* This was the very same chap whose giant visage had stared down upon my wife and I as we drank the Master's port at Jesus College. It struck Darwin at once that 'the struggle for existence,' which he had observed in all plants and animals, must set up a competition where favourable variations are preserved and unfavourable ones destroyed and that, 'the result of this would be the formation of new species'.

In another notebook, Darwin had already drawn a sketch like a branching tree, setting out how modern and separate groups of animals could be descended from a common ancestor.

So there you had it: the basis of evolution by Natural Selection — and essentially worked out by 1844, when he first confided his thoughts to Joseph Hooker at a meeting at Darwin's home of Down

House in Kent. (Hooker was the young botanist who sailed with James Clark Ross to the Antarctic on HMS *Erebus* in 1839–43 — the first person to see and name, if not to stand, on the place where I began this book.) In essence, Darwin's thoughts went like this.

All life is descended from common ancestors. New species arrive through a process of Natural Selection. This results from there being too many individuals that can possibly survive and reproduce in an environment, which in turn sets up a struggle for existence à la Malthus, or, as it has become popularised when referring to Darwin's theory, a struggle for survival, leading to *survival of the fittest*. Except that it is both a struggle for survival and a struggle for reproduction: because it is through the latter that those individuals with the variations that allow them to survive best in an environment, will be the *fittest*; that is, able to reproduce the most and pass on those favourable variations to their offspring. Conversely, those with unfavourable variations will be least able to survive and reproduce, and their line will not be preserved.

Darwin's concept relied on there being, first, natural variation in the population; second, a competition for survival and reproduction (differential reproductive success); and third, some mechanism of inheritance that would ensure offspring inherited the favourable variations of their parents. This was, of course, before Mendel, before genes and DNA, before Watson and Crick and the Double Helix. Which may all have accounted for why Darwin did not climb to the top of the dome on St Paul's Cathedral and announce to the world that they should abandon thoughts of a Creator and think only in terms of a natural process. For, such unknowns aside, if finches could beget different types of finches, wasn't it an inescapable conclusion that monkeys could beget men?

He confided his thoughts to Hooker, Lyell and Jenyns but otherwise kept such 'dangerous' ideas to himself.

– 31 –

Gower Street and
Domestic Matters First

I decided to go to Darwin's home, Down House in Kent, to immerse myself in the surroundings that Darwin found himself and see if I could not deduce something of the uncertainties that kept him so preoccupied. But I was getting ahead of myself. Darwin did not just step off the *Beagle* and then go into some sort of academic hibernation in the village of Downe, wife and kids instantly in tow.

Darwin's first love or, at least, the object of his first infatuations (as it remains unclear as to the extent that his affections were returned) was Fanny Owen. She was in Darwin's words, 'the prettiest, plumpest charming Personage that Shropshire possesses'. That was all in the period before Darwin boarded the *Beagle* and a hint that Fanny did not have her heart in the relationship in the same way that Darwin did, came when he arrived in Rio de Janeiro in April 1832. A letter from Darwin's sister, Catherine, broke the news that Fanny had accepted an engagement to a Robert Biddulph — a minor aristocrat and a major cad — within days of the *Beagle*'s departure. Darwin was heartbroken: 'if Fanny was not perhaps at this time Mrs Biddulph, I would say poor dear Fanny till I fell to sleep'.

In London, in the aftermath of the *Beagle*'s return, Darwin began to feel a keen sense of loneliness. He drew up a balance sheet listing the advantages and disadvantages of marriage: the result favoured heavily the benefits of getting married. 'My God, it is intolerable to think of spending one's whole life like a neuter bee living all one's days solitarily in smoky, dirty London.' With insightful thinking like that, it was no wonder this chap was destined to solve much bigger questions about the Universe and life, but for that moment it was enough that he had set his mind on getting a wife. With some fatherly advice to boot, Darwin settled on the notion of marrying his first cousin, Emma Wedgwood, the daughter of his mother's brother, Uncle Jos, and a close friend since childhood.

When Charles Darwin married Emma on 29 January 1839, they moved into a small cottage he had just rented in London. They christened the place Macaw Cottage on account of its gaudy colour scheme, reminiscent of the birds Darwin had encountered on his voyage. The cottage no longer exists, but how appropriate that the site should now be occupied by the Department of Biology of the University College London.

Once again, I found myself in London. I emerged from the cramped elevator of the Russell Square tube station into the pale English afternoon light. At the heart of the square lay gardens protected behind a high wrought iron fence and a cluster of much higher trees. A fountain played in its centre and paths criss-crossed the square; this was Sherwood Forest in the city and I was Robin Hood. I felt the jab of excitement that London never failed to give me — heroin to the travel-addicted. Leaving the sanctuary of the forest, I headed up Woburn Place in search of Gower Street.

The bland grey monster of a building that now claims 12 Upper Gower Street as its own is called — you guessed it — the Darwin Building. There is a small plaque that announces that to anyone with enough curiosity to go in its doors, but otherwise the connection with Darwin is not just downplayed, it is decidedly absent.

On the right, after entering the Darwin Building, I discovered the entrance to the Grant Museum of Zoology. You could be forgiven for thinking that this would be some sort of shrine to Darwin: it is anything but. Sure, there is the shell of a Galapagos tortoise, which the curators told me they thought was collected by Darwin — although records are so poor they don't really know, except that it is of the right era and who else was traipsing about the Galapagos in those times? There is a preserved and beheaded thylacine that belonged to Thomas Huxley, and a tuatara from New Zealand that Huxley also dissected.

One reason why Darwin is not linked so visibly with this site is that it's more famous as a site for the dead. At least, one dead Jeremy Bentham. Sometimes wrongly attributed as the founder of University College London, Bentham was a philosopher, known more now for his body than his mind. Upon his death in 1832, his will requested that he be preserved and put on display as an 'auto-icon' at the university. So, behind shuttered doors, he sits on a chair in a glass display case dressed in all his early nineteenth-century finery. Unfortunately, the preservation of his head did not go well and it was replaced with a model one — but for many years, bizarrely, he was displayed with the seriously deteriorated real head placed between his legs.

I had passed the shuttered doors and shuddered. I had no interest in seeing Bentham's dead body. When my father died, I could not bring myself to partake in the strange religious ritual of visiting the dead body laid out in the coffin — I wanted the memories of my father to be those of the living — so I was certainly not about to request a viewing of some fat pompous egomaniac that had been dead for donkeys' years. Personally, if I have to look at a grotesquely preserved and decapitated body, I'd rather it be that of the thylacine — but what I had really come to see was some recognition of Darwin and the time he spent sitting in a chair on the very same spot.

Yet, if anyone shines at the expense of Darwin in that dark little museum, it is Robert Grant himself. Grant was the chap who had befriended Darwin at Edinburgh University, introducing him to the Plinian Society and exposing him to ideas such as evolution. In those early years Darwin was a keen acolyte of Grant, helping him in his study of the marine life around the Firth of Forth. In 1828 Grant was appointed to University College London where he established England's first museum of comparative anatomy. But Grant's radical ideas on evolution were at odds with the established views of the Cambridge affiliated intelligentsia to which Darwin became associated. Although Darwin consulted Grant about how to preserve specimens before departing on the *Beagle*, Grant had so fallen out with the establishment that, by the time Darwin returned, it seems that Darwin did not want his material tainted through association with him. Although Grant offered to work up Darwin's collection of coral specimens, Darwin turned him down and, as far as I can tell, never spoke to Grant again.

A big dugong skeleton dominated the centre of the surprisingly tiny museum and clusters of skeletons filled every available space, every nook and cranny of the room. Dark wooden, glass-fronted cabinets were filled with more skeletons and animals floating in jars of formalin, like grotesque foetuses in see-through wombs. The people I encountered, squeezed into the remaining space, were fiercely loyal to Grant. They suggested to me that Darwin gets too much credit and that their man deserves more. An intriguing elderly lady, exuding in part the elegance of the English upper-middle class and in part the equally anachronistic eccentricities of an ancient hippy, sat with her long grey hair tied up in a wild bun, beaded tassels hanging from parts of it, as she painted the skeleton of an aye-aye. We introduced ourselves and I explained that I was looking for Darwin, or at least the evidence of him that I could find in his wake. She advised me that I was wasting my time at Gower Street and to go to his home in Down House, Kent. She confessed to being besotted with Darwin (a rare condition, as far as I could make out, at that address) and to having gone to Down House twenty-seven times.

I retreated to the outside. Twenty-first century London traffic and pedestrians went by me at pace, ignoring me, while I stood trying to imagine Gower Street in the nineteenth century without the buses, the black cabs and the black people; the complexion of London had changed, literally, since Darwin's time. Macaw Cottage may have given way to the bland white stonework of a new university, but across the road were some brick terraced houses that I thought might possibly have dated from those times. All in all, the street was quite boring whether one imagined it with horse-drawn carriages or double-decker buses and I could empathise with the Darwins' desire to get out of Gower Street and head for the countryside. Charles had asked his father for an advance on his inheritance (his father had duly offered three thousand pounds, but at four per cent interest!) that they might buy a home in the countryside. Emma would have preferred Surrey, but Charles discovered an old vicarage in the village of Down (later changed to Downe) on eighteen acres (seven hectares) of land. While he thought it 'oldish and ugly,' he recognised its potential and also a good price when he saw one: two thousand two hundred pounds.

Emma was less impressed than Charles with the place, but to no avail as by then they had two children and Macaw Cottage in Gower Street was becoming cramped, what with the servants and all. Charles was also sick with the stomach complaints — and worse — that would plague him till the day he died. Besides, Emma was pregnant again and they wanted to move before the baby arrived. It was time to head to the countryside.

– 32 –

Down House and a Balanced Life

Even with the horse power provided by a car, it is a surprisingly long drive from northern London, around the M25 motorway and across the gorgeously elegant Queen Elizabeth II Bridge (Europe's largest cable-supported bridge) to the village of Downe, where Darwin set up home in Down House. In this part of the world, the streets can have changed hardly at all from Darwin's times. The roads, squeezed between hedgerows, are just wide enough for a cart and too narrow for two oncoming cars.

First stop was The Queen's Head for lunch, a pub in the village that was used as a watering hole by Darwin. Built in 1558, the pub was already worthy of historic places protection by the time Darwin poured back his first pint. A brick building with flower planters on the walls, the doors were so low I had to stoop when going through them, just as Darwin must have done. I had a drink in the dark-timbered Darwin Bar, but ate my ploughman's lunch in the small room dedicated to Sir Francis Chichester, the first man to sail single-handedly around the world and who, remarkably, also lived in this village. How strange, I thought, that a little place that seemed like it could contain no more than a hundred or so souls at the best of times, should have hosted two of the world's most famous people to circumnavigate the globe.

I walked the kilometre or so from the pub to Darwin's house on the outskirts of the village.

This entire undertaking of mine had not been an *in the footsteps* type of mission as such. I was on a quest, but it had never been my intention to blindly go where Darwin went, to try to recreate his life. I was much more interested in finding the essence of Darwin's ideas. To that extent, I had travelled to many of the places he visited, but I did so to gain insight into the view of the world that he articulated. Nevertheless, what biologist could go to Down House and not be excited simply by the prospect of sharing the same space where such a great man had such great ideas? As I approached the large white two-storeyed house, my pace quickened, along with my pulse.

Down House, was where Charles Darwin wrote *On the Origin of Species*, and it is administered now by English Heritage. I entered its grounds by way of the car park. Most of the rooms have been returned to their original condition and there is an excellent audio guide, narrated by David Attenborough, that walks you through each of the rooms.

My favourite, somewhat to my surprise, was not Darwin's study but the drawing room: in it I sensed a sympathy with nature that accorded with my own. French doors opened out onto the garden providing a sense of indoor-outdoor living that seemed decades, if not centuries, ahead of its time. The blue floral wallpaper, the piano, the high-backed chairs, the fireplace and, especially, the light, all contributed to a feeling of luxurious comfort.

The study itself was interesting. A high-backed chair sat over near the window. It was here that Darwin used to write, with a board stretched across the arms of the chair and his feet resting on a footstool. Say what you like about Darwin, but he had an admirable sense of comfort. Although, as an admission that things were not always as comfortable for Darwin as his surroundings and furnishings might suggest, the opposite corner of the study was curtained off as a one-man ensuite, a sort of shrine to Darwin's troublesome bowel.

In the centre of the room was a table laden with papers, books and the paraphernalia of a working nineteenth-century scientist. I leaned across the rope barrier and touched the table. It was an act of worship, not vandalism, an involuntary acknowledgement that in looking for Darwin this would be as close as I would get, in concrete terms, to catching up with him: a finger alighting ever so gently on his work space, that some molecule of his genius, dished out so liberally on that very table, might still be there a hundred and fifty years later, and able to be absorbed through my skin.

It was a mistake: I set off some kind of alarm and a panicked attendant from the front desk rushed into the room ready to apprehend whoever had been stupid enough to breach the barrier. This coincided precisely with my decision to move to the billiard room next door.

There is something somehow reassuring to realise that Darwin wasn't some kind of pointy-headed nerd buried up to his waist in papers, burning the midnight oil and socially inert; that it wasn't just all work and no play for him. Darwin was apparently quite good at billiards and often played his butler. Other signs abounded that Darwin was a remarkably warm family man with what may be considered today a certain sense of balance in his lifestyle. It is true that it is easier to find such balance when the bank balance allows it, but it seems that Darwin used his wealth for the good of his family.

Darwin made several additions to Down House to accommodate his growing family and their servants, and, in all of this — the large dining room, the school room, the banisters down which the children slid — I found a sense of family and fun. Down House was really the opposite of what Charles's brother Erasmus — very much a city boy — called it: 'Down-in-the-Mouth.'

Darwin was at heart a man of routine and I was particularly keen to see the path that Darwin called his 'Sandwalk', around which he walked several times each day. It was on those walks that he did so much of his thinking. Often his dog, Polly, would accompany him. Polly was a white terrier with a patch of red hair where she had been burnt as a puppy. Darwin was devoted to her — it had been Polly's basket that I had noticed by the fire in his study — and she often lay on him and licked his hands.

The Sandwalk proved to be much longer than I had supposed, and above all else, was this revelation: it was beautiful. Even now, one-and-a-half centuries later, it is still a walk in the wilderness. There is nothing but trees and pastures. A densely wooded copse of trees hugs the path on the left side on its outward leg (many of the trees planted under Darwin's directions) while the views to the right are of rolling pastures, as rural an English scene as you could find this side of a John Constable painting.

It reminded me of the path near my own house where I walk my dog, a Labrador. Even on those days when I do not feel like going out, I know that if I do, the reward will be the time for reflection, the time to think. At Down House I had found insight not so much into Darwin's thinking about evolution and Natural Selection but in his attitude to life and family and especially the world around him. I felt a kindred spirit with Darwin that had less to do with our relationship to the Church and religion, less to do with our scientific views, than it did with the way we lived our lives. And it struck me then, that by going to Down House we could all learn a thing or two from the *way* Darwin lived his life as much as from where he lived it.

- 33 -

The Geological Society of London and a Striking Coincidence

Darwin's original intention in going to Downe was to have the benefits of both worlds: to enjoy a life in the countryside but, as it was only twenty-six kilometres from London, to be free to go there whenever he wished to interact with other scientists and attend meetings. In the event, his ill health made even the journey to London an epic — rather surprising for a man who had thought nothing of taking off at every opportunity into the high cordillera of the Andes for long treks. In fact, it may have been his very enthusiasm for adventure as a younger man that rendered him a near invalid later in life. Although there is a good deal of dispute and a good deal unknown about the causes of Darwin's illness, one favoured explanation is that while in Chile he had been bitten by insects known as benchuca bugs, which carry a protozoan parasite that causes Chagas' Disease, a South American version of sleeping sickness. Darwin had fallen seriously ill while on an expedition from Valparaiso to Santiago, consistent with the symptoms of a disease that was rampant in Chile at the time. However, it is also possible that Darwin had simply overdosed on poor-quality wine (indeed, that was his own explanation). Whether his being laid low in Chile was a short-term hangover or a long-term infection that would return to haunt him later in life, Darwin's ill-health while at Down House meant he journeyed to London hardly at all.

It would be wrong, however, to imagine Darwin cosseted at

Down House, a hermit from the academic world: he wrote prodigiously — it is estimated that in his life he wrote something like seven thousand letters — and received almost as many visitors as he got letters in return; well, maybe that is a bit of an exaggeration, but the poor man became so obsessed about being disturbed that he installed a mirror on the outside of his study window so that he could see when visitors approached the house.

Chief among his confidantes at the time were his old university mentors, Sedgwick and Henslow, as well as new friends and academic bright lights: Lyell, Hooker and Thomas Huxley. He also wrote frequently to family and even the luckless FitzRoy, to whom he penned the following:

> ... the little excitement of breaking out of my most quiet routine so generally knocks me up, that I am able to do scarcely anything when in London, and I have not even been able to attend one evening meeting of the Geological Society.

Earlier, even before moving to Downe, Darwin had tried to resign his post as Secretary of the Geological Society of London, a position he had accepted with some reluctance a year or so after disembarking from the *Beagle*. However, so keen were they to keep him on, the society bent the rules and suggested that he need only come to meetings when he could. Even that had proved too much of a struggle and Darwin had resigned as secretary of the society by 1841, the year before shifting out to Kent.

Still, I reasoned, a visit to the Geological Society might be worth it, if only because, for all his renown as a biologist, it was geology that Darwin set such great store by. An explanation of the Earth's biology was only possible, in his view, with an understanding of the geological context within which it occurred. Later, when suggesting an editor for his work, he considered it essential that the person, to be sympathetic to his views, must be a geologist first and a naturalist second. Hence, his preference for Lyell: 'Mr Lyell would be the best if he would undertake it'.

．．．．

I made my way back to London and found myself walking down Regent Street to the neon hubbub that is Piccadilly Circus. The skies were grey, threatening rain, and the constant flow of traffic made for lots of background noise, but this London was no longer the place that Emma and Charles had so readily rejected: it may well have been as noisy but it was nowhere near as dirty. The pavements were clean, the grey stone buildings freshly scrubbed, baskets of flowers hung from dark blue lampposts.

Eros stood at the confluence of what seemed like far too many roads, protected by fences and policemen as London sought to somehow show a stern face to terrorism. The statue of the nude god is actually meant to be Eros's brother, Anteros, the God of Love Returned, and in accordance with this it was called 'The Angel of Christian Charity'. But as I reflected on the need for the policemen and their flak jackets, on jihads and Orange Parades, on crusades and inquisitions, all conducted in the name of religion and the one God, I felt more at ease with the God of Love looking over us as I made the short walk up Piccadilly Street than I did with the notion of any kind of religious charity, Christian or otherwise.

About two hundred metres up Piccadilly Street was the cobbled driveway into Burlington House, which went through an ornate archway, easily the most impressive building in the street. The driveway opened into a large courtyard with Burlington House at the rear, now the home of the Royal Academy of the Arts. On the left side was the Astronomical Society and, a bit beyond that, the Society of Antiquaries. On the right, its entrance sequestered in the arch itself, was the Geological Society and, on the left side of the arch, were the doors to the Linnaean Society. It was a veritable playground for grey matter, a theatre for the brainy.

I had no appointment and, not being a fellow, I lacked the rights that would have guaranteed me entrance to the Geological

Society's premises. As I was contemplating just how I was going to overcome this minor technicality, someone came out of the locked door and I used the opportunity to let myself in, looking as fellow-like as I could muster. Not wishing to show any signs of hesitation that would have given my game away, I immediately walked up the blue-carpeted stairs, past the map room and into a dark dingy room that said, 'Library'. In the room, behind piles of dark and dingy books and a dark and dingy counter were two old people. When my eyes adjusted to the light, I realised that the male was only about thirty but already dressed for retirement in a cardigan and, I suspected, slippers, in the way that some Brits seemed to delight in making themselves look prematurely aged. I knew for certain that he watched *The Antiques Roadshow* on television, drove a Vauxhall and was probably a bellringer to boot.

The woman was lovely. She took time to explain to me how the Geological Society was at Somerset House when Darwin was its secretary, but moved to the present site in 1874. She did not seem to know whether Darwin had visited the present premises during the last eight years of his life but, given the difficulty he had getting to the society when thirty years younger, I reasoned that I should not take it as a given. I had to sign in and I couldn't help but notice that even though it was already well into the afternoon, mine was only the fifth name on the page: in other words, all this organisation, all these cardigan and twin-set wearing employees, were in place so that just four fellows and one faux-fellow could wander about its corridors and dimly-lit rooms, perusing maps of Uzbekistan or consulting manuscripts written by Lyell in his own hand. The main part of the Geological Society library is housed in what used to be the museum: a large, green room, with pillars and ornate ceilings. The shelves that house the books still have the runners on them for the drawers that held the rock specimens. The whole place seemed less like a museum than it did a morgue, with the society itself the deceased body. Had it become too hard for the fellows to attend, even those within twenty-six kilometres of London?

Having completed the first round of renovations at Down House and his book on volcanoes, Darwin threw himself into expanding on his initial pencil sketch, done in 1842, of his ideas for the transmutation of species — *evolution* by any other name. He completed a two hundred and thirty page manuscript by July 1844 and sent it away to be copied, but he was a long way from being prepared to publish what he knew to be radical and incendiary, if scientifically important, ideas. Instead he wrote a letter to his wife:

> My dear Emma
>
> I have just finished my sketch of my species theory. If, as I believe that my theory is true & if it be accepted even by one competent judge, it will be a considerable step in science.
>
> I therefore write this, in case of my sudden death, as my most solemn & last request, which I am sure you will consider the same as if legally entered in my will, that you will devote £400 to its publication...

So there you had it: the guts of *On the Origin of Species*, not just an idea fermenting in the travelled biologist's mind, but an actual manuscript, all dressed up and with no place to go. His books on the voyage had made him famous among the scientific community, so why not publish straight away? Why not a book on the transmutation of species? Why not a book that usurped the view of a world created by God and replaced it with one of a world formed by natural laws where evolution was as inevitable as ice below freezing? Why wait? Darwin clearly saw the academic merit in his idea — he was not backward in perceiving it to be the major scientific advance it would become — but like contemplating some nineteenth-century version of base jumping, he hesitated before taking the leap, unsure if professional exhilaration or annihilation lay before him.

Darwin discussed his ideas with a limited few. Among them Hooker and Lyell and, later, his god-fearing beetle-collecting mate who was offered the trip on the *Beagle* before him, Leonard Jenyns. In 1855, on Lyell's recommendation, Darwin read a paper by the naturalist Alfred Russell Wallace entitled, 'On the Law which has regulated the Introduction of New Species.' He noted some similarities to his own theory but was not particularly worried by it: 'it all seems Creation with him'. But on 18 June 1858, Darwin received the shock of his life. Wallace sent Darwin an essay written while he was recovering from malaria contracted while collecting specimens in what is now Malaysia: Wallace had independently come up with the basis for evolution by Natural Selection. As Darwin put it to Lyell, 'I never saw a more striking coincidence'.

This was not a particularly great time for Darwin even without Wallace to contend with. His daughter, Henrietta, was very sick, possibly with diphtheria, and his youngest child, named after himself, became ill with scarlet fever and died a few days after contracting the disease.

Preoccupied as he was with the grief for his son, Darwin was nevertheless devastated by the arrival of Wallace's manuscript in a way that must have been similar to the feelings experienced by Scott a bit more than half a century later when he should reach the South Pole only to discover Amundsen's tent there before him. Darwin sent Hooker an abstract of the Wallace manuscript plus a copy of his own manuscript completed in 1844: 'I really cannot bear to look at it. Do not waste much time. It is miserable in me to care at all about priority'. In fact, Hooker, along with Lyell, wasted very little time, convincing Darwin that he should prepare a joint paper with Wallace to be read at the next meeting of the Linnaean Society.

So it was, that I exited the doors of the Geological Society and headed straight for those of the Linnaean Society on the other side of the arch.

– 34 –

The Linnaean Society:
An Idea made Public

The rooms at the Linnaean Society may have been somewhat less grand than those occupied by their geological cousins, but the reception I received could not have been warmer or more welcoming. A lovely young woman, dressed trendily in black, let me in and ushered me into the Meeting Room, where I was left on my own to absorb it all.

A large room — perhaps twelve metres square with four-and-a-half metre studs and pink ceilings with gold filigree — it was the epitome of an environment for the erudite. A long table with a lectern ran along the front with a wonderfully ornate wooden high-backed chair: it seemed one didn't so much give lectures as make proclamations when speaking to the Linnaean Society. A portrait of the icon of the Linnaean Society, Carolus Linnaeus, sat behind the chair. And, like mug shots of the family — the royal line — around the room were other portraits; every one of them, I couldn't fail to notice, bigger than the one of Linnaeus.

On the right was a large painting: two along from the one of his friend Hooker was the original of the much reproduced portrait of Darwin standing holding his hat and wearing a cape. It was painted by John Collier in 1881 — not long before Darwin died — and, in one of those lovely bits of quirkiness, Collier was the son-in-law of Thomas Huxley, who had become Darwin's most ardent supporter once his theory became known. The painting is glorious: its background dark, with Darwin himself draped by the dark overcoat, from which his left hand extends holding his hat. His magnificent beard is full and white, and his eyes … they seem to look down below you rather than to you. He is solemn. He looks like someone's grandfather, but he certainly does not look in poor health.

Next to the portrait of Darwin was one of Wallace, done for the society posthumously by Roger Remmington in 1998. An afterthought apparently, it hardly seemed to make up for the slight against Wallace, for excluding him from the academic firmament for so long. It looked like a paint-by-numbers sort of effort. It seemed to be made of plastic, without the depth or subtlety of skin tones that the portrait of Darwin possessed.

Below the Darwin portrait was a plaque with the inscription: 'Charles Darwin and Alfred Russell Wallace made the first communication of their views on the origin of species by natural selection at a meeting of the Linnaen Society on 1st July 1858.' But I knew that at that time the Linnaen Society met elsewhere, that despite the loud clock ticking on the back wall — which seemed to be measuring time from that moment, *A.D., Anno Darwini* — that while this was now the home of the society, it was not the space in which those first words about Natural Selection had been uttered publicly.

Fortunately, that space was nearby and I made my way across the cobbled courtyard to Burlington House — built in the seventeenth century and now home to the Royal Academy of Arts.

It is a regal building befitting of royal occupants. Large banners hung down its sides announcing an exhibition of Chinese art, but I had come to see a room, not art. While the Linnaean Society now sits cheek by jowl with the academy, at the time Darwin was wrestling with the concept of Natural Selection that was not the case, and the meetings of the Linnaean Society took place in the academy. On 1st July 1858, papers by Charles Darwin and Alfred Russell Wallace were read to a meeting of the Linnaean Society in what is now known as the Reynolds Room.

It is a long thin room, all cream and gold filigree. Paintings line both the long sides. I recognised one by Sir Winston Churchill. At one end, almost inconspicuous, is a plaque that notes the event that took place in that room. It was an event that would have far more impact on the world than any of the paintings in that room, or, for that matter, the whole building. But the patrons seemed blissfully unaware of the history that lay so naked before them. They strode down the polished wooden floor, stopping to stand pensively before the John Singer Sargent or the Churchill or, just occasionally, before the pictures painted by lesser names now largely consigned to history's books. But nobody, not a single person, made any attempt to find a plaque on a wall. In an hour, no one but myself seemed to care that this was a room where great ideas — perhaps the greatest ever — were first liberated.

Part of that may well lie with the Royal Academy of Arts itself. Go to its website and you will be hard pressed to find any mention of Darwin. And Wallace does not get a look in either. The plaque was put up as recently as 2001 and maybe the academy's half-hearted and belated homage to Darwin stems from its own uncertainty? The lovely receptionist at the Linnaean Society told me that one of their historians reckons the meeting did not take place in the Reynolds Room but in a room that is now occupied by the men's toilets. To be on the safe side, I visited them too. But let me just say for the record, that if I had to pick the place where I would like to imagine Darwin's words being given flight, it would be the Reynolds Room and not some modern urinal.

Wherever it was, Darwin himself could not attend the meeting. He was in Downe burying his eighteen-month old son, Charles, in the local churchyard. Before leaving Downe, I had stopped at the church — St Mary the Virgin, a lovely little thirteenth-century church — and the thing that had struck me most was a sundial on the right-hand side up near the top with a plaque dedicated to Charles Darwin. It seemed an odd juxtaposition, this relationship between a church that said a virgin could have a child and a man that said all life could be explained through differential reproduction. It seemed an equally odd juxtaposition that Darwin's ideas, which would challenge the very basis of the teachings of the Church, were being aired in London at the same time he was engaged in committing his son to the Earth in a ceremony that said souls belonged to God — a god that created the Earth and all the plants and animals on it.

I walked back to the Linnaean Society and my friendly receptionist guided me up the stairs to the library and, once again, left me to my own devices. The library was spectacularly luxurious: two storeys high, perhaps a seven metre stud, the ubiquitous green on the walls but with the columns and ceilings highlighted in cream. Glass panels in the ceiling and on the Piccadilly Street side of the room let in light; four of them originals, the only ones to survive the German bombs during the war. Outside, sirens screamed along Piccadilly Street, the modern hysteria of a new war — this one on terrorism — the defining mark of the twenty-first century so far and the only thing to intrude into a room that otherwise had changed very little since Darwin's times.

There were four alcoves. In one was an etching of Down House and Darwin's study, looking much as it had when I saw it, and, on a shelf, a book I couldn't help but notice: *Sociobiology: The New Synthesis* by E.O. Wilson. Published in 1975, in many ways Wilson's book was a rallying cry, an offensive move (in both senses of the word to some); a piece of tactical brilliance in the war against Darwin's critics, as decisive as the D-Day landings on Normandy. But I am getting ahead of myself. The point was that Darwin's theory (and to be fair, Wallace's as well) did not change the world overnight. Even its staunchest advocates did not think it was without holes. There began a war of words, destined to last longer than any with bullets.

– 35 –

Reaction and Reception in the UK

In the wake of the Linnaean Society meeting, Darwin threw himself into writing up his theory fully and in November 1859 his book was published with the rather grand title, *On the Origin of Species by means of Natural Selection or the Preservation of Favoured Races in the Struggle for Life* — a mouthful destined to be known by its first five words. The publisher, John Murray, received orders for one thousand five hundred copies as soon as it was released, and the book has remained in print ever since.

There were those who immediately saw the import of Darwin's words. Included among them were, of course, Hooker (who was the Director of Kew Gardens) and Lyell. Thomas Huxley famously remarked upon reading it, 'How extremely stupid not to have thought of that!' But there was opposition too.

One of the first shots was fired by Richard Owen, the person who had helped Darwin write up the fossils collected during the voyage of the *Beagle*, and who was by then superintendent of the Natural History Departments at the British Museum. Writing anonymously in *The Edinburgh Review*, Owen reviewed *On the Origin of Species*. He began by damning Darwin with faint praise for his quaint writing style and then launched into an extremely detailed, exhaustively referenced, dissection of Darwin's theory of Natural Selection that was more *Texas Chainsaw Massacre* than it was little pricks with a scalpel. As Darwin himself described the review, 'It requires much study to appreciate all the bitter spite of many of the remarks against me'.

I made my way in the tube to Kensington, past the buskers, to the graciously curved entranceway to the Waterhouse Building of the Natural History Museum, which opened in 1881 as Owen's vision of a 'cathedral to nature'. The entrance hall itself was dominated by a monstrous dinosaur skeleton, as graphic an illustration as possible — if anyone needed it — that life on earth had changed, that forms existing in the past differ from those that populate the world now. Beyond the dinosaur and up some stairs, overlooking this whole creation of his, was a statue of Richard Owen. But as far as I could make out, that was his only triumph. Elsewhere, throughout the museum, it positively reeked of Darwin. From an exhibition on Darwin himself to explanations about individual specimens, inherent in them all was an implicit acceptance that evolution by Natural Selection was the basis for explaining the diversity and differences apparent in the museum's vast collections. The Natural History Museum may have been Owen's baby but it had grown up to be Darwin's child.

If assaults from fellow scientists came as somewhat of a surprise, Darwin should not have expected less by way of a reaction from the Church. As with much that was to follow the publication of *On the Origin of Species*, Darwin left it to others to fight his battles for him, content to observe the fray from the safety of Down House. One of the most famous battles took place in Oxford between The Bishop of Oxford, Samuel Wilberforce (otherwise known by the rather unlikely nickname, for a man of the cloth, as 'Soapy Sam') and Thomas Huxley. At a meeting of the British Association for the Advancement of Science, Soapy Sam turned to Huxley and famously asked whether it was on his grandfather's or his grandmother's side that he was descended from an ape. The exact words Huxley used to reply are a matter of conjecture, but the essence of it was that he would prefer an ape as an ancestor than a man that would squander his great intellect for the purpose of ridicule. Ouch! Darwin 1, God 0.

I drove to Oxford, in the Formula One mode in which I often find myself, not sure what I would find; and the answer was, not much. In my self-absorbed state, it was an indignity to ask any driver to park their car and ride a bus, but for one of Michael Schumacher's standing it seemed a particular annoyance to have to use the 'Park and Ride'.

As far as I could tell, even if Darwin had won the battle at the Natural History Museum and Thomas had pummelled Soapy into submission on 30 June 1860 (in what would become known thenceforth as The Oxford Debate) the Church had still won the war around Oxford. There were churches everywhere. Even walking through the grounds of the university colleges, God was palpably in the air: inserted into the play I stopped to watch, the songs of a choir and the way the whole town seemed to clasp its past, its history, like a child afraid to let go.

Throughout all the controversy that raged in the world outside, Darwin remained in Down House, where he continued to study and write books at a frenetic pace. These included one on orchids, another on climbing plants, two volumes on the domestication of plants and animals, *The Descent of Man*, one on emotions in animals and man, another couple on plants (their fertilisation and movements), one on insectivorous plants, and, finally, one on worms.

Yet issues remained with the fundamental theory of Natural Selection that underscored his life's output. For one thing, Darwin's mechanism of inheritance — the means by which the favoured characteristics of animals and plants could be passed on to succeeding generations — was flawed. Darwin had assumed that it must involve some sort of blending of the characteristics of the mother and father, with the offspring having characteristics that were somewhere in between those of its parents. The problem with that argument was that it inevitably would reduce the amount of variation for a given trait in the population, and it was variation in traits that was the grist of Natural Selection. If all individuals had similar characteristics, then differences between them in their reproductive success would be slight and the influence of Natural Selection would be correspondingly weak.

It took Gregor Mendel, with his experiments on peas and, later, Watson and Crick, to show us that fundamentally Darwin's concept of Natural Selection is correct: that heritability of traits is controlled by genes — coded parts of the DNA at the heart of all cells, and, importantly, all germ cells (the sperm and the eggs). Whereas bodies come and go, genes remain intact: the chemical messengers, the currency of inheritance. There is no blending as such, no watering down of genes. However, genes can be dominant or recessive or some complex combination in between. The important thing is that — mutations aside — genes retain their integrity. It becomes, then, like a lottery: which tickets will be allowed to go on in the next generation? And this is where Natural Selection is king: for those genes — tickets if you will — that facilitate an animal or plant's survival and reproduction, will be the most likely to be passed on and, therefore, there will be proportionately more of those tickets in the next generation, more animals and plants with the traits they code for.

I knew all this in a way that Darwin did not: that his theory had been vindicated by our knowledge of the actual mechanism of inheritance, the code written in the Deoxyribonucleic Acid, the DNA. Even so, I was troubled by the same issue that had most troubled Darwin about his theory: if the formation of new life forms occurs through Natural Selection, and this necessarily depends upon differential reproduction, whereby there will be winners and losers, and the characteristics of the winners — the *fittest* in evolutionary-speak — survive, how can one get specific life forms that do not reproduce? How can one explain the sterile castes of social insects? In such species, distinct forms such as worker bees exist but do not reproduce themselves. How could the characteristics that make them worker bees be favoured, as Darwin called it, if the worker bees do not reproduce? At first Darwin thought that this problem alone was, in his own words, 'insuperable' and 'actually fatal to my entire theory'.

The solution — alluded to by Darwin in *On the Origin of Species* when he said, 'This difficulty, though appearing insuperable, is lessened, or, as I believe, disappears, when it is remembered that selection may be applied to the level of the family, as well as the individual, and may thus gain the desired end' — would wait over one hundred years to be fully exposed: first by Bill Hamilton, the finger-deficient British whiz-kid with whom I had driven at great speed through Berwick Forest, and then, by Edward Osborne Wilson, the author of the book I had spied on the shelves of the library at the Linnaean Society. Their collective answer constituted what is now called Kin Selection, and was portrayed by them as just an inevitable consequence of Natural Selection.

Amongst mammals there is no better group in which to look for Kin Selection than the ground squirrels, which is how I came to be at Buffalo Airport with my family awaiting a flight to Calgary, Alberta.

– 36 –

Turner Valley and the Problem of Altruism

We had arrived at Buffalo Airport in our rental car well before what we believed our check-in time to be. Feeling hungry, we decided to pick up some lunch from a nearby Burger King. Returning to the terminal, I left the family to eat their burgers in the car while I sauntered up to the check-in to enquire about seat assignment, only to learn that the last boarding call for our flight had been given several minutes earlier. My travel agent had struck again: he had given us the wrong departure time for our flight. Like a puberty reversal, my testicles retreated to somewhere just below my ears as I felt the hand of panic seize me.

At Buffalo Airport rental cars have to be returned a good half-mile from the terminal. Beginning to act irrationally, I left all our passports and valuables with the check-in girl and ran out to get the family, ushering them along with our bags and my as yet uneaten Big Whopper and strawberry milkshake to the check-in to get their boarding passes. I told them the departure gate and sped off like Rubens Barrichello to return the car. Literally throwing the keys at the Budget lady, I raced back to the terminal, picked up my own boarding pass and ran to clear security. But much to my horror I observed that my wife and the kids were not waiting for me on the other side of security as arranged. When I questioned the security people — between gasps while hyperventilating — it became obvious that my family had never been through.

In a blind panic, I tore around the terminal. Buffalo Airport is laid out as two separate wings joined at a central hub. The other wing contained a completely different set of departure gates. I ran there thinking to myself that it was just too absurd that they could go to the wrong gate in the wrong wing. But there they were — not only in the wrong wing, but also on the other side of security.

I have seen families that row in public places like airports and who appear so perfectly dysfunctional that you wonder why they would even bother living together, let alone travel together. But at that moment I experienced a meltdown of my core nuclear faculties and I suddenly understood what it took to walk into a McDonalds and mow down everyone with an AK47.

'WHAT THE FUCK ARE YOU DOING THERE?!' I shouted. Rounding security, my wife did what probably any sensible woman should do in such circumstances: she threw my milkshake at me. Fortunately years of lying on the bottom of rugby mauls dodging kicks paid dividends and I was able to avoid the flying pink projectile. I was not so fortunate with the burger. With Michael Jordonesque-like improbability, the Big Whopper bounced off me and into a nearby rubbish bin. Half hesitating, I briefly considered whether to retrieve it, before rushing after my family.

If you ever want to get a bomb on board an aircraft I suggest that you pose as distraught parents. The security to our gate — when we eventually got to the correct one — faced with an hysterical woman, two bewildered children and a human version of Godzilla, let us through without checking a thing. We were ushered onto the aircraft and as I sat down in a pool of sweat, the fear of missing the flight drained from the pit of my stomach and was replaced by a new sensation: acute hunger.

Ironically, some sort of warning light in the cockpit had come on and that kept us sitting on the tarmac for over an hour before the pilot announced, 'although it can't be fixed right now, it is nothing critical and we are cleared to proceed'. At that moment I would have preferred that we had missed our flight and, from their concerned reactions, clearly our fellow passengers agreed. However, all went smoothly, although we missed the connection in Chicago and did not get to Calgary until around midnight, where we were greeted by Jan Murie, my supervisor from a previous life when I had been a graduate student at the University of Alberta.

Jan is ageless, which is to say that in thirty years he has always looked the same to me. He's wiry, with a grey beard, straight grey hair cropped fairly short and without any evidence of having encountered an experienced hairdresser; he wears boots, jeans, and a chequered shirt over a T-shirt, all of which is set off by a despicable floppy hat and, likely as not, a toothpick stuck between his lips.

Jan had come from Turner Valley to pick us up. There, at a nearby field station known as Gorge Creek, he had run a long-term study of Columbian ground squirrels. Under Jan's supervision I had also studied ground squirrels in the vicinity of Turner Valley, although mine had been of the Richardson's kind; the kind the locals call 'gophers,' the ones they make extravagant swerves at while driving just so they can run them over.

Turner Valley is the heart if not the brain of red-neck Alberta and I had come to love it and some of the people that lived there well. It is not too far from the place where the Oscar-winning film about two gay cowboys, *Brokeback Mountain*, was filmed and, although there were plenty of cowboys thereabouts, you would have been hard pressed when I was there (as the seventies turned into the eighties) to find a cowboy that would admit to being anything less than a raging heterosexual.

There is a certain faction of North American males who subscribe wholly to the cowboy form of dress without ever going near a horse in their lives. Larry was like that. Cowboy boots, Levis, big buckle, big sideburns, chequered shirt, leather waistcoat, Brylcream and a ten-gallon hat. That was his Sunday best and his Monday worst. For all I knew, that was what he wore for pyjamas too.

I met Larry when I was inducted, as an honorary member, into Hogstown. Finding Hogstown wasn't easy — it doesn't exist on any map — but my natural affinity for getting myself into peculiar situations led me right there.

I had been towing a trailer with a three-quarter tonne truck from Edmonton to the foothills of the Rocky Mountains south of Calgary to set up my study of ground squirrels. The thing was, I had never driven a vehicle that big before, I had never driven an automatic before, and I had never towed anything of consequence before. Given all that, I was congratulating myself, a twenty-some-thing student, on having done remarkably well, save for taking out an entire one hundred metre line of orange road cones when changing lanes in Calgary. It was getting late and so I decided to pull into a dusty little town for something to eat. I parked in what looked like an open field opposite what was then Turner Valley's sole fast food outlet.

Pat, the woman behind the counter, looked to be in her early thirties, with trim hair and a trim body. Her angular face, more pleasant than pretty, was completely devoid of make-up, as if she was saying to the world that what you see is what you get. I saw a woman for whom life was hard — someone who accepted her lot even if it was not a lot. What she saw in me I'll never know, but we clicked in the way that two people can click in the time that it takes to make a pizza.

That may well have been it, a brief flirtation between a counter girl and a foreign boy, had it not been for the inept way I had parked the pick-up truck and trailer. I was stuck. The wheels of the truck sunk deeper into the mud with each rev of the engine.

I retreated to the pizza parlour and my Pat. She said she'd call her husband ('Oh you have a husband?'). Ted arrived and the rest, as they say, is history. For that is how I came to be a citizen of Hogstown, along with Pat, Ted, Larry and the others. We met each week, when I would leave the ground squirrels and my camp in the foothills of the mountains and go into Turner Valley to engage in such memorable activities as injecting a watermelon with as much vodka as we could possibly manage and then drinking the contents through straws while snorting loudly.

On one particularly unforgettable occasion we had all travelled the sixty kilometres to Calgary to eat out at the city's best and most expensive licensed Chinese restaurant. Larry was strictly a three meats, potatoes and beans man and he had never gone to such a flash restaurant before. His one concession to its dress code was to put on his leather waistcoat with the sheepskin lining. I remember his look of horror when our waiter, dressed in a white dinner jacket and black dress trousers, brought out the won-ton soup. Larry had looked up at the guy, who was probably something like fourth-generation Chinese Canadian, and remarked of the watery soup without the faintest trace of mockery, 'No wonder you guys are starving to death over there.'

Mentally, if not physically, I crawled beneath the table. But not for long: there must have been something about eating so many vegetables or having his pork with cashew nuts that caused Larry's brain to divert from its usual topics of porno movies and badly mutilated bodies (Larry was an ambulance driver), because out of the blue he asked me to explain what I was doing with the ground squirrels. Except that he didn't call them ground squirrels, he called them gophers, and you could tell that the unspoken part of his question was, 'Why would anyone do anything with gophers other than run them over?' Except that he wouldn't have phrased it quite like that because Larry was incapable of using the word 'why' without adding the two words 'the fuck' after it.

So it had been that, in such an unlikely setting and with such an unlikely audience, I had launched into Darwin and the almost 'insuperable' problem with his theory. As they struggled to pick up tiny spring rolls with their chopsticks, I told them about the sterile castes of insects and how that was just the tip, the extreme end, of a much bigger problem with Natural Selection.

Worker bees forgoing sex to help their mother, the queen bee, have more babies may be the ultimate sacrifice in a Darwinian sense, but really it was just an extreme example of *altruism*, whereby animals appear to be doing something for the good of other animals at the expense of their own survival or reproductive prospects. And, on the surface at least, that should be a no-no under Darwin's theory. It is one of the undeniable consequences of the theory that Darwin dreamed up between circling the globe on the *Beagle* and circling the Sandwalk at Down House, that animals should behave selfishly. In the struggle for survival, the fittest should always be those that look after themselves and their self interests, because they will leave more babies and those babies will inherit the traits of selfishness. Conversely, individuals that hold back from reproduction, say, or put their lives at risk for another, would be bound to leave fewer babies, and therefore, the heritable bits — the genes as we now know them to be — that code for such selfless behaviour are bound to be swamped, selected out, by the success of the selfish.

Perhaps it was the difficulty of eating with chopsticks — which demanded their full concentration and left me by default with the floor — but none of the other citizens of Hogstown interrupted and I ploughed on, as much to fill the silence as to convince them that there was something to be got from gophers beyond the joy of flattening them.

I told them how Darwin had suggested that this difficulty with his theory could be lessened when it was remembered that selection may be applied at the 'level of the family'. He wrote that in 1859, and nobody else dealt with the perceived problem of altruism for over one hundred years. It wasn't until 1963 that Bill Hamilton — who had been a Ph.D. student just like I was when addressing the inaugural dinner meeting of Hogstown — solved the problem by formalising Darwin's notion of selection at the level of the family as an elegant and simple equation. What this student, who was one or two phalanges short of a hand, had so brilliantly proven, was that under Darwin's concept of evolution by Natural Selection there can be occasions when it will pay you to sacrifice your reproduction, and even your life, for the benefit of other individuals. It all depends upon how closely related you are to the animals that benefit from your *apparent* 'altruistic' deeds and how much it 'costs' you.

In fact, many years earlier, the British population geneticist, J.B.S. Haldane (who was as famous for his quotes — 'If one could conclude as to the nature of the creator from a study of his creation it would appear that God has a special fondness for stars and beetles.' — as he was for his science) apparently, one drunken evening (in the very bar in Cambridge where I had gone for post-coital drinks after being screwed over during my seminar by the Department of Zoology's academic hitmen), had grabbed a napkin and started to scrawl calculations similar to those that Hamilton would make later. Haldane addressed his drunken audience by announcing that he should kill himself if in doing so he could save more than two of his brothers or more than eight of his cousins. But Haldane quickly went on to dismiss the idea, recalling that on the two occasions he had jumped into a river to save a drowning person, he had never stopped to consider his genetic relationship to them before doing so. It seemed that my own audience concurred, as Ted piped up that he wouldn't kill himself if he could save a hundred of his cousins and that, frankly, he didn't care too much for his brother-in-law either. His indifference to the latter stemmed, as far as I could deduce, from the fact that his brother-in-law had snared his wife's very attractive sister who, in the wife-swapping, porno-consuming ways of small town Alberta, loomed large on Ted's radar as a potential mate.

I used the opportunity to point out to Ted that it all came down to the proportion of genes two animals had in common. That certainly, in an evolutionary sense, there was no reason for him to favour his brother-in-law because, apart from being as short as each other, they were completely different, unrelated, and should Ted, through some miracle of compassion, help his brother-in-law to have babies (which would have been the farthest thing from Ted's mind, with the possible exception of demonstrating the complete range of positions in the Karma Sutra with his sister-in-law), those babies would be unlikely to possess or pass on many of Ted's genes.

He would be helping the genes that constituted his brother-in-law to replicate at the expense of his own.

On the other hand, I added, as the waiter cleared away the last of the rice bowls, Pat *should* help her sister because, by virtue of both of them getting their genes from the same source (their parents), half her genes were the same as Pat's. If Pat could add to her sister's reproductive output, she would essentially be adding something to her own. It may not be as efficient as passing on genes by reproducing herself, because her sister's children (her nieces and nephews) would only have half as many of Pat's genes as her own children, but it would still be a pretty good return, especially if the costs to Pat of helping her sister were not too high.

Her cousins, however, shared a much smaller proportion, one-eighth, of her genes. (I did not bother to go into the process of *meiosis* and how each time we reproduce it is like a lottery with each of our sperm or eggs getting some random combination of half our genes, which are then joined through the process that, to give them their dues, all the members of Hogstown seemed to spend an inordinate amount of time studying, by watching videos with titles like *Deep Throat* and *Debbie Does Dallas*.) Drawing my monologue to its conclusion, I explained that for Pat to benefit from helping her cousins, the costs to her would have to be tiny, as the returns in terms of propagating her own genes would be meagre. And, as for second cousins, the benefits of her helping them became even more unlikely to be realised as they shared only one sixteenth of their genes, while for third cousins it was one thirty-second, and so on.

So that was it in a fortune cookie shell. Hamilton's genius was to recognise that when animals appeared to be behaving altruistically they were, in fact, still behaving selfishly; the benefits they derived in terms of passing on copies of their own genes outweighed the costs the behaviour incurred. Furthermore, for this situation to arise, for the benefits to exceed the costs by the required amounts, so-called altruistic behaviour was only likely to occur between closely related individuals.

That was where E.O. Wilson and the ground squirrels came in. Wilson recognised that Darwin's idea, and Hamilton's formulation of it, completely revolutionised our understanding of animal behaviour; that once we knew the relatedness between participants, we could much more readily understand how behaviour had evolved, how it had been selected through being advantageous to the individual performing it, in the same manner that long legs or camouflaged coloration may be advantageous to an animal.

That was also where my own research came in — as ground squirrels were renowned for giving alarm calls. Research had shown that individual squirrels that stopped to give alarm calls rather than take evasive action immediately, increased their risk of being eaten by the predator. If Darwin, Hamilton and Wilson were right, ground squirrels should, therefore, be most likely to call only when they had close relatives nearby. And that, largely, as it turned out, was the gist and sum of it.

If I had made any impression on the assembled citizenry of Hogstown, it was hard to tell. Larry immediately followed up with a story of how earlier in the week he had backed the ambulance over a gopher and it had exploded, showering the nearby building with blood. As the chorus of approving grunts died away, Larry yelled across the restaurant to our waiter, this time with a good deal of mockery in his voice, for another round of 'amaletto and wodkas' and, once again, I took up my station under the table.

• • • •

But that was then, and this was now, and I had wanted to know from Jan whether the ensuing research from that time when I was a student had continued to support Darwin's theory.

My family and I went up to Gorge Creek, where Jan showed us his study site and we watched the chunky Columbian ground squirrels forage among the meadows, while on one of the steep sides of the ravine that had given the place its name, two black bears foraged for ground squirrels. And, yes, the thirty or so years of study had revealed that Columbian ground squirrels favour their kin; that their society is based upon a system of matrilineal kinship, where daughters stick with their mothers and their sisters, their grandmothers and their aunts, and the males are reduced to little more than mating machines. It all sounded like a small furry episode of *Desperate Housewives*.

I took my daughter with me to see my old Richardson's ground squirrel study site in the foothills of the Kananaskis Mountains. In the mountains, close to where I had camped, we spied a grizzly and a pika — a sort of rodent of the rocks — but she couldn't have been less impressed with my campsite. She couldn't imagine staying there for more than a night, even if she were a cowboy, even if she were gay, and even if Jake Gyllenhaal were her companion.

We went to the towns of Longview, Black Diamond and Turner Valley and, if it was unfamiliar to her, now it was also unfamiliar to me. The place had changed. The pub at Black Diamond no longer looked like the sort of place where guys in baseball caps and cowboy boots would swing a girl about on the dance floor in a complex series of moves that substituted for conversation and foreplay.

In Turner Valley we found Pat's old restaurant, although now it had plenty of competition. It had been tarted up and I could not resist going in and asking the owner if he knew what had become of Pat. The owner had no clue who Pat was, let alone where she had gone. I asked a lot of people that afternoon in Turner Valley if they knew the various members of Hogstown and, in every case, drew a blank expression in response. That is, until I finally found a woman who knew Pat: she said that Pat had run off with Larry and was last seen heading for Calgary.

In some ways that brought closure for me. Hogstown was now disbanded; it was an idea that had officially died and no longer existed. Extinct. Kaput. It demonstrated, by way of comparison, the wonderful robustness of Darwin's own idea on Natural Selection, which seemed to have survived, relatively unscathed, against all the objections that had so far been thrown at it.

As we left on the drive to Edmonton, with me swerving — in complete contrast to the oncoming pick-ups — to avoid the ground squirrels, I couldn't help but reflect that Larry had been right about one thing: you could accuse him of being many things, but God knows, being a gay cowboy was not one of them.

– 37 –

Edmonton, Reciprocal Altruism and Perfection

We drove to Edmonton via what is undoubtedly the most beautiful piece of highway in the world: the road between Banff and Jasper with its unparalleled mix of mountains, rivers and lakes.

The chief attraction of Edmonton as far as my daughter was concerned was the West Edmonton Mall, the world's largest shopping centre. Quite honestly, having a place with eighty-four different shoe shops did little for me but, according to her worldview, that was as close to Heaven on Earth as it was possible to get.

I had come to Edmonton largely because it was the site of the University of Alberta, my *alma mater*, the place where I had been initially exposed to some of the extensions to Darwin's theory that kept it alive and well in the face of seemingly difficult problems. I knew that even though the evidence for Kin Selection and its effect on the behaviour of animals was convincing, there were still some troubling exceptions. Female vampire bats, for example, suckled infants that were not their own and that were not related to them. Why? Or, as Larry might have put it, why the fuck would they do that if the individual they were helping could not pass on their genes?

Driving along Whyte Avenue towards the university, I was reminded of my first Halloween party, which had occurred in 1978, soon after I arrived to start my Ph.D. (At that time Halloween was not celebrated at all in New Zealand.) I was reminded of my shock at the way I had been welcomed by one of my new friends — friends I had made quickly after we had all been put into emergency housing, twenty-three to a room, reminiscent of Darwin's days (and nights) as a boarder at Shrewsbury School.

'Lloyd, Buddy, come here and give us yer dick.'

It would take me years after that to get over the fear of ever being greeted in public by Paul again. Paul was one of the graduate students to emerge as an unlikely group of friends from our time together in the basement of Lister Hall; a group where the members were as strange and perverted in their own ways as any of the citizens of Hogstown.

There was Mark, the lawyer from New York, with the Sam Elliot moustache, cowboy boots, and a drawl as wide as Texas. There was The Nose, a short Englishman from north of Liverpool who pushed words through his giant proboscis in a way that made most of what he said incomprehensible. There was Red, a socially-challenged thirty-year-old virgin who, it seemed, had spent most of the previous several years living above the Arctic Circle, talking to no one, and thinking about nothing but sex 24/7. Jimbo hailed from Nova Scotia and was built like the proverbial brick shit-house: bearded, over six foot across the shoulders and weighing about one hundred and thirty kilograms, he had dislocated his right shoulder four times and the left one thirty-three times playing ice hockey. And then there was Jimbo's friend, Paul, a 'Newfie' with long blond hair and an eye for anything in a skirt.

Not one of them would win any awards from feminists. I only ever knew Mark's girlfriend as 'The Frenchwoman.' One day when I enquired after her, he answered in his slow drawl, 'I sent her out to get her legs waxed because it was like sleeping with a gorilla.'

Paul had been seated on a couch next to Jimbo as I entered the Halloween party and his shouted greeting brought the party to a halt. It worried me in part because I *was* wearing a skirt — well almost, I was dressed as Robin Hood — so I grabbed the arm of my companion (for the sake of decency, let's call her Beth). Beth had been a member of the British women's ski team and she possessed a body for which grown men would rip their own heads off.

At a certain point in the party I realised that I had been dancing with Jimbo's sister for a while. She placed her arms around my neck and kissed me softly whispering in my ear, 'You don't mind?' It was only then that I realised what was going on: Jimbo was with Beth and I was being offered his sister by way of exchange.

Unfortunately for Jimbo (one might say, fortunately for his sister), Beth did mind. But thinking about those carefree days of youth, which seemed as distant as Whyte Avenue seemed long, I could not help seeing them in a way that I missed back then: Jimbo's gesture, if proffering your sister for sexual favours can be considered as such, was actually an act of *reciprocal altruism*. In other words, a you-scratch-my-back-and-I'll-scratch-yours kind of carry on between animals, or as Larry would have put it: one good turn-on, literally, deserves another.

In this way, unrelated animals may help each other, even at some cost, as long as the favour is returned. The problem with this type of situation is that it is not considered by evolutionary biologists to be an evolutionarily stable strategy. That is, in most species such a system would be unlikely to work because it would be undermined immediately by animals behaving selfishly, by cheaters. An animal that only took favours but never returned them would theoretically do best, and it would be such selfish behaviour that would flourish at the expense of the altruistic one. Unless — and this was a big *unless* — the particular society of animals had a system for punishing cheaters, for deterring those that did not reciprocate. For that reason, reciprocal altruism is only ever likely to arise in species with big brains (advanced mental faculties) and a system of individual recognition that allows them to identify and punish those that do not pull their weight, so to speak. Therefore, the scientist in me reflected as I parked before the University's new sports stadium (which looked like nothing less than a slab of butter — hence, the nickname, the Butterdome) one should not look for reciprocal altruism in fruit flies or weevils, but rather in primates and parrots.

Advanced mental faculties was not a phrase that came immediately to mind when thinking about that group of university friends, but if one allowed that it didn't need to be advanced so much as adequate, you could imagine that reciprocal altruism might work for monkeys and men and, even, bats. Once again, as I strode past the flat-rooved red-brick buildings that pass for heritage in Alberta, it seemed to me that Darwin's theory had kicked butt. It had weathered the assault from yet another quarter as to whether some particular feature of animals really could be adaptive — really could be explained by its effect on the survival, or the reproductive success, of the individuals possessing it.

But there were other, more serious concerns, massing in the wings: other issues about Darwin's theory and its place in biology that were bothering me.

I arrived at the dark brick Biological Sciences Building overlooking the Saskatchewan River, which appeared to have been designed by three drunks let loose with a set of Lego. Whatever the administration squandered their money on at the University of Alberta, it apparently did not include architects.

It was funny going back to a place I had inhabited as if it were a ground squirrel burrow for four years, then abandoned for more than two decades. I knew instantly how to get in the back way through the loading dock; without realising I had the mental map still tucked away in the glove-box of my mind, I knew where every door and corridor led. In appearances, the building had changed even less than my supervisor, Jan, over the years, which was somehow discombobulating: it was like going forward in a time machine to a place you recognised, but which did not recognise you. For, apart from Jan, most of the people who walked the corridors or the faces that looked up from their computer screens in offices that had not seen a coat of paint since I was there, were unfamiliar to me. The place was like a nursery, taking in fresh-faced students and sending a new cohort of biologists out into the world a few years later — with Jan and his colleagues as the nursing staff.

The corridors were festooned with posters of the students' and staff's research. I read several as I whiled away my time waiting to see Jan. And, to a poster, they all had some spin, some angle, that said this feature of that animal, or that feature of this animal, was an *adaptation*, to use Darwin's words. In other words, every bloody feature they looked at in animals seemed to be the product of Natural Selection, to benefit the animal's survival and/or reproduction. That struck me as too perfect, too unlikely. It wasn't just that all these biologists and pre-biologists were singing off the same song sheet, they were singing the one and only note. How could *every* feature of an animal have so much influence on its survival or reproductive output that Natural Selection would weed out the wonky bits? It was just too perfect — and if animals were always perfect, how could an adaptation be distinguishable from the hand of God?

I thought back to those days when I was a student and how, when there was an issue, a conundrum, there always seemed to be an answer, a story, that could explain it as an adaptation. Reading the posters in the corridors, it seemed that nothing had changed: biological sciences departments were indoctrinating the babies under their care, inoculating them from contrary views, as thoroughly as any seminary.

When I was a student, the hot topic was infanticide. It was known that some animals killed young of their own kind, ground squirrels included, and, on the face of it, this did not seem to fit well with Darwin's mantra. Why would animals kill infants of their own species? Apart from seeming reprehensible, it just did not appear to make any sense from a Darwinian perspective. Initially, biologists, under the influence of Nobel Prize-winning ethologist Konrad Lorenz, proclaimed that animals did not willingly kill their own kind and that, therefore, instances that were observed were aberrations, weird mistakes, animals behaving badly.

But the more biologists looked, the more they saw that infanticide was not just a mistake, it was a regular occurrence in some species. The most high profile examples were in lions and monkeys. They were high profile because a chap called Brian Bertram and a woman called Sarah Blaffer Hrdy, employing a similar logic of selfish genes to that expounded by E.O. Wilson, came up with a novel explanation that could seemingly explain why infanticide should be adaptive, why it should pay big lions and big monkeys to kill little lions and little monkeys. Which was, in part, how I came to be sitting on the top of the cab of a safari truck with my wife and two kids, with nothing but a small iron bar to prevent us falling off, as we sped down a road in Zimbabwe.

– 38 –

Africa, Lions and the Fallacy of Group Selection

Either side of the road, there was the red African earth and, as far as the eye could see, the sparse trees that dotted the landscape like disused umbrellas that had seen better days. The din of insects could be heard even above the road noise. Of all the senses, however, it was the sense of smell that was most stimulated. The smell of Africa never leaves your nostrils: it is sweetly pungent, at once pleasant, yet like nothing you have ever smelt before. In many ways, Africa was the most different, most exotic place I had ever been to — more so even than the Antarctic or the Inca Trail. Women walked beside the road balancing large cans of water on their heads or bags of something like flour. One that I saw had a full bucket of water on her head, a baby strapped to her back, and she was reading a book while walking. Talk about multi-tasking: at least I could see the reason why they had the women doing it — that was well beyond the capabilities of any of the males that I knew.

We passed a couple of lads in a cart being pulled by a bullock: the cart had solid wooden wheels and looked like it had come right out of the Flintstones.

We were headed towards Mana Pools National Park. Apart from my family and the driver, there were two others on our safari and, for different reasons, we were nonetheless all after the same quarry: lions.

We arrived outside the park gates late at night and set up our tents there. We did not have permits to go into the park until the next day. As I lay next to my wife, with nothing but the thinnest piece of nylon separating us all from the wilds of Africa, I quaked as a couple of lions started roaring in a sort of feline version of duelling banjos. They might well have been hundreds of metres, even miles away — sound carries a long way in the still African night, especially when it is projected from a mouth that could easily open wide enough to encompass my head, hell, my whole body, and that of every member of my family as well — but they sounded like they were bellowing at each other from just the other side of our fire. I think there have only been a few times in my life when I have been more terrified.

Unscathed, unscratched, we arose in the morning disappointed not to find lion tracks all around our camp and pressed on into the park where we felt sure we should have an audience with the king of beasts.

Mana Pools is an unusual national park in that it does not give a damn about public liability — in fact it doesn't seem to do much for the public at all — it being one of the few national parks where you are not required to be in a vehicle, and where you are free to roam about on foot, at your own risk of course.

We set up our tent beside the Zambezi River, beneath a large, beautiful *Acacia albida* tree, and set out in search of lions. We saw impala, antelope of every kind, hippos, baboons and elephants, but not a sign of those that had been making the big cat calls the night before. At one point we did what, with hindsight, is probably the stupidest thing I have ever done in my life, and, as my wife is quick to remind me, for such an accolade there is a lot of competition.

We saw a female elephant with a young baby. They went behind some bushes and we abandoned our safari truck to sneak up on the other side of the vegetation so that we might get a better view and take some photographs. It was not a very sensible thing to do even if the elephant had gone where we thought it had but, unfortunately for us, it had not. We rounded a set of bushes only to come face to face with this giant pachyderm. Up close — and we were way closer than I ever want to be again to something that can stomp me into oblivion — African elephants are truly colossal, their ears massive. The female saw us, processed our approach as a threat, then threw her ears out and trumpeted loudly in preparation for charging us and, I didn't doubt, flattening us flatter than any gopher on the roads around Turner Valley.

My son and our driver were closest to the elephant, just metres from it. In a display that called into question the level of his concern for his clients, our driver ran past us towards the truck at a speed that suggested he could qualify for the Zimbabwean Olympic sprint team. My son, together with my wife, jumped behind a tree so skinny that even I could have pushed it over. I grabbed my daughter and, carrying her piggyback style, ran in pursuit of our driver. The elephant took a few steps forward but whether she did not wish to leave her young charge, or because she could see that the threat we posed was vanishing at speeds hitherto unknown in our family, she refrained from going farther.

Lionless, we returned to our campsite. That night we had a visit from another elephant, this one a large male with enormous tusks. The tree under which we had pitched the tent was as beautiful as any in the park, its green leaves offset by the orange fruit pods. Unfortunately, the elephants also found this an irresistible combination and, around two in the morning, my wife and I were awoken by a swishing sound. It was the sound a large bull elephant's trunk made as it was being dragged along the ground, literally inches from our tent, picking up fallen fruit. The massive legs were projected by the moonlight onto the thin layer of nylon that was our tent like the least appealing shadow puppet show you could ever want to watch.

The elephant moved around the tent and stopped with its left front leg not a toe's width from our sleeping son's head. Not wishing to make a sound and startle the elephant (or wake my son and, therefore, startle the elephant), my wife and I both put our fingers to our lips. But, really, it was a redundant gesture. Whereas the night before I had silently whimpered at the thought of being torn apart in a tug-of-war between two big cats, at that moment we were frozen with fear, incapable of making a sound even if we had wanted to; all we could do was watch and hope that the elephant did not turn our son's head into a pancake.

Then things got worse. There was a small earthquake and the thud of small bombs being dropped on the ground and on the tent: the elephant was shaking the tree in order to dislodge more fruit. He then proceeded to move about hoovering up all the fruit, stepping lightly around our tent like he was some sort of oversized ballet dancer before leaving us to move on to another tree. During all this, our son and daughter slept peacefully, completely unaware that they had come within a footfall of never needing their bicycles again.

When we emerged from our tent in the morning we discovered others had not been so lucky. A few hundred metres down the riverbank, an elephant had, when shaking a tree, pulled it down on top of what would be the newest vehicle we would ever see throughout our stay in Zimbabwe. The cab of the pick-up truck was completely flattened by the tree. We had, of course, heard the crash in the night, but there had been no way in Hell that any of us were going out to investigate.

A cape buffalo wandered into our campsite and it seemed such a benign creature by comparison — a big cow as far as I could see — that I saw no reason not to approach it to take its photograph. I managed to get two shots. The first was a beautiful portrait with the buffalo's yellow eyes in sharp focus, its head lowered slightly to reveal the horns that lay across its top like a bony skullcap. The second photo was a blur. The buffalo charged me and, practised from my training run with the elephant the previous day, I fled the scene in the one two-hundred-and-fiftieth of a second it took for the shutter to open and close. It was only afterwards, when I discovered that more people are killed by cape buffalo in Africa than any other animal that I realised this, too, belonged in the bag marked 'Most Stupid Things I Have Done'.

I was starting to appreciate why Darwin had, but for his brief stopover in Cape Town, not spent much time in Africa: it was too dangerous unless you had your wits about you.

Unable to find lions in Zimbabwe, we moved onto the Moremi Game Reserve in Botswana, where we were rewarded immediately: a pair of male lions, full of mane, sat like identical twins in the open grassland. They were bachelor males and they might well have been twins, waiting around for their chance to take over a pride: to become not just king of the beasts but leader of the pack to boot. They waited patiently it seemed, for throughout the long period that we watched them from atop our truck, they barely moved: a yawn here, a flick of the tail there, but really nothing to suggest that these were killers, especially not baby-killers.

In another part of the park, not too far away, we came across a pride that had just brought down a large cape buffalo (I cannot say that I felt sorry for the buffalo in any way). There were a couple of big males, four females and a number of cubs. The lions virtually ignored us as they tore into the buffalo, at times putting their heads right inside its belly to clean out the tastiest parts. This was literally nature 'red in tooth and claw' as Darwin's theory had often been caricatured. It exemplified the preservation of favoured traits that enabled a group of lions to bring down what is one of the most dangerous animals in Africa (cape buffaloes don't just kill more humans than any other animal, they also kill more lions than any other animal); it exemplified the weeding out of the weakest traits that enabled an animal like a buffalo to fall victim to its pursuers. The whole scene could have been a poster image for *On the Origin of Species*: a perfect illustration of all that Darwin's theory suggested.

But there was an unspoken narrative to the scene that was not immediately obvious to the casual observer's eye. The two brothers we had seen earlier would almost certainly make a play to take over this pride (or another) at some time, otherwise they could kiss their reproductive potential and their Darwinian fitness goodbye. Usually this involved a battle, a bloody coup, and, if successful, the brothers would drive out the resident males and establish themselves as interim leaders, because that was all male lions ever were, interim, their tenure at the top lucky to be three years. And this was the thing about lions — the gruesome thing: when they had such a change of government, often any young cubs in the pride would be killed, murdered, their defenceless little lives ripped from them by a quick, unprovoked bite. The same fate would befall any cubs born in the first few months after the reign of the new leaders began. Such observations put lions in a new light: more tyrants than monarchs, more beastly than king of the beasts.

Of course, all those profs and students in biology departments around the globe had to have an explanation that would concur with the message on the posters lining their corridor walls; they had to have an explanation that said this was adaptive. That was when some made a big mistake. They forgot that Darwin's concept of Natural Selection was about advantage to individuals; they resorted to species' advantage reasoning, aka Group Selection.

It is one of the most misunderstood aspects of biology, one of the most oft-repeated misconceptions, that animals in any way do things 'for the good of the species'. If I had a dollar for every time I had heard this phrase on television or the radio, or read it in books, I wouldn't just be rich, I'd be Bill Gates and Warren Buffet rolled into one.

These biologists suggested in their posters and elsewhere that the lions killed infants of their own kind to keep the population in check: to stop their reproduction running away from them in some Darwinian-fuelled bonking spree that would ultimately lead to a population explosion, where the likely fallout would be that they would outstrip the local resources and the ability of the environment to sustain them. If this happened it would lead eventually to starvation and, perhaps, even to their extinction. That is, by sacrificing a few babies, the species as a whole was better off, their future assured. Killing babies no longer sounded brutal, it sounded downright prudent. Except that there is a major flaw in such arguments that fall under the general umbrella of Group Selection.

If reciprocal altruism is mostly not an evolutionarily stable strategy, Group Selection (with the theoretical possibility that it might in some esoteric circumstances have some relevance for fungi or the like) is *never* an evolutionarily stable strategy. While it may sound reasonable, logical even, that animals should behave for the good of the long-term benefit or survival of the species or the group, that is not how genes operate, that is not how Natural Selection works. Any animals that in any way curbed their reproduction for the good of the group would pass on fewer genes than those that behaved selfishly and reproduced at the maximum rate they could. Of course, the offspring of those selfish breeders would inherit the genes that caused them to behave selfishly, so that, even if it is to the detriment of the group long-term, the selfish will always prevail. It is just the way of the world — the world according to Charles Darwin.

But Brian Bertram came along and provided an explanation that could seemingly explain infanticide, not as some sort of aberrant behaviour, but as really adaptive, really advantageous (in an evolutionary sense) to the *individual* animal performing the killing. Animals could kill their own kind and the explanation, it seemed, could sit satisfactorily on the corridor walls of any self-respecting biology department.

Bertram's insight rested on the killings being perpetrated by the incoming males, the coup leaders. He reasoned that by killing the infants — which were not theirs, and, therefore, did nothing to propagate the genes of the pride's new leaders — the females would become sexually active more quickly than if they had continued to nurse the infants that had been fathered by the previous males. The same applied to any cubs born within the ensuing few months (gestation in lions is about one hundred and ten days). Given the limited tenure that males could expect as the head of lion households, Natural Selection rewarded such murder because, by committing it, they produced their own cubs and replicated their own genes as soon as possible.

Had Darwin triumphed again? Had his theory been able to explain what was seemingly inexplicable? While in theory I should have been rejoicing in what I had seen in Moremi — the beauty of the pride, its cubs and their future killers — I went to sleep that night troubled by the thought that biologists had once again latched onto adaptation in a largely unquestioning fashion; by the way corridors everywhere creaked under the weight of posters proclaiming infanticide was the product of Natural Selection, Darwin's baby.

It had been my personal observation that the least discerning amongst biologists were often primatologists, who frequently could not help taking an anthropomorphic slant, which undoubtedly came from studying creatures that so resembled themselves. Sure enough, primatologists were quick to ascribe just about any form of infant killing in monkeys or apes as an adaptive strategy, whereby males killed to have sex more quickly and produce babies faster. One of them, Sarah Blaffer Hrdy, even gave such a strategy a name: she called it the Sexual Selection Hypothesis.

− 39 −

India and Infanticide

In the late 1970s, just as I was beginning to find out how to sneak into the Biological Sciences building in Edmonton by way of the loading dock, another graduate student, this one from Harvard, had been making a name for herself by employing the same explanation that Bertram used for the lions to explain the phenomenon of infant killings by Hanuman langur monkeys in India. Sarah Blaffer Hrdy had written a book called *The Langurs of Abu*. At the time, as a fresh-faced Ph.D. student, I had accepted the case she made. Years later, when I embarked on this journey and re-read her book, I was less convinced. The evidence was largely circumstantial and I was not sure that, in a court of law, I would have been prepared to convict the male monkeys of murder in the first degree.

To check out the scene of the crime for myself, my wife and I flew to New Delhi. We decided to go to Mount Abu — the site of Hrdy's study — via Agra, home of the Taj Mahal, the world's most celebrated monument to love.

My wife and I fought our way onto the train for Agra, through the throngs crowding the station in Delhi and past a line of blind men walking along the platform holding one onto the other like a line of elephants might walk trunk to tail. It turns out that there really is something to the expression about the blind leading the blind because, when the front person tripped over someone asleep on the platform, the whole lot of them tumbled down like a line of dominoes. It might have been funny in a sitcom, but there it reduced my wife to tears.

In creatures as patently social as primates, it might seem strange that some of us should murder each other or ignore the plight of those less fortunate. Surely we are meant to be lovers not infant killers, compassionate not mean? And watching the sunrise on the opalescent white marble walls of the Taj Mahal, it was hard to escape that conclusion. Built by the grieving Shah Jehan as a tomb for his much loved wife, Mumtaz Mahal, who died while giving birth to their fourteenth child in 1630, it was a wonder of curves, symmetry and detailed but subtle decoration. If a building could ever be feminine then this was it.

Back at our hotel, my wife and I enjoyed breakfast before heading out to look at carpets. We were ushered into a carpet purveyor's building with something of the reverence reserved for royalty. Bottles of Thumbs Up — a local rip-off of Coke — appeared on silver trays, brought to us by sycophantic servants, as did exquisite Indian tea, spiced with cinnamon and other goodies. Our host explained to us that his family had been the master stonemasons who had built the Taj. He showed us pictures of his ancestors, pieces of marble taken from the Taj, and intricately carved marble ornaments. We marvelled at pictures of his wife as a member of the Indian table tennis team, we accepted an invitation to his house for dinner the next night, we talked philosophy, we talked politics, we talked religion and we talked Darwinism.

It did not surprise me that our host subscribed to a set of Hindu beliefs, but he was remarkably well-versed in all religions and, even, the writings of Charles Darwin. Nirvana, being born again, and monkey gods — they were all concepts that did not sit well with the scientist in me, but I could not fault the depth or breadth of his knowledge.

He told us that according to the Indian epic story, *Rāmāyana*, Hanumān was a general in the army of King Rāma. Hanumān led an army of monkeys to rescue Rāma's wife, Sita, who had been imprisoned on the island of Sri Lanka. As a consequence, Hanuman langurs were revered in India, sacred. He seriously doubted that such a god-like creature was capable of infanticide, although he conceded that before taking Queen Sita back to India, Hanumān had set fire to the Kingdom of Lanka. This suggested, perhaps, that the monkeys were not without a violent streak.

The one thing we did not discuss in over two hours was carpet. Then our new friend — our new trusted friend — had his boys bring out some of his wares. While not experts, it was instantly apparent to us that these were vastly superior carpets to any that we had seen. Each one was more beautiful than the last. Always with an eye for a bargain I might have seized upon the opportunity to buy several carpets were it not for the fact that we were already overloaded with gear. No problem, our friend assured us, he could post them to us.

At this point my wife was poking me in my ribs — actually, it was more like punching my sides. But by then it was too late. I was on a roll. This was our friend, our philosophising master builder friend, husband of the captain of the Indian women's table tennis team. Who could you trust if you could not trust him? Besides, even with my limited knowledge of carpets, I knew that the prices we were being charged represented excellent value. As if sensing my wife's disapproval, our friend produced letters from happy customers extolling the service he offered. And so I opted for the four carpets we had liked most of all. I photographed the carpets and signed my name to labels that his boys assiduously attached to them before wrapping them elaborately in tissue paper, brown paper and string. We sat drinking more tea watching the boys address the packages and all the while my wife's fist continued to beat a tattoo on my side.

Back at our hotel, I discovered from our rickshaw driver that we had just been the victims of an elaborate scam. The parcels would never be posted. We would never see our carpets again. We would never see our money again.

I headed back to the carpet merchant's: the pretence of royal treatment had gone. I was shown the side door, through a quagmire of mud and dog shit. No one brought me any drinks, showed me any photos, or discussed Nietzsche, Taoism and Darwinism with me. I was kept waiting for forty-five minutes, and when someone finally appeared, I was unsure whether he was going to knife me or defer to me. In the end, he handed over the Visa slips and I ripped them up in front of him. Then my wife and I left Agra on the first possible train: the mail train — what it lacked in comfort, it made up for in the interminable time it took to get to Jodhpur.

• • • •

The train ride from Jodhpur to Mount Abu turned out to be even worse than the one that had preceded it. I had bought first class tickets for the night train but, when the train arrived, the stationmaster informed me that the train was full and that there was no room for us. I rarely lose my temper but, when I do, setting fire to small island countries should be the least of anyone's concern. Perhaps sensing this, the stationmaster relented and allowed that we could travel on the train, but only in third class where, it turned out, there were no seats for us: the train really was full. To make matters worse, my wife by then had diarrhoea. The toilet in third class on an Indian train consists of a small cubicle with a hole in the floor and a couple of foot pads either side, where one squats and, one hopes, discharges onto the train tracks; although from the condition of the cubicle, such accuracy had been beyond the skill of some. To make matters even worse, with the train so full, there were a couple of people desperate enough to want to sleep on the floor of the toilet cubicle; so each time my wife needed to go to the bathroom — which was frequently — she had to clear them out before they scurried back in to take up their positions as soon as she had left. Meanwhile, in the main carriage, we lay on the floor with those words *What the hell am I doing here?* taunting me in a way that they had never done before.

Mount Abu, on the face of it, might seem an unlikely place to go to see violence and infanticide. It is the site of the marble Dilwara Temples, built by the Jains between the eleventh and thirteenth centuries. Jainism is a famously non-violent religion. The Jains believe that the soul is a living substance and that nearly everything we see in the world is attached in some sense to our souls and is, therefore, alive. The worst sin a Jain can commit is violence against other living beings. In India, you will occasionally see grown men sweeping the ground before them — not for health reasons, but so they won't risk stepping on a bug and killing it. Some Jain monks even wear facemasks to avoid accidentally inhaling organisms.

Jainism — I had discovered from our erudite, if rude, carpet merchant — traces its beginnings to Var-dhamana Mahavira, who was born about six hundred years before Christ. Mahavira renounced his wealthy background and sought to discover the meaning of existence through fasting and, eventually, killing oneself. He never again lived in a house, owned property, or wore clothing of any kind. When he had completed his life's work — establishing the monastic order of Jainism — he began his final fast and died deliberately from starvation. By the first century A.D., Jainism had evolved into two sects that have persisted until today: the Digambara ('sky-clad' monks) who, true to their founder's fashion sense, wear no clothes, own nothing and survive on donated food that they collect in their hands; and the Svetambara ('white-clad' monks and nuns), who dress with a touch more modesty in white robes and carry bowls for donated food.

For the seven million or so Jains in India, the Dilwara temples make Mount Abu a site of pilgrimage. But Mount Abu has other attractions too. It is the only hill station in Rajasthan, sitting at twelve hundred feet above sea level in the Aravalli Hills. This makes it an attractive retreat from the heat and dust of the plains below. The cooler temperatures (nothing in India is actually cool: there is only not-so-hot, hot, and fucking hot), combined with its picturesque location beside tiny Nakki Lake, have made Mount Abu an extremely popular destination for Indian honeymooners. Throw in a mix of visiting foreign tourists and it is easy to see why the population in Abu at any one time far exceeds that of its twenty-three thousand nominal inhabitants.

But it was monkeys — not marble or matrimony — that had brought Sarah Blaffer Hrdy and, ultimately, my wife and I, to Mount Abu. To begin with, there were lots of them. Hrdy observed six troops around the township of Abu and another at Chippaberi, a bus-stop half-way up the hillside to Abu. All the monkeys relied to some extent on the locals for their food, with the monkeys of the Bazaar and Chippaberi troops obtaining a substantial proportion of their diet from people. This meant that the monkeys were highly approachable and Hrdy did not need to use binoculars. She claimed to be able to approach to within one metre of the Bazaar and Chippaberi monkeys, but she said she could approach even those of the other troops, to within three to six metres. Of course, that all started to sound less like surveillance and more like dancing with them.

To put things in perspective: the conditions under which the monkeys were living were not exactly natural. They lived either within or on the outskirts of a township fair bulging with people; they were fed by a population that regarded them as sacred; and they were maintained at high densities because of this. These could hardly have been regarded as natural conditions in anyone's book. Even so, as my wife and I stood observing a family of Hanuman langurs feeding beside the sculpted rock that had given their Toad Rock troop its name, with the grey waters of Nakki Lake sparkling below and the white walls of the palatial Jaipur House (where Hrdy had stayed at one time) to the right, it was easy to get a sense of what had attracted her to this study site. For me, the deciding feature would have been the concrete restaurant that jutted out into the lake in the shape of a boat. While architecturally questionable, there was no doubting that it served the best cappuccino in India — in fact, at that stage, as far as I could tell, the only cappuccino in India.

The outside of the Dilwara Temples looked even less inspiring than a concrete boat that could not float: they appeared to be little more than a collection of concrete domes. In deference to the religious beliefs of the Jains, my wife and I were asked to remove our shoes, belts and any other leather objects. I complied gladly — just happy that we did not have to do the full monty and go 'sky-clad.' But at the entrance there was a warning sign that read, 'Entry of ladies in monthly course is strictly prohibited. Any lady in monthly course if enters any of the temples she may suffer'. As luck would have it, although she would not have described it thus, my wife was somewhere midstream in her monthly course. Risking the wrath of the Gods, she entered the temples anyway.

The scale of the temples is immense. They cover an area, it seems, the size of a football field. Their interiors are carved entirely from marble. Every ceiling, every column, every arch — in fact, every square inch — is a three-dimensional storyboard of intricately and exquisitely carved figurines. In places the marble has been carved so thinly that it is translucent. It is a sight to rival the Taj Mahal.

According to my wife, after leaving the temple, she did indeed suffer, inasmuch as she remained married to me. But, while I don't want to be too dismissive of her claims, from my perspective, the thing that had suffered most from our trip to India had been the credibility of Hrdy's hypothesis.

How could one draw conclusions about the selective advantages of any behaviour by examining that behaviour in conditions that were so far removed from those under which it had evolved? Did I really think that hand-fed, human-habituated, overcrowded monkeys killing infants had any relevance to Natural Selection? Would Darwin?

The more I thought about it, the more it bugged me, and I determined that I needed to go back to India and observe the monkeys in as natural an environment as I could find.

• • • •

I flew into Bombay, or Mumbai as it is now called. The plane arrived at two a.m. and, rather than getting a room in the city, I decided to go directly to the train station and catch the early train to Ahmedabad, from where I intended to figure out how to get to the Gir Forest National Park.

India had changed not at all in my absence. The same old heat, which would wilt tomatoes in seconds, greeted me as I stepped off the plane. There was the same old herd-like shove to get through immigration. There was the same old peeling grey building trying to pass itself off as an international airline terminal. The same old taxi drivers trying to rip me off at every turn.

During the taxi ride into the station, I discovered that in contrast to the rest of the world, the twenty-first century still hadn't quite arrived in India. People still lay sleeping in the streets: in doorways, on traffic islands, on the bonnets of cars. It still stank of faeces and urine. Dogs still roamed among the garbage that lay strewn everywhere. Precarious buildings, forming a sort of tarpaulin city, clung together for support. The more substantial buildings looked neglected and broken down. Humanity filled every nook and cranny in what was clearly a city of cracks.

The station, too, was little different to those in Delhi or Jodhpur. By then it was three-thirty a.m. and, as the ticket office did not open for nearly two hours, I joined the rest of the throng lying on the concrete floor, my three bags beside me. When the ticket office opened, I went in to make my reservation.

It was at this point that a man asked me for my pen while, I realised an instant too late, an accomplice swiped one of my bags. I ran after the man who had distracted me and, catching up with him in the main part of the terminal, I grabbed him by the throat, held him against the wall and yelled until I attracted the attention of a couple of policemen.

After telling my story to the uniformed policemen and a plain-clothed officer who had appeared, the accused man and I were led up a dark alley beside the station to a grubby hut; not, it has to be said, before the plain-clothed officer had taken the trouble to punch the accused a couple of times in the head.

The hut contained four people dressed in dirty trousers and singlets. Another wore shorts to complement his singlet. A sixth person lay on the floor, his leg manacled to the leg of a bench. This, I was told by one of the original policemen, was the Detectives' Office. Tall, dirty, hot, and in two shades of peeling yellow and green, it looked almost as far away from being an office as these guys had looked from being detectives.

The investigation, such as it was, was handled with a sort of sado-masochistic glee. The accused was yelled at. He responded by yelling back, somewhat plaintively. His pockets were emptied. And then the detective in shorts produced a vicious leather strap, about two centimetres wide and more than half a metre long, which was attached to a wooden handle. With both hands, he wielded this over his head and brought it down on the accused man's back. The scream it elicited only encouraged another blow. Next, the accused was made to hold his hands out. He whimpered and then he received two or three lusty blows, swung with the full force of the detective's weight. Whatever information the detectives were after was not forthcoming, so the man was made to sit on the floor with his legs straight out in front of him, his shoes off. The detective in shorts struck the soles of the accused one's feet with repeated blows using the strap. The screams were sickening.

I was repulsed, experiencing disbelief that this could be happening. It was like being in a Quentin Tarantino movie, with all the disgusting bits from *Pulp Fiction*, *Reservoir Dogs* and *Kill Bill* rolled into one.

Those screams must have contained some information, because suddenly one of the detectives left and returned a short time later with my bag. At last I was free to go, to catch a train to a forest that contained monkeys that had set fire to Sri Lanka and possibly killed their infants to boot — but at that moment, all that seemed a much less dangerous prospect than continuing to deal with the Mumbai police.

Eventually, I arrived in Sasan-Gir by way of a train from Ahmedabad and a long taxi ride. I opted to stay at the lodge with its big wide verandas. Sitting in the rattan furniture and downing gin and tonics, it had more than a vestige of colonial Britain about it.

Each morning, with driver and jeep, we headed out to explore the national park. There were seven distinct routes that we could take and the park ranger assigned the day's route to the driver. This was not a random process as, for some perverse reason, he always assigned a different route from the one we had requested.

Gir is not just home to monkeys: it is one of the last remaining refuges of the Asiatic lion. We came across two groups of lions. The first looked somehow less regal than their African counterparts: skinnier, smaller, hungrier — as if in the heat of India everyone had to eat sparingly whether rickshaw driver, Jain monk or big pussycat. It struck me that, should they commit infanticide too, Indian lions would be advised not to waste the food. The second group was in the process of eating one of the local's cows.

We encountered the main object of our searches — troops of Hanuman langur monkeys — feeding high in the trees, the features on their black faces barely visible in the dim forest light. They swung between the trees acrobatically, whooping and jumping, each troop clearly led by a single male. The sizes of the troops seemed smaller than those I had seen around Mount Abu and Jodhpur.

I did not, of course, see any infanticide. It is a rare event. In fact, during the four years of her study, Hrdy didn't see any actual infanticide either. What she gathered was circumstantial evidence: the disappearance of infants coincident with take-overs of troops by males. Like lion prides, langur monkey troops consist of a group of females and their young with an adult male monkey as the head of the troop — although, tellingly, this can sometimes be two or, even, three males. I say tellingly, because in the northern regions of India, where the monkeys are at their lowest density, multi-male troops are the norm and, in these circumstances, it seems that infanticide is exceedingly rare, if it occurs at all. Whereas, in the rest of

India, where densities are unnaturally high because the locals feed the monkeys and put offerings out to the gods that the monkeys are quick to claim as their own, one male is able to successfully commandeer a group of females. Bands of all-male monkeys roam about, somewhat akin to the pair of lions we had seen in Botswana, looking for the chance to usurp the male leader of a troop. The battles to take over a troop can be prolonged, lasting several weeks or even months. In this heightened state of aggression, which is fuelled by the unnaturally high population densities, it struck me as understandable, excusable even, that males might strike out at other monkeys and, of course, with infants being the most vulnerable, surely they would be the most likely to be injured or even killed?

I had analysed all the evidence I could find on reported cases of infanticide in langur monkeys. If the Darwinian-based Sexual Selection Hypothesis were true, then the one incontrovertible prediction it must make is that the time between births (the *inter-birth interval*, as primatologists call it) for mothers that have lost their babies to infanticide should be less than that for mothers that have not. Otherwise there would be absolutely no advantage, in a Darwinian sense, for males to kill infants with respect to increasing the pace at which they could father their own offspring. That is, if the act of killing did not accelerate the rate at which males could pass on their genes, then how could those genes that code for such behaviour proliferate in the population at the expense of genes that did not cause male monkeys to act infanticidally? What I found was that the average inter-birth interval did not reduce. What I found was consistent with male monkeys simply being hyped by the aggression that accompanies take-over bids, striking out at all and sundry like a Bombay detective, and likely in the process to damage the most vulnerable: the young.

The manager of the Gir Lodge had invited me to have tea with him, sitting perched on the tiled three-storey roof. We watched the sun go down. From our vantage point I could see turbaned villagers trooping home, single-file, as they emerged from the forest and headed across the fields, many with a bullock or two before them. Peacocks called loudly. A troop of monkeys next to the hotel squawked at each other and danced through the trees, using their long tails as a fifth leg. It could have been a scene out of a Rudyard Kipling story.

And that too, I reflected, was the problem with Hrdy's hypothesis, with many primatologists and biologists in general: they were often too quick to accept Darwin, too quick to accept that everything about animals and plants had to be adaptive, the product of Natural Selection. Faced with a lack of evidence, they made up plausible stories — *Just So* stories — no more based on fact than any of Kipling's. And the greatest collection of *Just So* stories, I decided, could be found in the corridors of biology departments, where in the absence of evidence to the contrary, the authors held forth reasons why Darwin's theory of Natural Selection could be used to explain every facet of an animal's biology.

The langur monkeys of India had been a lesson to me. Many aspects of animals are unlikely to be as finely tuned by Natural Selection as biologists would have us believe. And, if the 'principle of selection' as Darwin called it, were not as pervasive, not as controlling as Darwin's self-appointed disciples made out, then maybe the direction that evolution took could be more of an accident.

This didn't make me more inclined to accept religious versions of the world — be they from Hindus or High Anglicans — but it did make me wonder whether Darwin's concept of Natural Selection produced an inevitable pathway. If the implication were that Natural Selection may not always lead to the perfect solution, was there room for believing that what life forms prevailed was all just an accident?

– 40 –

Venice and the Spandrels
of San Marco

If you are going to have an addiction, you should make sure it is a good one. Some have the good fortune, apparently, to be addicted to sex. For me, the dice have not fallen so kindly: I am addicted to coffee. So, when I arrived in Venice it never occurred to me not to have coffee at one of the outdoor cafés that line opposite sides of the Piazza San Marco.

The setting was magnificent. My family and I sat in the sun listening to a string quartet play Vivaldi, while pigeons played bullrush with the feet of tourists that criss-crossed the square in search of the better view, the better photo, the better souvenir: when all they had to do was sit at our table and they could have had it all. Behind us was the Procuratie Vecchie, a three-storey structure built over an arcade that makes up the northern side of the square. Opposite was the Procuratie Nuove with its competing café — although because it sat in the shade at that time of day, it was less populated with customers — and, completing the enclosure of the square on its western side was the Napoleonic Wing of the Procuraties. Together these three buildings did little more than constrain, providing a super ornate fence around three sides of the piazza that focused the gaze and forced the feet down to the other end where there was the building I had, like so many in the square that day, come to see.

The Basilica di San Marco is a bravura piece of architecture. Capped with a series of multiple ornate domes, it began life on the site in its present incarnation nearly one thousand years ago. As I wiped the frothy milk from my lips and summer moved to autumn for the string quartet, I marvelled at the tall and striking Campanile, or bell-tower, to the right of the Basilica. It dominated the skyline of the square, indeed of Venice itself, standing like a sentinel or protector over the canals and this area so prone to flooding by the *acqua alta* or spring tides.

My main interest, however, was in the cathedral itself, and my reasons were probably a little different to those of most visitors. I had come not to see the bejewelled and famous Pala d'Oro behind the altar, I had come to see the spandrels.

The biologist Stephen Jay Gould had made the spandrels as famous as the altar's jewel-encrusted 'tapestry' in the narrow but hallowed halls of evolutionary biology. I had come to San Marco to look up at the mosaics that adorned its central dome. The dome was held up by four arches. The spandrels were the tapering triangular spaces formed at the intersections where two rounded arches were at right angles.

When you look up at the spandrels, like the rest of the ceiling, they are adorned with mosaics, and these fit so perfectly into the tapered triangular spaces provided by the spandrels that the initial impression is that this must have been the designer's purpose in creating the spandrels. But as Gould and his co-author, the geneticist Richard Lewontin, pointed out, that perception is misleading because spandrels are 'necessary architectural by-products of mounting a dome on rounded arches'. In other words, the spandrels were the inevitable product of a design constraint. They were not designed, primarily or otherwise, to be a canvas for a mosaic depicting a man pouring water into the narrowing space beneath his feet, however clever that use of the space may be.

The implication for evolutionary biologists, for our view of Darwin and his process of Natural Selection, is clear: we should not be fooled by the current utility of a particular aspect of an animal or plant into assuming that its usefulness is the reason it has evolved that way. Put another way, current use does not necessarily provide evidence that any structure or trait of an animal evolved by Natural Selection; that it is an adaptation; that it somehow influences the animal's reproduction and survival to such an extent that animals without that trait do more poorly. To the contrary, as Gould maintained, many aspects of the biology of animals and plants are simply the consequence of design constraints similar to those that affect the spandrels.

He reminds us that Darwin was never the rabid pan-selectionist that the majority of biologists, in his wake, have become. They have grasped his concept of evolution by Natural Selection rather loosely, yet run with it and applied it to explain nearly every single possible feature of animals and plants. As Darwin wrote in the very last edition of *On the Origin of Species*:

> As my conclusions have lately been much misrepresented, and it has been stated that I attribute the modification of species exclusively to natural selection, I may be permitted to remark that in the first edition of this work, and subsequently, I placed in a most conspicuous position — namely at the close of the introduction — the following words: 'I am convinced that natural selection has been the main, but not the exclusive means of modification.' This has been of no avail. Great is the power of steady misinterpretation.

Steady misinterpretation: is that what we biologists are guilty of? Making too much of a good thing? Darwin had a great idea, but even he saw its limits. If the unseen hand of Natural Selection did not produce some of the changes in the creatures that exist on Earth, what did? What were those other 'means of modification'? The opposite of deliberate or purposeful? Accidents? Could it be that the forms we see on Earth have as much to do with some statistical improbability, some accident, as they do with the design of a winning combination? Is life really just a huge game of Lotto?

I was engrossed by those questions as I left the piazza that day, as a church with design constraints — which Gould reckoned were a metaphor for life itself — receded behind us. It was only later that I realised I had been charged over forty-five dollars for two cappuccinos and a couple of very small carbonated orange cordials. To be honest, I could have been charged twice as much and I would still have come away happy. Such is the price of an addiction. I console myself with the thought that at least I don't have to pay for sex.

$- 41 -$

The Burgess Shale and
Good Design Versus Luck

The Burgess Shale is a fossil-bearing area in the Canadian Rocky Mountains. It was discovered in 1909 by a palaeontologist with the unlikely — but likeable — name of Charles Doolittle Walcott. The story goes that Walcott's horse stumbled and, when he dismounted to examine the stone it had dislodged, he discovered the first of the many fossils that would make this the most important site in the world for Cambrian fossils. The Cambrian is a geological period, a time slice from the history of the Earth over five hundred million years ago, when life did not exist on the land and, of that which existed in the sea, much consisted of creatures with soft bodies. Typically, it is the hard parts of animals that get fossilised, if any parts at all, but the Burgess Shale, apparently, was in an area prone to rapid mudslides, which killed and preserved the soft-bodied and hard-bodied animals alike, creating impressions of them that became fossilised in the rock.

It was Stephen Jay Gould who made the fossil animals of the Burgess Shale really famous. He championed them as evidence that Natural Selection was not the only game in town, that the forms that life on Earth took were, to a certain extent, controlled by Lady Luck. He argued that during that period, half a billion years ago, there were many more basic body plans than those that exist in animals living today or, indeed, soon after what became known as the Cambrian Explosion. The latter refers to the proliferation of animal forms that occurred in the seas at that time, as evidenced by the Burgess Shale, but it could just as easily, in Gould's mind, have referred to an explosion of the physical kind. According to Gould, it was not Natural Selection that determined which forms persisted, but whether they were fortunate enough to survive some catastrophic event such as a comet hitting the Earth and wiping out most other forms of life. Periodic catastrophes that happened on a scale of hundreds of millions of years (such as the impact of a comet said to be responsible for the demise of the dinosaurs), were not something that Natural Selection could prepare an animal for: in such cases being a winner meant simply being in the right place at a bloody awful time.

As surely as Gould had pointed me to Venice, I knew that I must return to Canada and visit the Burgess Shale in Yoho National Park. Why were so many of the creatures of the Burgess Shale no more? Were they the losers in an evolutionary battle waged under the flag of Natural Selection, or was Gould right and, irrespective of their design, were they just accident victims, the collateral damage from cosmic events too mighty to defend?

My daughter agreed to accompany me, and one morning, we found ourselves in the small British Columbian town of Field, waiting to join an exclusive guided trip into the fossil beds. Access to the Burgess Shale is strictly controlled: a guided party of fifteen is allowed but only a few times a week for a very limited number of weeks in the short alpine summer. I estimated that, in all, only four hundred or so people were allowed into the site each year. And maybe that was enough? Maybe that was all the people who were stupid enough to bust a gut over twenty-two kilometres and eight hundred metres of elevation just to see a few stones — at least those stupid enough to pay sixty-nine dollars for the privilege of doing so?

A latte and cinnamon bun served as breakfast at the quirky Pig Truffle Café. At eight a.m., we met up with our guides, Paul and Kimberley, who had both conducted research on the Burgess Shale fossils. Paul had also been the curator of invertebrates at the Drumheller Museum in Alberta for twenty years.

Leaving Field, we drove some sixteen kilometres to the base of the Takakkaw Falls. The hike that followed was much more gruelling than I had expected. The initial part of the track went through forest, with a series of switchbacks zig-zagging up the steep terrain and providing excellent views of the Takakkaw Falls, which were distinguished by having a ledge about one-third the way down that the water hit and bounced off like a Las Vegas fountain.

We stopped briefly at the serene Yoho Lake with its turquoise water surrounded by conifer forest and a backdrop of mountains that could only be glimpsed through the rain and cloud that had enveloped us. It felt more like a winter's day than the height of summer.

Moving upwards, we passed a number of bear droppings. Paul had warned us about bears when we set out, suggesting that we stick together as there had been no known instances of a bear attacking people in a party of more than four. Not all that reassuring, really, as who was to say if any bear we met could count? We passed a mound where a bear had been trying to dig up a Columbian ground squirrel, and I thought of Jan and his squirrels that day at Gorge Creek as they had tried to avoid the black bears — I didn't doubt that, like them, I would alarm call to my daughter in the event I saw a bear.

When we eventually made it to the Walcott Quarry — as the part of the shale that has yielded the most fossils is known — it was decidedly underwhelming, not much bigger than the fireplace in my dining room. But it was brilliant too, in a way that transcended all that. There was something about being up there, so isolated, standing on rocks that were more than half a billion years old, and being able to fossick among the slivers of shale and find the telltale marks of creatures that had lived way back then. The most amazing thing from my perspective was the realisation that these creatures did not live at over two thousand metres gasping for air as we were: they lived on the sea floor. As if to emphasise the enormity of that, the clouds pulled apart and we looked down — way down — on the aptly-named Emerald Lake, while across the valley, mountains with glaciers barely able to cling to them stood even higher than us. And it hit me, like a thump in the stomach of the brain: someone, some thing, some power had to have pushed those giant slabs of rock from sea floor to mountaintop.

What made the Walcott Quarry so special was that, for whatever reason, it was a place where soft body tissues were fossilised. At a time on Earth when most life had yet to develop backbones or, indeed, bones of any kind, here the floppy bits had been able to leave their marks in rock. Paul handed me a flat piece of rock. On it was a dark grey smudge, as if someone had drawn on it with a pencil. With the use of a small magnifying glass, I could make out the banana-like shape of *Ottoia*, an ancient member of a group of marine creatures that go by the colourful name of penis worms. Paul showed us another piece of shale, no more than ten centimetres across, and etched onto it I could make out the perfect impression of a *Marrella* (a lace crab), just a couple of centimetres long. I recognised its head shield and, on one side, the long antennae that bent backwards from the front end, around the head shield. *Marrella* were card-carrying members of the Phylum Arthropoda, ancestors of a lineage of animals that would eventually give rise to the insects.

All the specimens of *Pikaia* recovered from the shale had already been taken to museums, but Paul showed us a picture of what is the oldest known member of the Phylum Chordata — a lineage that would, in time, give rise to all the animals with backbones, including us. It looked like a little eel, less than five centimetres long, as unprepossessing a creature as you could imagine.

But there were other creatures not so easily classified: they did not conform to any readily recognisable forms known today. One was *Anomalocaris*, an animal that apparently swam by using flexible lobes on the sides of its body to propel itself through the water. It had a big head with two large arms covered in spikes and, by Cambrian standards, it was enormous, the blue whale of the Cambrian seas at about sixty centimetres in length. Another was *Wiwaxia*, a sort of slug-like creature covered in spines.

There were many others, too, which when they were named had to be assigned to a brand new biological grouping at the same time. While a few recent taxonomists have reassigned some of these creatures to known groups — casting doubt on Gould's assertion that many of the animals of the Burgess Shale Formation have no affiliation with modern groups of animals — it seems that the more fossils that are unearthed from the Walcott Quarry, the more animals are found that do not belong to any known lineages.

My daughter picked up some stones and discovered a beautifully preserved specimen of *Olenoides*, a trilobite. Seeing this daughter of mine — this lineage of barely a few years — holding that splinter of rock, I was dumbfounded by the enormity of it all: she held in her hand the fingerprint, as it were, the forensic leftovers of a creature that had died more than half a billion years before. That life had somehow progressed from it to her seemed not to be in doubt, but why some lineages should have done well while others had died out, well, that really was a mystery.

As we sat eating cookies, made by Kimberley in the shape of trilobites, it seemed possible that Gould was right: that Darwin had shown us a mechanism by which the lineages of life could evolve, but Natural Selection didn't necessarily help you when it came to understanding why particular lineages prospered at the expense of others.

My daughter and I left and headed down the mountainside, with the rain coming in and our view becoming more obscured with every tired footstep. This trip had been a revelation, I reflected. Just then I saw some bear scat and realised we had dropped to a party of two, which meant that the numerical skills of the bear did not count. We were fair game. And I realised that I wanted to continue living and breathing, that I did not wish to become a fossil — even my soft parts — mangled and mauled by some fucking bear whose ancestors had given rise to seals, and all because of some *Pikaia* that had won out in the crap game of life with the *Marrella* and the *Anomalocaris* and the *Wiwaxia*.

– 42 –

The United States, Again, and Intelligent Design

For some reason, my search to find the truth about Darwin, about life, kept drawing me back to the United States. It was not a country onto which Darwin had stepped even once. Of all the Western nations it seemed like the one in which he had made the least impression, where the foothold of his ideas was hardly more evident than any of his footprints. The United States may be the country that has given us more Nobel prize winners than any other, but it is also the country in which, according to an article that I was reading in *Time* magazine, fifty-four per cent of the people do not believe that humans have evolved from an earlier species and, screw the nuclear physicists, potassium-argon dating, and all that those prize-winning scientists have found out about the age of the Earth, fully forty-five per cent of Americans believe that 'God created the world along with all creatures big and small in just six days'.

That seemed mindbogglingly irrational to me. You could question the concept of Natural Selection and liken it to an Italian cathedral, you could lay the blame for the path that life took on comets and other freakish events, but you could not walk in the Rockies and not be struck by their great antiquity, in which the six thousand years suggested by the Bible must seem like the twinkling of an eye. You could not look at the pattern and distribution of animals on Earth and conclude that they had not evolved, one from the other; you could not look at a chimpanzee and not recognise parts of ourselves.

Yet somehow, those Americans — and not just in their ones and twos, but millions of them — had bought the biblical story, the one told by God, lock stock and fucking barrel, in the face of overwhelming evidence to the contrary. Indeed, I reminded myself, this was the same country where O.J. Simpson had been found not guilty; but the unthinking acceptance of a story with precious little evidence in its favour — not even a glove that don't fit or otherwise — seemed even more absurd.

There were plenty of places I could have gone. I could have gone to Dayton, Tennessee, site of the Scopes Monkey Trial, where in 1925 high school biology teacher John Scopes was charged with illegally teaching evolution under Tennessee's anti-evolution statute. That statute said:

> That it shall be unlawful for any teacher in any of the Universities, Normals and all other public schools of the State which are supported in whole or in part by the public school funds of the State, to teach any theory that denies the story of the Divine Creation of man as taught in the Bible, and to teach instead that man has descended from a lower order of animals.

Sixty-six years after the publication of *On the Origin of Species* and the good people of Tennessee were not having a bar of Charles Darwin. Or at least, the bits of Darwin that related to humans.

I could have gone to Pennsylvania where, eighty years after the Scopes trial, parents sued the Dover Area School Board in York County for requiring a statement about Intelligent Design to be read by science teachers when teaching evolution. The statement said:

> Because Darwin's theory is a theory, it continues to be tested as new evidence is discovered. The theory is not a fact. Gaps in the theory exist for which there is no evidence … Intelligent design is an explanation of the origin of life that differs from Darwin's view.

I could have gone to any number of states that make up what is known as the Bible Belt, where church on Sundays isn't so much an option as it is a bylaw. Instead, I chose to go to the place where one state, aided by the Religious Right and some dubious counting practices, would rob a nation of its true election result and thereby do nothing less than change the course of history for this planet: I went to Florida.

On the way, as a sort of concession to the Bible Belt, my family and I flew through Charleston, South Carolina, part of the world where Protestant fundamentalism isn't just practised, it's made perfect. However, we stopped for not much longer than it took for me to send a few postcards with messages like, 'Be glad you are not here.' For, while I had a lot of time for people who sought the spiritual side of life and a God they could turn to as a chum, as I neared the end of my journey I was becoming increasingly intolerant of the self-inflicted blind: those that will not see because they will not look.

If Charleston had not seemed to my liking, the United flight from Charleston to Orlando was like going to Hell. By a long shot, it remains to this day the worst flight I have ever taken in an adventure that has accrued more frequent flyer miles than I ever anticipated at its outset.

Somewhere mid-flight we hit the worst turbulence I had ever experienced and, according to the flight attendant, the worst she had experienced too. She said this just after she had poured coffee all over my lap. Not that she did it deliberately: we hit an air pocket and the plane dropped so suddenly, so violently, that my coffee cup literally shot up and hit the ceiling before bouncing back down on me. Not even the air-hostess's attempts to wipe it up were enough to bring some cheer to me as the meal service was cancelled and we settled down to a bumpy ride that would have done DisneyWorld proud.

At a certain point, I turned around to converse with my family, who were occupying the three seats behind me. I noticed the elderly woman asleep in the seat across the aisle from them. Her head was resting on what I took to be the shoulder of her daughter and, as

I turned back, I couldn't help but reflect that she reminded me of my grandmother just before she died: her skin had that same waxy appearance and her mouth was open.

It had been just a casual observation, a brief reflection, but when, some minutes later, I heard the daughter scream, I knew instantly that her mother was dead. The air-hostess rushed to help and called out for any doctors onboard to help. Two came forward.

The three of them tried to give the old woman CPR, but they did so while she was still sitting upright strapped into her seat. I knew enough from my first-aid training required for going to Antarctica that, for CPR to be effective, the patient had to be lying on her back. My wife, the nurse, knew the same: but the doctors, the medical ones, had taken charge and were insisting that they do it their way. Perhaps they were just doing it for show, to assuage the daughter, to show they cared?

Certainly the flight attendant cared. As we came into land at Orlando airport, the pilot barked an order over the intercom that they were to desist from their attempts to breathe life into the woman's unresponsive body and strap themselves into their own seats. To her immense credit, the air-hostess ignored the captain's request and kept the breaths and the chest pumps going throughout the bumpy landing and taxiing. Perhaps by then she was doing it for herself?

Once on the ground we waited while a crash team came on board looking like something out of the television show, *ER*: youthful, attractive medics in blue fatigues, with a stretcher and drips, and a get-out-of-our-way sort of attitude. They carted the old lady off the plane, laying her body out on a trolley before putting it in an ambulance and screaming off.

In all this, the daughter was largely forgotten. At one moment she was going on a trip with her mother, in another moment she was left alone in a plane of strangers, motherless and dazed. To her immense credit, for the third time that day (I count her earnest attempts to wipe the coffee from my lap as the first), the air-hostess remembered the daughter and went back to put a comforting arm around her, leading her away before the rest of us disembarked, happy to be off the damn plane, happy to be alive.

That air-hostess could have been as ugly as sin (and she was not), and she would still have been my hero: I would have her any day before the floozies on Aerolineas Argentinas.

The surprise for me about Orlando, about Florida in general, was that the people all seemed pretty much like me. They may have been somewhat fatter on average, and I hope, that were I to die on a plane landing at Orlando, my obituary might record that I was somewhat better dressed, but overall these were pleasant human beings. Almost to a person they were courteous and cheerful. They did not come across as ignorant ogres. Being God-fearing, it seemed, did not make you something to be feared — at least not as you went about your day-to-day business.

Yet, if I was struck by one image from Florida, it was that captured in the Michael Moore film *Fahrenheit 9/11* — of the stupefied look on President George W. Bush's face as he was told of the terrorist attack on the South Tower of the World Trade Center. His Chief of Staff whispered in his ear, 'A second plane hit the second tower. America is under attack'. President Bush continued to sit there before the students of the Emma T. Booker Elementary School, as paralysed and dumbfounded as any of the students would have been had they just been told they were about to be examined on trigonometry. And in that moment, the Religious Right — because make no mistake, George was their man, their can't-use-foetuses-to-do-stem-cell-research-but-can-kill-criminals man — must have wondered if they had backed the right horse.

The President was later to come out swinging: with God on his side, he launched shock and awe against Baghdad and the world became, almost overnight, a much more dangerous place to be — at least if you were an American soldier or an Iraqi citizen.

Wars fought on religious grounds are not new. People being killed for their religious beliefs is not new. The Holocaust — do I need to say more? How many had died in Ireland, even in my life-time, as Catholics and Protestants killed each other for believing in the same God? In Israel and Palestine, the blood of Jews and Arabs marred a landscape where opposing religious factions resented the other's right to be there. I had watched in sorrow as the Taliban bombarded the two thousand year-old giant sandstone statues of Buddha in Afghanistan. And it went without saying that there were few things more reprehensible than the attacks on innocent citizens — such as at the World Trade Center, and the like — by Muslim terrorists in their supposed Jihad, or Holy War (now there was an oxymoron). Sadly, this litany seemed to know no end.

When I thought about the great iconic images of my lifetime, they were all associated with the United States in one way or anoth-er: the assassination of JFK, planes flying into the Twin Towers of the World Trade Center, a man landing on the moon. If I had been older — as old as the lady who had passed away on our flight, say — I didn't doubt that I would have added the anguished looks on the faces of gaunt people wearing striped clothing in a place called Auschwitz, or a mushroom cloud over Hiroshima — but both those events were before my time.

It seems an awful shame that so much of what we dwell on as human beings is death and destruction. Vietnam. Rwanda. Cam-bodia. Serbia. Somalia. Place names that conjure up not images of landscapes or wildlife or plants or rocks that may have so fasci-nated an itinerant young Darwin, but place names that are buz-zwords for genocide, for man's seemingly inexhaustible capacity to inflict misery on other men. And let's not beat about the bush, they were largely men. Put my United flight attendant in charge of the world and you could be sure it would be a much better, much safer place.

We waited for over an hour in a line at Universal Studios to take a boat ride that included one terrifying moment when Jaws reared out of the water unexpectedly, much as the southern right whale had startled my wife when in Argentina. And in that moment I was struck by a thought: that it was not some shark, not some faction of nature we needed to be scared of — it was us. So much suffering in the world was inflicted in the name of God, or gods, or political beliefs propped up by religious beliefs, nearly all of which, ironically, supposedly admonished us to love thy neighbour and turn the other cheek.

It seemed that one had only to invoke God and the religious would follow, irrespective of the logic, if there be any at all. It was what scared me about the rise of the Religious Right in America more than the rise of a fibreglass shark. 'Intelligent Design' was no less than a slogan to not use your own intelligence, to subjugate reason to a set of beliefs that would enable you to plunder the Earth as your own, to punish people for their sexual orientation, to take an eye for an eye, and a country for a building.

Intelligent Design is nothing more than Creationism in drag: a belief, masquerading in the clothes of science, that God created the world and all the creatures in it. It is a way of having religion taught in supposedly secular curricula without ever mentioning the word God: for if what we observe can only be explained by an intelligent designer, who might that designer be? No second prizes, no second guesses. But it's like *MASH*'s Klinger trying to pass himself off as Marilyn Monroe: no amount of make-up and wigs can hide the ugly face or the five o'clock shadow. Intelligent Design does not even get close to passing itself off as a science. There are no testable hypotheses. In his 2005 ruling that the Dover Area School Board in Pennsylvania could not teach Intelligent Design as part of its science curriculum, United States District Judge John E. Jones described the proposal as 'breathtaking inanity'.

The scientific methodology is not the only way that we can gain knowledge about the world around us, but it serves no purpose at all to confuse what is science by including aspects that do not conform to its methodology. My world would be a pretty limited place if I only got to know it through the testable hypothesis, but equally, science would be much the poorer if we compromised the hypothesis testing and rigour upon which it is based. Yet none of that, not even the rulings of courts from Dayton, Tennessee to Harrisburg, Pennsylvania have deterred the advocates of Intelligent Design from pursuing their agenda.

Their arguments fall into two main categories: *irreducible complexity* and *gaps in the fossil record*. The first goes largely along these lines: many features of animals and plants are extremely complex and yet, to be effective, they need to have all the elements present that make up that trait. In other words, half the trait would be of no use, no advantage to the animal at all. A favourite example is the human eye. They liken the chances of Natural Selection producing an organ as complex as the eye to a tornado passing through a junkyard and assembling a bus. But of course, that is all hyperbole, all bullshit. Unlike a tornado (or for that matter, Creationism), evolution does not take place over a single moment but over long periods, often slowly, where one thing is built upon another. And yes, it is possible to see how a rudimentary light receptor could evolve, over time, into a complex light receptor like an eye.

In my travels I had come to see the Earth and appreciate it as Darwin had: as immensely old, with mountains that had once been under the sea and with rocks that went back billions of years to a time when life wasn't some primordial soup, it wasn't even on the menu. I had come to see how some forms could change, one to the other. How, for instance, many of the animals roaming the pampas of Argentina have fossilised ancestors that were a bit different to them. How the finches, tortoises and iguanas on the Galapagos Islands exemplified the mechanism by which such changes could take place, whereby animals placed in different, reproductively isolated places, could become adapted to the local conditions. In England, between a portrait of Malthus and a tour of Darwin's study at Down House, I had learnt to appreciate how the selection of favoured traits could come about as a result of a competition between individuals to stay alive and reproduce. As a consequence, because traits were heritable, the proportion of animals in the population with the more successful traits would change over time, so that to an outside observer it would appear that one form of a trait had been modified into another. It was this working-with-the-bits-you-have approach that was the real evidence of evolution, to my mind. It was why the flippers of a penguin were fundamentally the same as a flying bird's wing and a seal that propels itself on its belly should still have the remnants of a bear's or otter's legs.

The *modus operandi* of the practitioners of Intelligent Design has been to scour the natural world looking for complex things and then to ask the biologists to explain how they could have evolved in steps. Any hesitation, any inability to do so, is immediately taken as evidence for their supposed alternative hypothesis: that the thing must have come into being all at once, and therefore, by implication this suggests the existence of a manufacturer with purpose, a so-called Intelligent Designer, aka God. But they can only get to their answer by default; there is no way of testing their hypothesis, no way of testing God.

Some have painted Darwinism with the same brush: saying that there is no real way to falsify it and, therefore, no real way to properly test it. But as J.B.S. Haldane — the chap who accused God of a preference for beetles and came up with the logic that would be the basis of Kin Selection before dismissing it — once said: 'I will give up my belief in evolution if someone finds a fossil rabbit in the Precambrian'.

And that is the thing about the fossil record and our dating of it: it is consistent with a progression of life on Earth from the simple to the more complex, just as evolution by Natural Selection would suggest. So it seems like grasping at straws when the Intelligent Designers argue that gaps in the fossil record detract from the Darwinian explanation. In fact, it seems to me that the fossil record is remarkably consistent with the evidence of an evolution of life over long periods. Yes, species do sometimes change suddenly in the fossil record, from one to the other, but in the Galapagos and in the mountains of New Zealand I had seen species that could change in geological time frames so short as to be but heartbeats in the history of the Earth. Also, it is a bit rich of the Creationists from behind their pseudo-science lipstick and Intelligent Designer mascara to expect perfection from a record that was bound to be fragmented: only a fraction of animals and plants are fossilised, and we uncover a much smaller, infinitesimal fraction of them. It would be like looking back over the places I had visited on this journey and trying to reconstruct both the path I took and what I did. There might be my name on an airline manifesto here, a hotel booking there, perhaps the odd restaurant reservation that could be pinned to me; my name scrawled in the visitors' book at Down House, the logbook at the Royal Geological Society or on a card given to the lovely receptionist at the Linnaean Society — but it would all be pretty piecemeal and, though I don't doubt it would be possible for a detective or the police, say, to reconstruct my movements in a broad sense, there are bound to be holes, periods when I apparently did not exist, gaps in their knowledge.

In a sense, Intelligent Design does not deserve to be given the time of day, let alone for me to have spent as much time thinking about it as I have. And it would certainly be wrong and unfair to tar all Christians similarly, to regard them all as equally unthinking. But it would be a risk, too, to dismiss the threat the advocates of Intelligent Design pose to the advancement of knowledge, to finding out what the hell this is all about, and, as a consequence, to how we should live our lives.

As my family and I drove along a ruler-straight divided highway, with trees on either side creating the impression of an avenue, I couldn't help myself thinking, *if there is life on other planets, you'd hope that it would be more intelligent than some of it on ours.* Fifty-four percent of Americans believed that they had been created by an Intelligent Designer, forty-five per cent believing it happened in just six days along with all the rest of God's creatures, in the face of what — as my journeying had revealed — was overwhelming evidence to the contrary.

I was driving slowly, seldom venturing into the passing lane. I wasn't in my usual Formula One mode. A close encounter with death — not even my own, but that of an old lady on an aeroplane — had that effect. I realised just how tenuous was our grasp on life, how easily we could be stopped dead, a Darwinian casualty. I was driving as Ayrton should have done.

I recognised, too, that for all of this, I had come up against the biggest limitation of Darwin's theory: it explains how life on Earth evolved, but not how the Earth got here, not how the Universe began. If we couldn't explain that — and science seemed to have no definitive answers — were we left, as an act of *faith*, believing science will eventually provide those answers, simply because to date it has explained things like why an apple falls, why continents drift, and how we can go from amoeba to men?

Was that any better, any more reassuring than having faith in a Creator? In fact, quite the opposite: faith in a Creator makes things plenty reassuring for Christians. You can more readily accept a mother dying or a World Champion motor racing driver putting a steering wheel through his head if you believe in a God, in a Heaven and an afterlife. Which was why, at that particular moment in time, we were travelling sedately in our Dodge Neon towards Cape Canaveral: the birthplace of that one iconic lifetime image that did not involve death.

This turned out to be a much more exciting, much more rewarding experience than I had anticipated. To marvel at the cramped conditions and the apparent primitiveness of the early spacecraft, to tour one of the space shuttles up close, why, you could see a form of evolution in that alone, how one thing had been built on what had gone before.

Most amazing to me, however, were the mock-ups of the Mars robots: small craft sent out to our nearest planet in order to search for signs of life. They were ingenious in their design, transforming from a bouncing ball before spitting out a little range rover. It could have been a child's transformer toy, the perfect gift for Christmas.

They were equally ingenious in their operation. Cameras, oscilloscopes, measuring devices of every kind to sample, fondle, X-ray and analyse the Martian surface.

As far as I am aware, they have found nothing conclusive to date: evidence of water (a vital ingredient of life, for sure) and some telltale marks in rocks that could be, wishful thinking, the indicators of life's first stirrings. I have absolutely no doubts that were life to appear on Mars it would evolve according to those principles first deduced by Charles Darwin on his voyage on the *Beagle*. It would certainly evolve along different pathways, the Burgess Shale had taught me that, but it would be subject to Natural Selection all the same.

But as I continued to explore the exhibition space at Cape Canaveral that is where I became unstuck. For if Darwinism could explain the evolution of life so neatly, it did nothing to tell me about how the universe was formed, about how those ingredients for life were first brought together, first made available.

I read about the Big Bang. That did little for me. My child-like mind (for, intellectually, a child is what I am when it comes to astrophysics) demanded to know what was there before the Big Bang. And if all the universe's ingredients were condensed into a little dense pinprick of a ball, what was outside of it? How big was Space? Were there universes beyond our universe? Could science explain that? Could Darwin? Could God?

I had reached the limits, not just of the known limits of our universe but of our Knowledge with a capital K, because, really, science did not yet have convincing answers for how the universe came into being, or even, what were its limits. I have read Richard Dawkins and his suggestion that to believe in God is to be deluded, but equally I have listened to a lecture given by the Nobel prize-winning physicist Sir Paul Nurse in which he said that on this point science and religion are as one; both are equally inadequate explanations for the origins of the universe; that to believe science can explain our universe's existence involves an act of faith as much as believing in some supreme being. Dawkins suggests that you are wiser to bet on science, that its track record is so much better. Any system of knowledge that can give us Darwinism, that can reveal to us how life itself evolves, can surely, given enough time and the right measurements, tell us how the universe came into being.

I looked out at the launch pad, the place from which we humans propelled ourselves into other worlds. Some might well ask, *Why the hell are we doing that?*, but I have never doubted for one minute the importance of space exploration. It is the *Voyage of the Beagle* for the new millennium, where perhaps among the planets and stars and space, some new Darwin will find the ingredients for a new explanation, a new story, which will prove as incontrovertible as that of Darwin's. As we explore the universe, so we may come to understand better our place in it.

– 43 –

The Sea of Cortez and
the End of a Journey

When I started this journey, indeed, even when I started writing this book, I did not know where or how it was going to end. It would never have occurred to me in a million years that it would end near the tiny Mexican resort of Cabo San Lucas — a place never visited by Darwin, nor ever entertained by me as a possible destination (although given my travel agent's proclivity for unexpected itineraries, there is no place in the world that I ever rule out completely).

I had received an invitation to attend a conference in the village of Los Cabos, just up the road from Cabo San Lucas at the end of the long peninsula that is Baja California. The conference was entitled 'Defying Ocean's End' and it was being convened by legendary marine biologist Sylvia Earle and Gordon Moore, co-founder of Intel, and the originator of 'Moore's Law' (which says, essentially, that the power of computer chips will double every eighteen months along with his bank balance).

There were one hundred and fifty of us, so-called experts from a variety of fields, brought together in the super luxurious surroundings of the Westin Spa and Resort to see if, through our collective wisdom, we could identify solutions and map out a plan of action to save our oceans; because — the one thing about which there could be no disagreement — we were killing them.

There has probably never been a conference more well-intentioned, nor a conference with loftier ideals: this was nothing less than a gathering of rich, powerful and well-informed men and women wishing to save the planet (as I was demonstrably not of the first two categories, I figured it was intended that I try to fit into the third). Yet there was still something incongruous about it, something removed from the real world as only a group of multi-millionaires, politicians and scientists can be. In the break between sessions, I went for a walk around the hotel grounds.

The hotel had been designed by prominent Mexican architect Javier Sordo Madaleno to pay homage to the natural rock arch at Land's End near Cabo San Lucas, which separates the Pacific Ocean from the Sea of Cortez. The main part of the hotel consisted of a sweeping building that hugged the bare coast. It contained a dramatic arch that, when viewed from the landward side, framed views of the Sea of Cortez. The Sea of Cortez is that body of seawater sandwiched between the arm of Baja California and the rest of Mexico's body. It is one of the most biologically rich marine areas in the world, containing thirty-one species of marine mammals (including one-third of the world's whale and dolphin species), five-hundred species of fish, four thousand eight hundred and forty-eight species of marine macro-invertebrates (those animals without backbones that are large enough to be visible with the naked eye), and six hundred and twenty-six forms of macro-algae. The problem is: it is sick.

As I walked through the arch and down onto the beachfront, with its seven different swimming pools, there was nothing overtly obvious about the sea from its surface to suggest that it was not well. But I knew that below the surface it was being ravaged by the combined effects of over-fishing and pollution, and that the cumulative effects of prolonged abuse spelt death for any system. Take Darwin himself.

Darwin had died on 19 April 1882, following a period of vomiting and nausea, which had been his constant companions pretty much since he stepped off the *Beagle*, and, if you included motion sickness, you might well say, since he stepped onto it too. There is only so much one body can take and, after spending more than half his life battling attacks on his alimentary system, be they from protozoa imbibed with the bite of a benchuca bug or whatever, he succumbed at around four in the afternoon in his house at Downe, surrounded by his family.

There is an urban legend that Darwin somehow recanted his views on his deathbed and embraced the views of the Church. Nothing could be farther from the truth according to his daughter, Henrietta. Darwin's last words, uttered to his wife Emma, were apparently, 'I am not in the least afraid to die'.

It is true that Darwin wished to be buried in the grounds of the little church, St Mary the Virgin, I had visited in Downe. But that was understandable: it was much more about staying close to his family than seeking to be closer to the Church. His brother Erasmus had been buried there the year before, his wife would be buried there later, as would four of his children, including the hapless Charles who had died of scarlet fever and been buried just as Darwin and Wallace were having their great discoveries read to the world in the Reynolds Room.

It was Darwin's scientific colleagues and the government of the day, not Darwin, who had insisted on marking his funeral with pomp and ceremony befitting of his contribution to our understanding of the world. A week after he died, then, Darwin was laid to rest in Westminster Abbey, so that nearly a century later some long-haired graduate student, and thousands like him, could stumble across Darwin's gravestone in the gloom of the High Anglican's holiest place and be reminded that there are some questions so big that they are worth not just asking, but spending a lifetime seeking to answer. Among Darwin's pallbearers that day were his friends and avid supporters Joseph Hooker and Thomas Huxley, and Alfred Russell Wallace, co-discoverer of Natural Selection, but destined to be a paint-by-numbers figure who in life and death would always exist in the shadow of Darwin.

Emma Darwin had stayed in Downe, preferring to mourn the loss of her beloved Charles in private. After his death, the deeply religious Emma discovered amongst Darwin's notes a letter she had written to him soon after they were married, anxious should his wavering views on religion mean that they could not share the afterlife: 'everything that concerns you concerns me and I should be most unhappy if I thought we did not belong to each other forever'. She found Darwin had appended to the letter these words: 'When I am dead, know that many times, I have kissed and cryed over this'.

Darwin was always good with endings. He demonstrated this when he wrote the final paragraph of *On the Origin of Species*. Its first sentence was a masterpiece:

> It is interesting to contemplate an entangled bank, clothed with many plants of many kinds, with birds singing on the bushes, with various insects flitting about, and with worms crawling through the damp earth, and to reflect that these elaborately constructed forms, so different from each other, and dependent on each other in so complex a manner, have all been produced by laws acting around us.

It was a statement of elegant beauty, a metaphor for the world. The diversity of life all around us, Darwin was saying, is nothing less than a testimonial to the powers of Natural Selection.

I paused before leaving the beach, looking up at the admittedly impressive buildings, but being far less impressed with how they sat in their environment. This was a desert: the surrounding ridges were completely bare save for the odd cactus. Yet, the previous evening, we had sat out drinking our margaritas and piña coladas, immersed in what was essentially a false world created entirely by man.

The brown, pink and yellow stucco walls of the buildings had a sort of pastel charm, but there was no way that this was camouflage, no way that we were saying — like the leaf-mimicking butterflies and moths that Darwin had marvelled at when first arriving in South America — that we were blending in with our environment. The lawns were beautifully green and manicured with impressive cacti growing in their centres. But if you thought about that for even a minute, none of it made any sense.

This was a desert, the average rainfall in Cabo San Lucas is only twenty-five centimetres per year: manicured lawns, even unmanicured lawns, cannot exist without water. So where were they getting the water from, and what source in that parched landscape could sustain such pillaging long-term? And big cacti? Hell, irrigation is not for them: the Cardón cactus is the world's largest cactus species and is pretty much endemic to the deserts of the Baja California peninsula, where these very slow-growing plants are also extremely long-lived, with many specimens living well over three hundred years. Three hundred years! They made even the giant tortoises Darwin had ridden on the Galapagos seem like babies.

So how had we created this vision of the world that was more akin to Disneyland's garish topiary, where giant cacti grew in lawns that were flushed with water three times per day? If you watched the gardeners at the resort long enough you saw: the cacti die, of course, under an onslaught of water for which Natural Selection has not prepared them — and the gardeners sneak around and replace the ones that have died in their infancy, so that when we pull back the curtains, the view from our all-white king-size beds is of a perfect world of our making, a false world in which nothing dies.

To anyone looking from the outside with even the flimsiest knowledge of biology, it had to be plainly obvious that this resort did not belong in this environment. And if we could stick it there on that land, like a boil on a bum, what hope was there for the seas, where everything we do is hidden beneath the waves from all but the likes of the Sylvia Earles? We use bottom trawlers that bash and break the sea floor in our quest for fish. The fish and the shellfish: we don't harvest them as an orchardist might tend a crop of apple trees, we clear fell, taking every last one if we can get it. We set long nets that kill many species other than the ones we are after, even though we are supposedly not allowed to take the dolphins. We kill sharks just for their bloody fins. And it's not just what we take out of the water: nobody seems to care or notice what we put into it either. We throw our oil, our garbage and our turds into the sea.

The seas are sick. The coral is dying. The fish are dying. Each year, perhaps each day, the Earth has fewer species, and the seas fewer still. And it is not like those becoming extinct have lost some competitive battle that is Natural Selection and are being punished for poor design and a failure to adapt: they are the innocent casualties, the unforseen body count resulting from the way we choose to treat this world.

What is this biodiversity — in the sea or otherwise — that Darwin had alluded to with his entangled bank, if it is not some marker for the action of Darwin's Natural Selection; a snapshot of Natural Selection's changing face at a point in the history of the Earth?

I joined the others for the conference dinner, but I couldn't escape the feeling that there was a cruel irony to this conference, which was being held on the desert margins of the Sea of Cortez — probably the place in the marine world where biodiversity was most under threat. The conference was rallying against the negative impacts of human-induced environmental effects, exemplified by the likes of the tourist developments at Cabo San Lucas: by holding the conference at the resort, we were helping to propagate such effects, if not sanction them.

And that, I mused, would seem to be symptomatic of the human condition: our power for conscious thought, our power to do good, is nowhere near equal to our power for destruction.

I sat at a table with Dee, who had taken me to South America when I had sought to follow Darwin there, and Claudio, smiling as ever even though away from his dear elephant seals. As we sat feasting away on a variety of exquisitely prepared sea foods and meats in our surreal Salvador Dali-like environment with its multi-coloured stucco and cacti-adorned lawns, I contemplated just where all my journeying had led me.

Had I finally reached my South Pole, the answer to '*What the hell am I doing here?*' — and yes — I realised I had. We are not the ultimate product of a supernatural Creator but the incidental by-product of a natural process; a process recognised by Darwin, which he called Natural Selection. But I'd also come to realise that there was a second answer to that question, and that was that we were systematically destroying the diversity that was a consequence of that process — *that's what the hell we are doing here*!

I wondered what Darwin would think if he were *here* — now. For in a strange kind of way, through undertaking this journey, I had come close not just to Darwin's ideas but also to Darwin the man. I felt I knew Darwin, in the same way that I knew friends like Dee and Claudio, and I would have been very comfortable had he been sitting at our table, wiping the soup from his beard. And I think I know what would have been going through his mind: he would have been disgusted. Not just with Cabo San Lucas, but with what we have done to the world. His idea of evolution — that sketch first scribbled in a notebook not so long after getting back on the *Beagle* — was of a branching tree, a bush, not a mountain. By implication, humans are but a twig on that bush, no more important than any of the other branches down which life has evolved, be it to barnacles or bristlecone pines. We are not at a pinnacle, some peak that we should feel compelled to conquer other life forms like Hillary atop Everest.

For the first time in the history of the Earth, Natural Selection has given rise to a single species that has the capacity to destroy the biosphere, to do no less than destroy life on Earth. In that sense I figured it didn't really matter whether you believed we were forged by the hand of God or the equally incredible march from single-celled ciliate to bipedal primate. Either way, it was a bloody tragedy — enough to drive anyone to drink.

Just then the waiter brought me my fillet mignon and I auto-matically asked for a glass of red wine. 'Una copa de vino tinto por favor.' And then, struck by a sudden childhood flashback — and to the waiter's obvious dismay — I added, 'No, he cambiado de parecer, todo un puto caliz' — which, with my limited Spanish, was as close as I could get to, 'No, I've changed my mind, bring me a whole fucking chalice.'

Acknowledgements

This book began as an idea, no better formed than a bit of primordial goo: that it should eventually evolve to take wing has as much to do with the support I have received as it does with my own creative abilities.

The research and writing of *Looking for Darwin* was generously supported by a Copyright Licensing Ltd Writer's Award. I am grateful to CLL for initiating this award and their support of nonfiction writing in New Zealand. I would like to thank all involved with the CLL Writers' Awards, including Kathy Sheat (CEO) and Jenny Jones (Chair of the Awards Panel).

I am thankful to Andreas Schroeder and the creative non-fiction writing programme at the University of British Columbia, to the Banff Centre for a writer's residency and for the enthusiastic support and gentle prodding of Geraldine Cooke from the UK.

I thank all those who assisted me with the various parts of this journey and in particular: Andy Wroot, Sarah Wroot, Jan Murie, Dee Boersma, Claudio Campagna, Dave Houston and NHNZ (including its film crew: Robert Brown, Adrian Kubala, Andrew Penniket and Ed Jowett).

I am indebted to Longacre Press, and in particular to its managing director, Barbara Larson. Barbara has been a long-time advocate and supporter, encouraging me well before there was anyone else willing to do so. My writing has been made immeasurably better by the abilities of the world's sharpest editor, Emma Neale. Thanks, also, to Christine Buess for her design and Annette Riley for her marketing.

When you buy a book like this, you are not paying for costs that have been underwritten by others. My family bore, undoubtedly, the most significant costs, which aren't factored in to the sticker price — if they were, this book would be unaffordable by all but billionaires. Not only have my family had to endure being trucked over much of the globe, accompanying me like my baggage (although in South

America and India, at least, more inclined to stay with me), but they have had to suffer through equally long periods of my absence, both physically and mentally, as I became pre-occupied with this quest. And — perhaps most difficult of all — they have had to suffer through what have become years of living in a house that is in the ruinous state that accompanies renovations, without it ever showing signs of advancing much at all. In fact, largely because of this, I do not take evidence for the great antiquity of the Earth as necessarily negating the possibility of a Creator: based upon the rate at which I have been able to remodel our small abode, I would say that four-and-a-half billion years would be a conservative estimate of how long it would take me to create the world. So to Frances, Daniel and Kelsey: you have my unreserved thanks, admiration and love for your ability to tolerate me and the ways I have unfairly disrupted your lives.

For more information, please see: www.lookingfordarwin.com